WILLIAM EVERSON

The Life of
Brother
Antoninus

WILLIAM EVERSON

The Life of
Brother
Antoninus

By Lee Bartlett

A New Directions Book

Book design by Sylvia Frezzolini. Manufactured in the United States of America. New Directions Books
are printed on acid-free paper; clothbound editions are Smyth sewn. First published clothbound by New
Directions in 1988. Published simultaneously in Canada by Penguin Books Canada Limited.

LIBRARY OF CONGRESS CATALOGING-IN-PUBLICATION DATA
Bartlett, Lee, 1950–
    William Everson : the life of Brother Antoninus.
    Bibliography: p.
    Includes index.
    1. Everson, William, 1912– —Biography. 2. Poets,
American—20th century—Biography. I. Title.
PS3509.V65Z56   1988   811'.52[B]   87-11034
ISBN 0-8112-1060-X

New Directions Books are published for James Laughlin
by New Directions Publishing Corporation,
80 Eighth Avenue, New York 10011

CONTENTS

PROLOGUE   1

1 The Valley   3

2 Waldport   33

3 The Fine Arts Project   59

4 Berkeley   80

5 Conversion and The Catholic Worker   111

6 Brother Antoninus   128

7 Kentfield, Breakthrough, and "Prodigious Thrust"   148

8 The Rose of Solitude   168

9 The Spirit and the Flesh   193

EPILOGUE: The Integral Years   217

APPENDIXES   235

ACKNOWLEDGMENTS   243

NOTES   246

BIBLIOGRAPHY   261

INDEX   266

ILLUSTRATIONS   FOLLOWING PAGES 110 AND 192

PROLOGUE

On Monday, December 8, 1969, the front page of the *San Francisco Chronicle* served notice to its readers that one of the most colorful and energetic decades in our history was crashing to a close. Much of the lead space was devoted to the violence which had erupted two days before at the Rolling Stones' concert at Altamont Speedway, on the western rim of the Great Central Valley. A quarter million fans had descended on the rolling brown grasslands for an afternoon concert featuring the "world's greatest rock-'n'-roll band," and by dark four people were dead and thirty more were injured. There was a story about the massacre of civilians by American troops at Song My in Vietnam, and another recounting the murder of Fred Hampton, the young Illinois state chairman of the Black Panther Party, during a police raid.

Next to these events the marriage of a poet would seem of little moment, and yet such an announcement was thought noteworthy enough to hold a place alongside these reports on the *Chronicle*'s front page. "Brother Antoninus to Marry," read the headline, followed by a story from an unnamed correspondent who had attended a poetry reading at a small university town seventy miles north of the city the afternoon before:

Brother Antoninus announced here yesterday that he is leaving the Dominican Order of the Catholic Church to marry a 22-year-old woman. The 57-year-old monk and poet made the revelation dramatically, during a reading of his poetry on the University of California campus here.

Brother Antoninus began the reading with a series of poems on Pluto and Persephone, the mythological king and queen of the regions beneath the earth. Then, he told an audience of 300 persons, "By now, you probably realize I am not writing about Pluto and Persephone, but about myself. My life longs for simplicity, for truth."

"At the end of this reading I will take off this habit and I will be married." Antoninus did not reveal the woman's name, but said she was 22 and they met four years ago. "She came to me for counseling," he said. "Now I go to her for counseling."

When the reading was over, the best-known living Catholic poet slowly removed the black and white Dominican robes he had worn for over 18 years. "This is my habit," he said, "and when I take it off, I take off my own skin. But I have to take it off to find my heart."

vvvvvvvvv
ONE
vvvvvvvvv

The
Valley

William Oliver Everson was born on September 10, 1912, in a
small rooming house on an oak-lined street in Sacramento, in
northern California. A quarter of a century later, he remembered
of his parents, "In the world of myth, my mother was a goddess
and my father was an ogre. So I took her away from him—right
out of the womb. There is something strange and intangible about
what the young mother pours into the psyche of the first son.
Heroes are made, according to both Freud and Jung, on the breast.
And my father never forgave me."

His father, Louis Waldemar Everson, was the son of a
Norwegian shoemaker, who was also an evangelist and founder of
the Protestant sect the Iversonians. His own mother had died at
his birth in 1870, and at the death of his father 11 years later he
was sent to live with relatives in the port city of Christiania, now
Oslo. One morning playing on the docks, he slipped aboard a ship,
and, while he was exploring the engine room, the vessel, loaded
with immigrants, pulled out of the harbor for New York. The ship

arrived on July 3, 1882, and the boy went over the side onto an Italian lighter carrying bananas, then under the docks where he hid for a time. For the next few years he lived a homeless existence with a group of other boys on the New York streets, selling newspapers and stealing to get by. By the time he was twenty, he had held all sorts of jobs—traveling with carnivals, working as a ham actor, typesetting for newspapers. He never had any formal education, but he taught himself English and, according to people who knew him, had an impressive vocabulary. As his son Lloyd remembered, "Dad spoke without a trace of an accent. He made no attempt to teach any of us Norwegian, though most of our family's social contacts were with the Danish community. He admonished the Danes for continuing to speak Danish among themselves. He said, 'If you're going to be American, speak American.'" According to William, "He was self taught as a musician and really had a gift for this, though he never experienced a substantial breakthrough. He wrote music, especially marches and bandmusic, and wrote many popular songs which never quite took hold. He was also a singer and was most famous in the San Joaquin Valley for his classic yodeling—on Saturday nights people would come from miles around to hear him perform. This is my first memory of my father: standing on a lighted bandstand constellating a tremendous psychological force with his person."

Francelia Marie Herber was 15 years younger than her husband. She was born in Adrian, Minnesota, one of many small farming towns founded in the nineteenth century by the Catholic Church to get immigrants out of metropolitan areas. Her family was very large, and when she was 15, following the death of her mother, her father arranged for her to live with an older childless couple in town. Soon she got a job typesetting for the local newspaper, and it was there she met Everson, who for some years had been traveling around the country working as a musician and bandmaster. He had taken a temporary job working for her newspaper, and within a few weeks she was in love. Louis Everson had been married once before and now, because Francelia was a Catholic and he was divorced, they couldn't marry in the Church, or of course in Adrian. Everson decided to leave for the West, and soon she followed him; they were married in Yuma, Arizona a few months later.

Not long after the couple's first child, Vera Louise, was born, they packed their few belongings and left for the promise of California. For a time they lived in Sacramento, where William was born, then moved a few miles south to Turlock, where they had their last child, Lloyd Waldemar. Louis could get no steady work during these years, though finally, in 1914, he was offered a job as bandmaster in Selma, where the family took up permanent residence. Fifteen miles from Fresno, Selma is at the heart of the great San Joaquin Valley. It had been founded only thirty years before, like Adrian as a new farming community along the railroad line, and kept a fairly constant population of 3,000 until the Second World War. By the time the Eversons arrived, it already had a reputation as a prime peach-growing area. From childhood through adolescence William's life would be thoroughly rural and, given his father's previously peripatetic existence, thoroughly stable. The family would live in only two houses in 30 years, both modest, woodframe structures, and it is of the first of these that Everson has his earliest memory:

I was two years old and we were playing in the yard. I cut the little toe on my left foot on a piece of tin. Somebody brought a pan full of water and I put my foot in it. It was a white enamel basin, like you'd use on the back porch. As I watched, I could see the blood turn to water, the beautiful slow emergence of the blood. There was a sense of beauty about this: the instantaneous attention of the group, the aesthetics of the experience. But it was also a victimization. The strangest thing is that I don't associate my mother with it at all.

His mother had early on doted on his father, an attitude the elder Everson not only encouraged but required from the much younger woman. When her son was born, however, she immediately began to transfer her attention from her husband to William, and each passing year Louis grew more resentful. To make matters worse, he was a rather short man, standing only about five feet, four inches, while Francelia was taller. William grew quickly, and by the time he was into adolescence had already reached six feet. "The omnipresent hatred in the air in the Central Valley surrounding the First World War was a blight on my early life," he recalled. "The paranoia was amazing—we couldn't eat peppermint candy because we were told German spies had put arsenic in the color." This "threat of evil in the air because of the war was maintained by the hostile attitude of my father. When the Oedipus complex should have been resolving itself between the ages of seven and twelve, it simply wasn't possible."

To further complicate matters, his first sexual experience was also problematic. When he was just six, two neighbor girls who were a bit older took him and his brother out into a field near their house and undressed for them. Seventy years later he would recall, "I can still see them standing there, undressed. It was like a rite, a ritual, with archetypal resonance in my imagination. The focusing of sexuality in terms of secrecy, nastiness." This happened only once, and the girls soon moved away. And yet it served as a profound introduction for Everson to the woman as temptress, over against the idealization of his mother, a perception which would haunt him throughout his life.

William was not a good student. He learned to read and write quickly enough, but he was prone to daydreaming and had particular trouble with mathematics and science. According to his sister, "He became fascinated with airplanes and Charles Lindbergh, and he drew countless pictures of airplanes and made model planes. He signed his drawings with a W.E., adapting his initials to the 'WE' title of Lindbergh's book about his historic flight, wherein he referred to himself and his plane as 'we' as if they were as one." By the sixth grade, he failed to maintain passing marks and he was held back a year. This meant not only the obvious humiliation with both his classmates and his family, but the loss of his girlfriend of two years who when she moved on without him broke off their friendship. Still, later he was popular enough to win his eighth-grade election for class president, much to the chagrin of his school administrators.

He entered Selma Union High School in 1926 and continued to have academic problems. As he wasn't planning to go to college, he took the easiest courses allowed. "The ethos of my family was not oriented around academia," he later recalled. "My father was self taught, and my mother's education was very minimal. The expectation was that I'd be a musician, or maybe an artist. I took art all the way through high school, and did fine at that." Here he also discovered sports. He had always enjoyed sandlot football, but now because of his height the football coach encouraged him to play. "I came into my own in football when I was a junior. I made the first string as a tackle. By my senior year I was carrying my own weight. One day in practice that year I hit a dummy so hard that I broke the pulley holding it up. The coach stopped everything and said to everyone, 'Look at that. Bill has drive.'" In the first game of that season he blocked a punt, which set up his team for a touchdown, and for a day at least he was a hero. "The biggest event of that year was our first matchup against San Jose. They came down with their razzle-dazzle plays and their Stanford coaches, and we beat them. Selma celebrated for a week." During that game, however, Everson's kneecap was dislocated (an injury that would plague him into old age), and he had to be carried off the field.

Interestingly, though his grades remained poor and he had little interest in his studies, during Everson's junior year an intelligence test was given at the high school, and Lloyd and he ranked second and third respectively among a group of 130. Everson's father was astonished. Lloyd, his brother thought, had become his favorite, and he expected good things of him, but he always assumed William was slow. Once he got the results of the test he took him aside and told him that if he didn't make the honor roll he couldn't play football. "When it first happened," Everson remembered, "I went to tell the coach and broke down crying. Football was all that was important to me then, and I thought I was doomed. But somehow I managed to do it, so I was able to keep playing."

This ultimatum only served to widen the gap between Everson and his father, however. The strain was always psychological and emotional; never was his father in any sense abusive physically. And even the psychological strain was not readily apparent to others in the family; in fact, in later years Lloyd Everson was surprised to learn from his brother that there had been any strife at all, or that he felt he was somehow favored by his father. "Every semester," for example, "Bill would bring home a certificate attesting to his having read so many books—usually a lot. I would bring home a certificate awarded for not having been absent or tardy for the whole semester. My father would say, 'Any dummy can get one of those—look what Billy got.'"

Still, following the football incident Everson began to spend much of his time wandering the fields near his home hunting, and soon on weekends he was going off on hunting trips by himself or with friends. His great delight was to hunt on the west side in the salt flats. Earlier in the century the area was known for its wheat, but when the valley irrigation system was constructed, the alkaline level in the soil was raised to a point where great stretches of field were no longer usable for farming. "I became a crack shot with a .22 Winchester pump. I'd get the rabbits running, and sometimes quail or squirrels. I think I had an unconscious omnivorous appetite for hunting as a way to get out of the whole home situation with my father. It was an alternative of stability and inner peace in a natural world which made few demands on me. That was my obsession with nature. It didn't demand responsibility. I could lose myself in it."

vvv

Louis Everson's Saturday night band concerts were extremely popular. As his daughter remembered,

Dad was quite handsome in his white bandmaster's uniform and cap. He had intense blue eyes and his glaring glance when he was displeased could be withering. He had a great zest for life and the endurance to keep going 18 hours a day when necessary. He could parade march for miles and even when he was older could end a march not the least bit tired, while some of the younger men would be ready to collapse.

Not only would most of Selma turn out on those warm valley evenings, but families from the outlying farm areas would come into town during the day to get their week's supplies, then stay on for the music into the night. There was of course little radio, and no television, so that for a farming community these weekly concerts were big events. "The town was filled with people from as far away as Hanford," Lloyd recalled. "You couldn't walk across the park there were so many people sitting around. The sidewalks were jammed. Before we were old enough to play in the band, Bill and I went early and placed programs on all the benches, then went over to the fountain and handed out programs to the people who were streaming over from across the street." Later, the poet "was always there with everyone else, the guys and the girls eyeing each other." And it was on one of these evenings, in the summer of 1930 just before his senior year that Everson met Edwa Poulson.

Until this time he had generally felt awkward around girls, and had never dated. Edwa was a year younger, but fairly mature. Her father, a banker, had been one of the wealthiest men in the community, but with the collapse of the stock market in 1929, he had lost most of his money. Her mother, who, like Everson's mother, was many years younger than her husband, had died when Edwa was just twelve. She had one younger sister, and essentially took over the maternal role in the family throughout her adolescence. "She always regretted the termination of her youth like that," Everson recalled.

But it made her more mature than other girls her age. She was robust and maternal, and I was in love. School started and one evening we were sit-

ting on a porch swing outside her house. I could tell she wanted me to
kiss her so finally I worked up courage and did. The next night I saw her,
we walked over to the school grounds and, in an alcove behind a stair-
case, fell to making love. It was a first for both of us. I had been living
a fantastic sexual life in my imagination, but that was the first time I
touched a woman erotically.

From that point on, the two were inseparable, spending every free
moment at school together, walking home together, passing their
evenings in each other's arms.

In his sophomore year his English teacher, Helen Schafer, had
assigned the writing of poems in various forms. At this time
Everson was an avid reader of hunting magazines, and had just finished an article on peregrine falcons. For his assignment, he wrote
a long poem called "To the Duck Hawk." His first published
poem appeared in *The Magnet*, his high school yearbook, the same
year, along with a letter to the editor and an advertisement for his
father's print shop. A dozen more short poems appeared in the
next two numbers of the yearbook, all doggerel:

> The months of pep and spirit and sport:
> We won from Kingsburg and Clovis;
> From Fresno High we did victory court,
> But to bitter defeat they drove us;
> From hardy Madera and Lemoore we won;
> Fresno Tech we barely nosed out;
> With a victorious month very nearly done,
> We smashed over Reedley, a rout.

And now he took to writing a love poem a day to Edwa, though
unfortunately those poems, like "To the Duck Hawk," have been
lost.

Every summer from age 12 on, Everson worked at the local cannery. The area was famous for its large peach crops (one of Louis
Everson's most popular songs was "Selma, Home of the Peach,"
written for the San Francisco International Exposition of 1915),

and Libby's cannery was the area's largest employer. Technically, Everson wasn't allowed to work full days because of his age, but because of his size he was able to pass for a sixteen year old, and worked sometimes as many as 60 hours a week. He was stationed in the cookroom, keeping the capping machines stocked with lids, and his pay went to buy his clothes and provide spending money through the school year. According to Lloyd,

Libby's played a large part in shaping the fortunes and complexion of Selma and her environs. Bill worked there a few seasons before I did and in 1931, through his efforts, I was hired to operate a capper, putting lids on cans like he had done before he moved on to the syrup room. The pay for men was 30¢ an hour (in those days gas was as low as 9¢ a gallon, and you could get a rib steak and fried potatoes at a diner for a quarter). The capper was a hot job. You stood between two exhaust boxes at 210 degrees each. The air temperature was 120 degrees. They had to put one kid down by the door at the first machine because he passed out. You spent 10 hours on the capper, then stayed another 2 or 3 cleaning up capper alley. A big hose was attached to two pipes, one water, one steam, and we hosed down the cappers, floor, under floor conveyors, and etc.

Everson often used his breaks to write, and as Lloyd recalled, "One day the fellow who kept the equipment greased came by and told me 'the big shots are coming through. Try to look halfway decent and halfway intelligent.' Bill wrote a poem, 'The Big Shots Are Coming,' describing how the excitement rippled through the plant. We were told the poem was typed up and displayed in the main office of Libby's in San Francisco." Everson held the summer job all through high school, and continued to work there occasionally after graduation as a syrup maker throughout the thirties.

Everson graduated from high school in 1931, into the Depression. The crash didn't hit the San Joaquin Valley as hard as many other places, mainly because when the bottom fell out of the peach market, the farmers were able to shift over to the growing of grapes for raisins, which weren't viable crops in other areas of the country. The cannery, however, closed up for a time, and there were no real jobs available. Everson's father had always opposed the idea of his going to college. "My mother's attention to us only grew stronger and my father resented it, resented the fact that we didn't have to engage life in the same way as he did as an adolescent. This became a very difficult situation. My sister went to a business college and got a job. Before too long, my brother broke loose and went to work in the aircraft industry in Los Angeles. But I just clung there, waiting."

Almost from the start Everson and Edwa had talked of getting married, once they were able to support themselves. Unlike Everson, however, Edwa was a good student, and their plan was for her to go straight from high school to Fresno State College to get a degree, and then a good job which would enable them to marry. She spent the following four years at Fresno State, first as a physical education major. She had always been athletic and was an especially good tennis player, winning the college championship one year. After a time, however, thinking of employment after graduation, she shifted her emphasis to elementary school-teaching. And during this period, Everson actually did more than "cling" at home. First, he tried a semester at the college, catching a ride with friends up to Fresno each day. Though he didn't do particularly well and dropped out at the end of the term, the experience was not a disaster, and the campus literary magazine, *The Caravan*, published his poem "Gypsy Dance." Then the following fall, he traveled to New Mexico with two friends whose family had country property covered with piñon trees. The three hatched a scheme to harvest piñon nuts commercially. "After a lot of driving we finally found the property," he recalled, but the whole adventure failed. "We thought it was a matter of just picking up the nuts. The Navaho had it down pat, picking the nuts for candy manufacturers, but we didn't know what we were doing, and nothing came of it. My companions were really harebrained. We ran out of money for gas and I wanted to wire home. But they insisted we steal gas all the way. We were lucky not to be shot because those hombres in New Mexico didn't fuck around, but it was a marvelous trip, my first trip out of California."

vvv

When Franklin D. Roosevelt won the 1932 Presidential election, he inherited a country three years into its worst depression, with over 13 million unemployed. "I propose," he told Congress on March 21, 1933, "to create a civilian conservation corps, to be used in simple work, not interfering with normal employment, but confining itself to forestry, the prevention of soil erosion, flood control and similar projects. . . . I estimate that 250,000 men can be given temporary employment by early summer." By April 5, Roosevelt had established one of the earliest of his New Deal Programs, the Emergency Conservation Work agency (known popularly as the Civilian Conservation Corps, or the CCC), providing national conservation work primarily for young unmarried men. Recruits lived in camps, usually not too far from their homes, under semimilitary authority; they were given $30 a month, plus housing, food, and medical care. Each recruit signed up for a six-month hitch at a time, and by the close of the program in 1942, the CCC had employed 3 million young men.

Everson wasn't aware of the first call for recruits in the spring, but one afternoon in the fall, while he was in Fresno, he read an advertisement for the second six-month call-up. He rushed to the downtown CCC office and signed up immediately: "I didn't even get a chance to go home. I went in my street clothes into an Army truck right on the spot, and they drove us down to Sequoia National Park. I called my mother and told her what I was doing, and asked her to send my work clothes. There were supposed to be clothes for us there, but the camp had just opened up and there were none waiting. Just dormitory buildings with tarpaper roofs. It was on the road to Mineral King, a place called Cain Flat." He didn't have a chance to call Edwa, who spent the next week wondering what had happened to him. When she got the news, she wasn't pleased, and the next semester started a brief affair with a fellow student at Fresno State, where she was now living.

This was obviously an impulsive act on Everson's part, one that a year later would have been impossible. Usually, after applying, an enrollee would have to wait up to two months for the processing of his application, then go to a conditioning camp (often an Army post), where he received a medical examination, vaccinations, and a kind of boot camp initiation, running over many weeks. But when Everson applied, the program was still new; "the impasse in my home had grown very ferocious, the tension between my father and me. I needed to get out, to make a statement, to do something purposive. So I just grabbed the opportunity."

That time was very important to me, away from home and women, among my peers. It was an important crystallizing experience, especially to be thrown out into the expanse of nature like that. It was my first prolonged experience of nature outside of the farmland. We did road work, cutting a road to a fire lookout at the top of a peak. We had no bulldozers or jackhammers—just shovels and blasting powder.

Everson worked on his trail crew eight hours a day, five days a week, and most of his monthly salary was sent home.

The work was often grueling, but he enjoyed camp life enough to re-enlist for a second six-month period, and he was made the leader of his crew, which meant a raise of $6 a month. In May, the group's work completed at Cain Flat, they were first sent to Hockett Meadow to attempt to destroy an infestation of beetles in the lodgepole pine. Once fire season arrived, they moved on to build a ranger station, fence pasture, and construct stone fireplaces for campers.

Everson had entered the CCC on November 1, and during the following nine months he saw Edwa only twice, once during Christmas furlough and once during the short break between hitches. By late summer he could stand the separation no longer, and applied for early leave so that he might return to Fresno State, where she was still enrolled. By this time Edwa was a senior, while

Everson entered as a second semester freshman. She had ended her
affair some months before, and they picked up their relationship
as if there had been no break. Additionally, beyond his recovery
of Edwa, Everson was now better prepared for college:

Now, what college did for me was to introduce me to a body of men my
own emotional age who were thinking. This produced an intellectual
awakening. My break with the CCC gave me a distance from the family
and my father's attitudes, but I remained a little retarded in intellectual
matters. Suddenly at Fresno State I was awakened. It was my association
with three young men there—Stuart McKelvy, Andrew Curtin, and
Hubert Buel, which allowed me to step out of the family and adopt a
pose of critical objectivity.

Everson had been raised a Christian Scientist. As Vera remembered, "Our mother was born into a Catholic family, but when
she came to California from Minnesota she became a Christian
Scientist. A friend had introduced her into that faith because her
eyes were giving her a problem. Mother's eyes improved and she
credited Christian Science for their being healed. We children
attended the Christian Science Sunday School in Selma for several
years, until a rift occurred in the group (about 35 or 40 members,
if that), and mother withdrew from the Society. There were so
few children in this group that we really stood out in the strongly
orthodox community, and we felt like oddities, at times." Still,
according to Lloyd, "even though Dad was then a self-professed
agnostic, he was respected by most of the local ministers and some
of them used him as a soloist occasionally in their Sunday services.
Dad took Bill and me once in a while to those services."
At the time they stopped attending the Christian Science
Sunday School, Everson had adopted his father's "nineteenth-
century Ingersollian agnosticism," and when he returned to
Fresno, he was undergoing a spiritual crisis. Early on, Edwa took
him on Sundays to her First Christian Church, though he didn't
feel in any way drawn to her religion. His months of relative seclusion in the Sequoia forest, however, had made him feel uneasy,

somehow certain that his agnosticism paled before the vast rich-
ness of the natural world. One afternoon in the campus library,
completely by chance, he happened upon a collection of Robinson
Jeffers's poetry: "I took it home," he told a group of students in
1975, "and devoured it. Suddenly the whole inner world began
to tremble," as he experienced not only an aesthetic breakthrough
but also a religious revelation. "The entire structure up to that
point began to shudder, and then the tears were pouring down my
face. The words in that book were just hammering into me, one
after another—terrible, devastating blows. I picked up my pen and
began to write this jagged poem, my first true poem," "October
Tragedy":

Do not sing those old songs here tonight.
Outside, the buckeye lifts nude limbs against the moon.
Outside, the heavy-winged herons
Are scaling down into the misty regions of the marsh.
Bitter is the wind, and a mad dog howls among the withered elderberry
    on the ridge.
Bitter is the quiet singing of the cricket,
And silent pools lie black beneath still reeds.
Go away, follow the spoor of a wounded buck
Over the marsh and deep into the desolate hills.
You must never sing those old songs here again.

"No concepts, pure mood," he continued. "It was as if suddenly
all those years of trying to write were coming together. I couldn't
believe it. I began to write other poems and by the end of that
semester I knew what I was going to do." And at the conclusion
of the spring semester, Everson left college to return to the land
and write poetry.

vvv

Edwa graduated in 1936, and in the fall began teaching at a primary school in Tranquility, a small town 75 miles from Selma.
Over these months in the good weather Everson worked as a pipe-

layer, often traveling as far as 40 miles for his day's work in the grape fields; during bad weather he would stay at home and write. Every weekend Edwa would return to Selma to see him, and they tried to save as much money as they could to set up housekeeping. The following year, she was able to get a position at the primary school in Dinuba, much closer to home, and finally, on the Memorial Day weekend of 1938, after an eight-year engagement, the couple got married.

The wedding was held at Edwa's father's house. Hubert Buel, Everson's close friend from Fresno State, was the best man, and many relatives and friends from both families attended. Both his parents were pleased at the marriage—his mother had always gotten along extremely well with Edwa, while his father was relieved to have him move permanently out of the house. Following a reception, the pair left for their honeymoon, a drive down the coast through Big Sur to Los Angeles, with a two-day stay at the Highlands Inn in Carmel. When they returned to Selma a week later they took up residence in a rented house in town, though by the end of the first month they had discovered a small ranch house for rent on East Dinuba Avenue and Mill Ditch Road beyond the outskirts of town. Eventually, they purchased an eight-acre parcel of land nearby for $800. Their plan was to grow muscat grapes, which were already established on the property, and sell raisins to the Sun Maid Company. In time they hoped to buy an adjoining piece of land and build a house on it. For the next five years, Edwa regularly continued teaching at the Dinuba school, while Everson worked summers at the cannery, occasionally continued to lay irrigation pipe in the winter, and, with Edwa, began to establish his crop.

One of the poet's best friends during this period was Lee Watkins, whom he met in the Selma Public Library one autumn afternoon. The Watkins family were well-known as beekeepers, and because he worked for his father, Lee was able to spend much of his time in the library. He was older than Everson, married, and he and his wife Milicent had two children. As the poet remembered, "He was a totally different kind of mind. I was introverted, he was extroverted. He had read absolutely everything, and became the dominant influence on me until he left for the Bay Area near the start of the war." Everson and Watkins spent at least two afternoons a week together in the library, reading and talking, and they saw each other often socially with their wives.

Watkins and his wife had decided against having any more children, and to that end he had undergone a vasectomy, a rather rare operation in the thirties. Neither Everson nor Edwa wanted children, yet both were unhappy with the available methods of contraception, as they seemed unnatural and disruptive. Everson simply couldn't see himself as a parent, especially given his difficult relationship with his own father. Edwa felt that teaching kept her close enough to children, and after helping so fully in the raising of her own sister, valued her time away from youngsters. The subject came up in a discussion with Watkins, who convinced Everson that a vasectomy was the most viable solution to their problem. In February of 1940, Everson and Edwa drove to Ione for an appointment with Watkins's physician, who performed the surgery in his office with a local anesthetic.

Everson had discovered Robinson Jeffers's work in October 1934, and by the end of his spring semester at Fresno State had completed the poems that would be published in his first short book, *These Are the Ravens*. Soon after he started writing seriously, he began submitting to magazines, though without much luck. In 1935, for example, he sent poems to *Scribner's*, the *Saturday Review*, the *Atlantic Monthly*, and *Harper's*, and all were rejected. A small magazine called *Westward*, located in San Leandro, accepted two poems, "Do Not Brood for Long," and "Winter Plowing." The editor, Hans A. Hoffman, had just started a series of chapbooks called the "Pamphlet Series of Western Poets," and in August Everson decided to submit a collection called *The Blue Wind of September*. Hoffman wrote back accepting the poems, explaining, however, that the author should provide $30 to help defray publication costs. He offered a royalty of two cents a copy, which would sell for ten cents each. A thousand copies would be printed, with Everson taking half the edition. Hoffman suggested a slight reordering of the poems, with "These Are the Ravens" coming first; he also suggested the final title of the collection. The pamphlet appeared in November, and for many months Everson carried copies with him everywhere, selling them and giving them to friends.

In September of 1935 he gave his first talk on writing poetry, to a class at Selma High School, and in December gave his first public reading, to ladies of the Selma Wednesday Literary Club. For the next two years he sent poems to magazines regularly, and was just as regularly rejected from *Esquire*, the *New Republic*, the *Yale Review*, the *Atlantic*, and *The New Yorker*, though in the summer of 1937 *Poetry* magazine published his poem "The Watchers," and the *Saturday Review* accepted "Sleep":

> The mind drifts warmly, focused on farther dreams.
> There comes over the eyes a vast and immeasurable tide,
> With no shore breaking, the lift of a darkening sea,
> And the mind goes down to it gently, lapped in the lull.
>
> Now from the sunken brain the freed flesh throbs the deep song:
> The bone and the fiber hark the same music;
> The blood pounds cleanly, pulsing wantonly through the slack and
>   indolent limbs,
> Loosed from the mind's hand, the nerve's dominance,
> Sprung to the secret joy of release.
> It comes to the eyes as a moving tide,
> With no shore breaking, the lift of a darkening sea,
> And the mind goes down to the depth and the silence;
> The loose blood pounds the deep song.

In April of 1938, he submitted a manuscript of new poems to the Yale Younger Poets Series called simply *Poems*, but without luck; the award that year went to Joy Davidman.

During these years Edwa was the poet's primary reader, and was

extremely supportive of his writing, as Everson was of her newly
discovered artistic talent. As he recalled,

When we first got married, and I was spending a lot of time writing,
Edwa got restless and decided she wanted to try sculpting. We began to
order books from the library on sculpting and got hold of some clay. She
began to mold, then soon moved on to wood and stone, and she began
to get very adept. In the fall of 1942 Fresno County had an art show,
and she had two pieces shown there. When we visited the show she was
much made over; no one knew anything about her and suddenly here
was this fully-bloomed talent. I'm sure it was this artistic atmosphere we
had in the home that was the cutting edge of our evolving perceptions.

Other readers of manuscript work included Hubert Buel and
Lee Watkins, as well as Everson's new friend Lawrence Clark
Powell. A mutual friend who was a librarian at Fresno State had
suggested to Everson that he write Powell, then a journeyman
librarian at UCLA, who had published a book on Jeffers. Everson
did, and the two hit it off immediately. While in Los Angeles for
his honeymoon, Everson met Powell for the first time, and a short
time later, when Powell traveled to Selma to do research, he
stayed for a number of days with the poet. During the Christmas
holidays of 1938, Everson and Edwa made a second trip to Los
Angeles, and Everson carried along with him the manuscript that
Yale had rejected, now called *San Joaquin*. Powell had read most
of the individual poems before, was immediately impressed at the
strength of the collection, and offered to write a foreword. He
introduced Everson to the publisher Ward Ritchie, who had a reputation for doing very lovely editions, and on the strength of
Powell's recommendation, he accepted the manuscript. Like
Hoffman, Ritchie required a subsidy, this time $125, a rather large
sum in 1938. Everson and Edwa had received $100 as a wedding
gift from Vera, and Edwa insisted, that there could be no better
use for the money than the production of this book; and by early
July the 100 copies of Everson's first full-length collection were
ready. Under the terms of the contract, Ritchie kept 50 copies to

sell, while Everson was given the other 50. In fact, he decided to send out only one review copy, to *Poetry*, which mentioned the book along with the work of three other poets in July 1940.

In later years Everson remembered of Lee Watkins that "he was the only other intellectual in Selma. They left the central valley as soon as they could get out." Living in Selma in the late thirties as he became more and more preoccupied with his poetry, Everson felt that he couldn't be more cut off from the intellectual and cultural life of the country if he had been living on the moon. In a way, even San Francisco was as far away and magical as the literary meccas of Paris, London, and New York. Edwa, Buel, and Watkins all offered a community of readers, but they were not writers themselves, and Powell was not a poet. What sustained Everson's sense of deepening vocation, nourished it beyond measure during these crucial years, however, was a correspondence started by chance with a poet seven years his junior.

In 1940 Robert Duncan was still Robert Symmes. He was living in Woodstock, New York, writing poetry, and helping James Cooney produce the final issue of *The Phoenix*, then editing *Ritual*, and *The Experimental Review*. Everson had published "Orion" in the third issue of *The Phoenix* in 1938, and Duncan ran across other work of his while rummaging through Cooney's files; he initiated their correspondence with a request to consider this poetry for his new journal:

Your "POEM" in Phoenix is very sensitive, a real ritual aware and breeding awareness. The feeling which POEM FOR THE DAY OF THE FEAST gives of the autumn entering of The Tropic of Capricorn is very fine. You have the craft to begin with and that is a godsend for while Jimmy often seems to be able to overlook entirely the matter of craftmanship (I might as well say always) when the writing has stirring meaning to him . . . I can't do that.

Ecstatic over this contact with another serious and publishing poet, Everson sent off an immediate reply, not only giving Duncan permission to publish "Feast Day," but remarking of the younger writer's own "We Have Forgotten Venus" and "Persephone" (which appeared in the spring 1940 *Phoenix*) that

I am glad to see somebody writing like this. I get so goddamned sick of seeing this thin metallic stuff in Poetry every month: well-wrought, carefully manufactured,—and dead. We have to get back to the living language. . . . There will be no poetic revival until we make of poetry a live and resilient and urgent thing. It makes me feel very good to read these poems of yours. I like your intuitive handling of free-verse rhythms. The conception of balance and counter-balance of the weight of the phrase.

For the next year and a half the two corresponded animatedly, exchanging manuscripts, using each other as sounding boards for the working out of their aesthetics. "You write letters which make mail worthwhile," Duncan wrote. "Your criticism is a challenge . . . because you are tackling your own existence: and I too am doing that—I use these letters as an explanation board in a way. You are a citizen of countries I know." And Duncan's replies often helped Everson come to terms with his own misgivings. In July of 1940, for instance, he complained to the younger man that while the work of Robinson Jeffers was central to his heart, he worried about being "derivative." "Certain matters of composition are learned yes," Duncan replied, "but your power tho it is aimless is not derivative. That is why you feel the integrity of your work—because the power rises from you—you have let loose a life stream of creation but you don't know what to do about it. Right now you register the fact that you have such powers, and that you have the added advantage of knowing about the craft of writing and on top of that: of being honest. But you have a responsibility beyond that. . . . You must be fully aware of the roots of compulsion— none of us are but we recognize the terrible duty of destroying ourselves to enter what must be called libido consciousness."

Further, Duncan introduced Everson to the work of Ezra Pound. While Duncan was attracted at this period to Pound's *Cantos* especially, he suggested to Everson that he read Pound's lyrics carefully as a corrective to Jeffers. In these earlier poems

Everson discovered not Pound's allusiveness or architecture, but the music of his ear.

Duncan's sending me to Pound's short poetry had a great disciplining effect on me. I was so heavily oriented to sensation, as if I believed everything was physical. I hadn't yet emerged from the maternal into a sense of the patriarchy. I was belatedly trying to get loose from the umbilical cord, the heavy breasts of the mother, the heavy thighs, the female belly. The identification between woman and nature had me enthralled and Jeffers just reinforced this. Pound began to civilize me, for it didn't seem that he was trying to prove so much in the earlier poems, not like in the *Cantos*, where he kept trying to elevate his aesthetic into a cry of anger and anguish. But for me those earlier lyrical poems were of great value and I have Robert to thank for my discovery of them.

In Everson's early poems like "Lines for the Last of a Gold Town" it is difficult to see beyond Jeffers. But once the poet got hold of *Personae*, and especially "The Return" and "The River Merchant's Wife," which he read again and again, both his sense of the image and rhythm were drastically altered. In 1941 he would write "The Approach," his own version of "The Return," and it was indicative of what would follow—a sharpening of the image, a tightening of the syntax, and especially the elimination of enjambment.

In November, Everson sent Duncan his radio verse play "The Masculine Dead" (which remains unpublished), and the following month Duncan responded stressing the bardic. The poem's ending, he argued, "seems to rise from the deepest centers":

> Go down into darkness with hardly a sigh.
> We are the tortured and the damned,
> Forever doomed to rise through the autumns,
> Hungering the wealth of the broken lives we never fulfilled,
> O far and far the violence of earth opens before us,
> The torrent—

"This is real—it ceases to be good or satisfactory—it is living. . . . I want to tell you that I have gone back to your work hungrily.

I have been impatient with your fillers. Why in a stage play for radio then does the thing burst into the deep heart utterances? Why not go away from radio plays, from poetic stories into the final utterances, clairvoyance, inspiration itself?" Duncan and Cooney had published excerpts from Lao Tze. "Your world seems close to his—and your feeling out toward a seed-force is like his feeling out toward the TAO."

As war grew more likely daily, the two young poets, separated by three thousand miles, shared through the mail their sense of the secret and subversive nature of the poet's vocation, a hermetic and religious brotherhood. "I want to talk with you about this period which we have entered," Duncan wrote at the end of 1940,

it is the Human Winter—let us remember that—and hold no foolish hopes. I feel it as a greater cycle in our lives in so far as they are lives of love we shall be persecuted, in so far as they are dedicated to creation we shall be hunted down at last—in so far as we would give life—we cannot take it—and we have entered the criminal world. Yet how much can we see clearly even in the tortures. We live in a country where in the shadow of tremendous forces—consider the great extrusions of granite, consider the terrible face of the desert at noon—the human race has destroyed slowly its awareness. The last religions flicker and go out, the last masters are mocked—and we who begin the new awakening here—we are considered insane—that we believe in any force beyond us.

Everson had just registered for the draft, and was depressed and confused. "Let us at last be ready to give everything away," Duncan consoled him.

Let us be ready to become of the lowest order. In prison I shall learn the importance of the body; in death I shall learn the gesture of death-crossing. . . . The Poet is the redeemed man. He attempts to awaken his fellow man to the infinite joy of the God-self. As such he cannot but reveal the true nature of war, of property, of government.

Although Duncan had been born in Oakland, a few hours' drive from Selma, the two men had never met, something both very much wanted. Finally, in the summer of 1941, Duncan decided that he was "sick enuf of coterie living and New York culture," and he returned to Bakersfield to see his mother. After a few weeks he decided to hitchhike up the valley to Berkeley, and stopped off in Selma and spent the day with Everson and Edwa.

Throughout these years Everson regularly continued to send off poems to major magazines, and just as regularly his work was rejected. In the summer of 1939 he sent "a group of the best poems" he had done to *Poetry*, which under the editorship of Harriet Monroe had accepted his work three years before; now, the new editor George Dillon rejected the work with a printed rejection slip, which sent the poet into a fit of "anger and humiliation." As he wrote Dillon in early 1940, Monroe's acceptance had given him "strength, coming at a time when my writing was regarded with indulgence it justified me, and I settled down to production with a confidence I had not felt before." Now, with the rejection, he was confused by "the consistent stream of material entering the magazine on no other discernible grounds than that it dealt with the class struggle. . . . I sat down and scrawled a facetious, hurried scrap with a social message, concocted a fantastic letter," and, adopting his mother's surname, signed the submission "William Herber." *Poetry* published "The Sign" in its February 1940 issue (a number which led off with Gertrude Stein's "Stanzas in Meditation"; see Appendix), with the following contributor's note:

William Herber sent us a letter with his poem: "I am writing from a camp fire near a small town between Bakersfield and Tulare, Calif. I have had no address for three years . . . have just finished working the fruit in Imperial Valley and am on my way to Oregon. . . . Before I became a 'fruit bum' I had a couple of semesters in college and got interested in poetry there." He adds that he reads Poetry in the public libraries, so we hope he will see this issue. We have his signature and will send his check when he writes for it.

As Herber, Everson then sent a second poem, which *Poetry* again accepted immediately. "My friends received your acceptance with great glee," he continued to Dillon.

They saw immediately the possibilities of the situation. Young genius killed under a freight train. (And certainly one dead poet is worth a dozen live ones). Gradually more poems are found. A book is produced. Biographies appear. Tears are shed lamenting the untimely death. A legend springs up. All the slobbering sentimentality of the literary tapeworms is evoked.

But with the acceptance of the second poem, Everson felt a pang of conscience. "The sending of that second poem is one of the really contemptible acts of my life," he confessed.

I mailed the first in anger, and it served its purpose. It showed me all I wanted to know about you. I sent the second in meanness, deliberately debased myself, deliberately joined the host of panderers and double-jointed pimps that make the age what it is. . . . Condemnation of me in no way absolves you. Whatever repercussions the incident is liable to gather, you most fully deserve. As editor of the one journal upon which American poets heavily lean, at a time when poetic expression needs the most rigorous preservation of its ideals, to let yourself be swayed by the extraneous political mess speaks eloquently for itself. . . . However, I come later to regret the arrogance and the presumption of this letter, I say now that it is becoming more and more apparent that *Poetry* died with its founder.

However, following the letter, which was printed in its entirety under "Correspondence" in the May 1940 issue of the journal, Dillon got in the last, biting word: "We still think the poem signed 'William Herber' the best we have seen by Mr. Everson. It is certainly true in his case, as in the case of so many poets today, that 'l'indignation fait les vers.' And if a few rejection slips are all he needs to get going, that is easy." Obviously the second Herber poem never appeared, and though *Poetry* continued to review his books fairly regularly, he submitted no poems to the magazine again for three decades.

For the next two years Everson published nothing more in journals at all, though by November of 1941 he had gathered enough
poetry together to make a third collection, *The Masculine Dead*.
He sent this group of a dozen new poems, most of which had been
approved by Duncan, to James Decker, a subsidy publisher in
Prairie City, Illinois. Decker accepted the manuscript immediately, and offered to publish the book in an edition of 200 copies
if Everson would contribute $85 to production costs. The poet
agreed with the understanding that he would receive 50 copies,
plus royalties. At first, Decker promised to get the book out in
February or March, but there were delays, and the collection
finally appeared in late September. When his copies arrived,
Everson was devastated—he had not been shown proof, and there
were myriad typographical errors, and errors in line breaks. In a
letter, he exploded: "It is unthinkable that the book should be
released as it now stands. . . . The injury is beyond remedy." He
insisted that an errata sheet be inserted immediately. Decker
responded that his sister had set the type and was a neophyte; he
agreed to include the errata slip and to send review copies wherever Everson wished. On September 28, the poet, now a bit
calmer though still thoroughly disheartened, replied that the
review copies go "to all the magazines and journals that review
poetry"; further, he asked that copies be sent to his brother and
sister, Duncan, Josephine Miles, Anaïs Nin, Harry T. Moore, C.
F. MacIntyre, Hans Hoffman, and Robinson Jeffers.

Later, Everson would come to call the body of work written
between his discovery of Jeffers and 1941 "single source," that is
poetry that took its impulse from the landscape of the region.
"Muscat Pruning" (from *These Are the Ravens*) is indicative:

> All these dormant fields are held beneath the fog.
> The scraggy vines, the broken weeds, the cold moist ground
> Have known it now for days.
> My fingers are half-numbed around the handles of the shears,
> But I have other thoughts.

> There is a flicker swooping from the grove on scalloped wings,
> His harsh cry widening through the fog.
> After his call the silence holds the drip-sound of the trees,
> Muffling the hushed beat under the mist.
> Over the field the noise of other pruners
> Moves me to my work.
> I have a hundred vines to cut before the dark.

The narrator thinks about the valley fog and the vines, about working in the fields, about a bird's cry; then the sound of other pruners brings him back to himself. Often meditative like "Muscat Pruning" and with titles like "Fog Days," "We in the Fields," "Winter Solstice," and "Coast Thought," the poems of the first volumes are generally short lyrics that attempt to set a mood or capture an emotion. They are set against Eliot's sense of the impersonal, and are neither paradoxical nor ironic in the fashion of the day. Rather, they look through Jeffers back to both Whitman and Wordsworth in their celebration of the natural world. This is not, however, to say that these early poems are either trivial or sentimental. Through poems like "Who Lives Here Harbors Sorrow" and "The Knives" there runs a dark melancholy and a recognition of the occasional fierceness of a sometimes difficult landscape. Also, at times there wells up a barely muted rage at man's environmental and political stupidities, as in poems like "Attila" and "On the Anniversary of the Versailles Peace, 1936."

Despite Everson's dissatisfaction with the production of *The Masculine Dead*, however, of the three first volumes it is the most ambitious. While these poems continue to be rooted in the landscape, their imagery and rhetoric reflect Everson's growing concern with the worsening world situation. The lead poem, "Orion," sets the tone for the rather less pastoral poems that follow: "The weight turning on the tipped axis hangs to that line; / Atom-smashing pressures war at the center / Straining the charged and furious dark." Further, the volume contains two long poems, "The Sides of a Mind" and the reworked radio play "The

Masculine Dead." The first is a meditative sequence, a form Everson would return to again and again throughout his career, focusing on the end of both a decade and a phase of his life. The poem's nine sections open with a dialogue on the role of the poet in the world—must he turn into himself for some kind of true sensibility or must he go out into the political or religious sphere, the world of action, to effect his art? Neither, a third voice answers. Rather, he must listen to the natural order "leaning for music" from the earth for "the vision." The following passages constitute both a kind of autobiography and a confession, as Everson ranges through his broken relationship with his father, his love for and attempt to move beyond his mother, his vasectomy, the relationship of man to other creatures, birth, death, and meaning. While rather grim, the poem concludes on a mildly hopeful note on the last day of the decade, as "the decade that tempered the shaft of our lives / Wanes to the past / . . . The wind's with the runner, / Throwing its weight through the last hour."

The final "single source" poem, "The Masculine Dead," is even more experimental and certainly bleaker. Following a prologue which outlines the movement of a storm south from Alaska, there is a series of monologues by female voices—an old woman, a girl, a widow, a wife, and others—interspersed with commentary by a chorus of "the masculine dead." In dramatic evocations of powerful scenes, the women remember husbands and lovers now dead: "And bearing him up that heavy hill his head rolled back, / The throat strained upward, white and weak, / The cords standing under the clear skin, / And the bruised mouth open." Yet the deaths seem to have little meaning, and have come too soon ("For we are the men who, young and hot-blooded / Fell under the blow, / Were knocked speechless and stunned, / Our dead eyes and our open mouths / Facing the sky"), as the women without men are left only with their memories and the ghosts of the dead beating their "boneless hands on the air." The war in Europe has erupted and for the poet even the quiet hope of the earlier poems

in the volume seems to have drowned in "the grinding rivers of
the world."

vvv

Everson saw his mother less after his marriage and his move out
of town to the ranch, though they continued to be close, and she
got along very well with Edwa. In the mid-thirties, having developed trouble with one of her lungs, she soon started coughing
blood. At first, her physician diagnosed this as tuberculosis, and in
1937 she went into a sanatorium near Fresno, where she was confined for a year. Everson visited her as often as possible during
these months, and eventually, taking the tuberculosis precautions,
she seemed markedly improved, though this didn't last. At the end
of a year, the sanatorium doctors felt that there was nothing more
they could do, that the problem was caused not by TB but by a
deformed lung, and she was sent home. Her health continued
gradually to decline, and by early 1940, while no one thought the
condition to be fatal, it was decided that surgery was needed to
correct it. She traveled to San Francisco for the operation, which
seemed to go well, but suddenly during her recovery period she
developed complications. Within a week, without warning, she
died.

Not only was this a devastating blow for Everson, but it immediately led to an even greater estrangement from his father. "Her
funeral was Masonic Rite in Selma," he recalled. "My mother was
an Eastern Star, and it was an Eastern Star ceremony. But to me
it was appalling. I just couldn't see my mother going out without
something more emphatic. In the church I began to cry out and
began to beat my hands on the coffin lid, just after the ceremony
before they carried the coffin out. Everyone in town was there,
and many people tried to quiet me. Finally, when I sat back down,
crying, my father's eyes just rested on me, glaring." Everson was
profoundly disturbed by his father's attitude, though his brother
regarded it differently. "As I see it, it was Bill who was creating
a real scene and Dad spoke sternly to him as any father would."

After this Everson and his father didn't talk for a number of weeks, and to complicate matters further Louis Everson remarried an old family friend within just a few months of his wife's death. Ever since their first meeting when he was a boy, Everson had not liked this woman, who was a Christian Scientist and fairly unstable. When he was in his twenties, she was confined to an asylum, but not long after Francelia's death she was released and returned to Selma. Everson was totally unprepared for the sudden marriage, and he refused to attend the ceremony. Outraged, he wrote his father and told him that he wasn't able to face the situation of his remarriage, that it was simply too soon and that he had loved his mother too much. To try to involve himself with a woman who now held the position his mother had held with his father was something he just couldn't do. In an accusatory and harsh tone he railed, "When a man has reached your age he shouldn't have to jump in bed with the first woman who passes by." His father's reply was forthright—"Don't judge me," he wrote, "until you've been in my situation. Your accusations are vile! I have no obligation to answer them."

Thus, for the next year Everson did not see his father, save for once when they chanced upon each other in a bank, and he simply brushed his father aside and stormed out. In early December of 1942, Louis sent Everson and Edwa a Christmas card and a few small Christmas gifts in an attempt to reconcile, but Everson, while moved, was incapable of it. He replied in a letter on December 22:

Dear Dad—
    Your card and packages have arrived, and both Edwa and I want you to know how appreciative we are of the impulse of generosity and forgiveness that prompted them. I am sincerely sorry this rift has come between us, and I want to apologize for my arrogant letter, and for the unfortunate incident in the bank. But I do not feel, things being as they are, that I can pick up the threads where they were broken. There is so much of the situation that I cannot explain, that I can hardly account for

in my own mind, that goes back through years into childhood, and is all mixed up with the remnants of many things that are gone now—there is so much, that if I am to have any peace I have had to sever completely all the associational ties, and go on to what lies ahead. Perhaps I have been brutal and callous in my treatment of the whole situation, and am sorry and want to cover whatever foolish or immoderate thing I may do in the ignorance and blindness of a particular moment. I remember that today is your birthday, and wish you many more, many good seasons, and wish deeply that things could be other than what they are.

—Bill

The marriage, in fact, was over in less than two years. The elder Everson continued to be extremely demanding, and perhaps this aggravated his new wife's psychosis. One evening, for example, as the two of them were sitting at the table after dinner, his wife looked at him and said, "Isn't it strange that we are sitting here like this when we both know that I am going to kill you?" Further, she would wake screaming in the night that the Japanese were invading; in one dream in particular she imagined herself to have killed scores of soldiers in the front yard through a window with a machine gun.

In early January of 1943, Louis went out to the ranch to try once again to talk things out, but Everson refused. A week later the poet was drafted, and he never saw his father again.

vvvvvvvvvvvv
TWO
vvvvvvvvvvvv
Waldport

On October 6, 1942, Everson was classified IV-E by the Fresno
draft board. He had registered two years earlier, at age 28,
applying for CO status. His problem was similar to that which
many young men would face during the Vietnam War—according
to the Selective Service Act, CO classification was tied to specific
religious belief, and he had none in the traditional sense. In filling
out his forms he was forced to try to couch his Jeffersian pantheism in religious terms to make it acceptable to the board.
Unfortunately this initial document has been lost, though Everson
later remembered making a rather vaguely worded argument
based essentially on a combination of Western humanism and a
Buddhist's sense of the sanctity of all living things. Further, at this
time he became a vegetarian. More than likely it was the fact that
his father served as a justice of the peace in Fresno County (though
he was personally opposed to his son's move) rather than the force
of his written application that aided in getting his CO classifica-

tion. Interestingly, he was never called up from Selma to the Fresno office to verbally defend his request.

In the summer of 1942, however, as the war effort intensified following a number of setbacks for the United States in the Pacific, the draft was stepped up and Everson was asked a second time to defend his position to the board. "It is true that my underlying conviction against the necessity for or the justification of war has remained unchanged," he began, in the seven-page handwritten explanation that does survive, "yet my attitude in the past two years has undergone a considerable shift in emphasis."

The war caught me in the last phase of the intense state of religious feeling common at one time or another to young men. With some individuals that feeling finds its mode in the orthodox forms of religious practice. I, who had never received a thorough Christian training, found it in a response to Nature. It seemed to me that everywhere I might turn my eyes I beheld in the tangible forms of the natural world the illumination of a divine and benevolent Being. And nowhere was it more evident than in the manifestations of life. A living thing became the very incarnation of God, and when the War began with its vast slaughter, its unspeakable crimes, its appalling degradations, I knew no feeling so powerful as that of outrage at this profanation of the very essence of divine presence.

And it was this essentially Emersonian position that he outlined in his first application, a position that he discovered "not uncommon in the people I found around me." In 1940, much of the country remained isolationist, and many people gravely disapproved of America's drift into war.

But the attack on Pearl Harbor suddenly changed the entire outlook of a great number of pacifists and isolationists, he continued, as "they were plunged into a struggle as titanic as any that had ever gripped the world, they felt the stakes to be as great":

they felt an immediate and impending danger, and sensed that it would be only by an enormous effort, a momentary stooping to the animal levels of savagery and ferocity that would save all they had gleaned from a past which was itself a long struggle toward enlightenment. And so it was that the men who, ever since the Armistice of 1918 denied the right of armed force, did not hesitate to put their trust once more in the sword, and to take their morality with them as they did so. They took their morality with them; they would suffer immediate degradation to achieve future elevation, and never before, at least in my remembrance, has there been as much public emphasis placed upon morality, the principles of righteousness, as there has been in American discussion since the Hawaiian attack.

The debate itself he found to be a good thing for the moral and spiritual life of the country, but he found himself "in the unfortunate position of commending the ends while deploring the means." As his youthful religious zeal began to wane, he "turned, in the Wordsworthian sense, from exaltation to reflection":

from the concerns of the appropriate worship of a deity to the concerns of human existence in a precarious world—it was just as that shift was being finally established that I was confronted with a moral debate the issues of which were not removed to the abstraction of hypothetical conjecture, but were as immediate and as vital as the very choices of death or survival. And I no longer had the comfort of a considerable minority to sustain . . . many who could defend me when the planes were over remote Warsaw were inclined to think I was both deluded and a fool when the planes were over San Francisco. My closest friends were one by one joining the army. I lost one at Java and one in the Atlantic, men whose integrity and conviction I have every reason to admire, and I found myself faced with the personal problem of meeting these men, who were willing to die for their beliefs, on their own terms, the terms of moral speculation, of human implication rather than the terms of divine ordination. . . .

I was, under the shift of standards, forced to concede the logic and true morality of men fighting for survival. I was forced to decide whether or not the prospects of life under what is reported to be the most brutal and tyrannical political regime in centuries were preferable to the terrible ordeal necessary to overcome it. From a personal standpoint I had to visualize in applications all that we know of Nazi subjugation: see myself in

bondage, or before their firing squads, see my wife sold into their broth-
els, my family murdered, or scattered to the ends of the earth; the land
I love visited upon by rapine and famine and enduring a bondage the cost
of which could only be repaid in the future centuries.

Although Everson argued that once the question was stated in
these terms his first impulse was to "seize arms and fight to the last
ragged edges of endurance," upon reflection he realized that the
final worth of a people is not determined by later generations
according to their physical accomplishments but rather by "the
character and the quality evidenced within the way it meets the
prime ends of life, by the scope of its conceptual awareness of the
fundamental issues involved in the existence of humankind in a
chaotic universe, and by the tenacity of soul with which it adheres
to those concepts." The values of Greek civilization survived
Roman conquest, he continued, and indeed triumphed, "for they
were accepted at last by the men who called themselves the con-
querors of the world, and have persisted through the enormous
welter of war and confusion from that day to this."

I saw that the highest things my people purported to be fighting for were
the things that could not be won on the field of battle, and could not be
lost on it: that only the outer forms of these things could be won or lost;
their essences remain unchanged in the shiftings of victory or defeat, and
only those who have earned them in their souls possess them. . . . The
men who stir a hundred million people to hate are unable to stir one soul
to love. Their own fires consume them, as the fires of all the long-gone
wars have consumed those who set them, or consumed their children, or
their children's children. Who can read the past, can read the future; and
the wars of the future, when the B19 is a midget, and the 5,000 dead in
the shambles of London, and the 8,000 dead in the shambles of Cologne
are a mere pinch in the heaps of the shattered slain—such a one, in the
mutual anguish of his soul, is more than willing to accept upon his flesh
and in his blood whatever the sacrifices necessary to bring peace to the
earth, and to bring it now.

Therefore, Everson concluded, while the world would more than likely suffer for the moment were America to pull out of the war, in the long run its suffering would not be in vain—"we may even die, but our ideals and our concepts would not die, and the men of the future would say: here was finally a people in all the bloody past who loved peace too much to fight for it." He would not, in short, modify his stance. Certainly today, given the historical hindsight of the revelations of Dachau, Auschwitz, and Belsen, his position seems perhaps naive, yet it is lyrically argued and obviously deeply felt. His local draft board, under pressure to fill new quotas, was sufficiently convinced, even though the argument did not rely on an established religious approach to the problem, to uphold his classification. And thus on January 8, 1943, Everson received his "Order to Report for Work of National Importance."

When France fell to Hitler in 1940, America had instituted its draft. In response, the three historic "peace churches"—the Quakers, the Church of the Brethren, and the Mennonites—joined with various other pacifist organizations to found an umbrella group called the National Council of Religious Objectors (NCRO). At this time the government was in the process of dismantling the CCC, and it soon became apparent that a program of a similar type might be useful in dealing with the CO problem. Where in the CCC the responsibility for the camps was divided between the Forest Service (which ran the work projects) and the Army Reserve (which oversaw administration), under the new Civilian Public Service (CPS) the daily camp administration (termed "overhead") would be picked up by the NCRO, which ensured civilian control. Funding the camps fell to the NCRO and thus as the war progressed whenever the government had problems with the CO situation, it could not interfere directly but had to negotiate with the umbrella religious organization. Obviously, some COs, including Everson, objected to being affiliated with a religious body in this way, though until later in the war there were really few other options for men designated IV-E, conscientious objectors to both combatant and noncombatant military service.

By the end of 1941, about 25 CPS camps had been established

across the country, a number which increased to 67 by the end of the war. Between 1941 and 1947, the camps held 11,950 COs, all working primarily on tasks which had previously been the province of the CCC—tree planting and soil erosion, firefighting, and trail clearing in their generally rural settings. Additionally, about 500 COs volunteered for medical experiments, while another 2,000 worked in mental hospitals. Three of these camps were situated in Oregon: Camp Number 21 at Cascade Locks (which opened December 5, 1941), Camp Number 56 at Waldport (opened October 24, 1942), and Camp Number 59 at Elkton (opened November 7, 1942). Like the other camps, these three were charged primarily with forest reclamation work, projects that were overseen by both the Forest Service and the Oregon and California Revested Lands Administration.

Everson's "Order to Report for Work of National Importance" instructed him to report to the Fresno draft board for his papers and transportation to Camp 56 at Waldport at 2 p.m. on the 16th. According to the document, "willful failure" to do so would subject him to a fine and imprisonment. Attached to this notice was a note explaining that he would be expected to leave Fresno the following day. An enclosure outlined "supplementary instruction for campers": a description of the project, an explanation of camp financing (including the fact that "the individual camper is asked to give his services to the project without compensation"), and a description of clothes and linen to be taken to the camp by the CO. Everson remembered in a later letter to Edwa their last morning together—her packing his suitcase, his waving goodbye to her from a rear window of the Greyhound as it pulled out of Fresno on the 17th: "As the bus rounded the corner you stood on the curb looking across the car, and I shall never forget your face. It was swollen with grief. The wind had scattered your hair, and you were staring into my passing bus as if your very life depended on that one last glimpse. Though the passengers must have gaped I stumbled out of my seat and half-fell over an old man to wave my hand at the glass; in a second, in less than a second, you were gone."

Actually, in the confusion of the Fresno station where Everson and Edwa sat in silence pondering their separation, neither heard the call for the bus to Oregon, and thus Everson was forced to take a later departure. This meant both that the administration at Waldport had to be notified of the delay and that rather than traveling with fellow COs he had to make his way north without like company. When the bus arrived at San Francisco and he had to make a transfer, Everson again became confused, missed his connection, and finally was forced to stay overnight in Berkeley with Lee and Milicent Watkins. The next day Watkins got him on the right bus, and he finally arrived at Waldport on January 21, a day late.

The trip was hard. Besides the missed connections and confusions, the weather was bad all along the coast. Once in Waldport, he realized he had overshot the camp by four miles and telephoned for a ride in. As he wrote Edwa that night,

I must have stood about there, being eyed, for about two hours, when a closed-in pick-up, the laundry-wagon type, came up. It was full of new arrivals being driven to the doctor, and I was taken along. We spent the afternoon at the doctor's, a residence and office combined, though the exam took only a few minutes. Then we headed for camp, picking up my box on the way, which had come in earlier, and pulled into the place about dark. Supper was about to begin so we hustled into the mess-hall, and had a very good meal. Everyone was seated when I walked in, and necks were craned. And it was certainly an unusual gathering. The faces were largely of the plain, placid farm-boy type, with beards and off-style hairdos noticeable, but here and there a fine brow, or nose, or a sensitive mouth. Some of the men seem to be of a very high type, and many are the simple fervently religious. I had to stand up and be introduced.

After dinner, he was given two blankets, sheets, a pillow, a sewing kit, and a Bible. He was shown to his bunk, then asked to see the Camp Director for a consultation.

On his first meeting, Everson found the Director, Richard C. Mills, to be "calm, sane, intelligent, considerate, and sympathetic." Like other camp directors, Mills himself was actually a drafted CO. He had taken administrative training at the Brethren Service Committee's special school at Elgin, Illinois, and was afterwards posted to Cascade Locks. When Waldport opened, he was sent down as Director, along with a crew to set up the camp. During their conversation, Everson told Mills of his hope that he might be returned to his farm where perhaps he would be of more value to the country, and Mills was sympathetic. Still, regarding COs, the government was not known for a particularly wise policy of labor distribution. A high proportion of men in the CPS camps had either professional or technical training, and yet the work offered them was largely unskilled. Thus a typical trail crew at Waldport might include a machinist, a lawyer, a farmer, and an engineer. There had been talk of allowing those COs whose occupations in civilian life might be crucial to leave the camps very early on, and Mills responded with a glimmer of hope. He explained that although no work furloughs were to be granted from the CPS until they were also granted from the Army, this might happen in the future. Generally, however, he was pessimistic about the possibility of early release, and Everson returned to his bunk depressed, wrote his letter to Edwa (he would write her a letter, and sometimes two, almost every day through the year), and drifted off to sleep. That night a rare snow fell, "the most snow in the chronology of the white man hereabouts."

▼▼▼

During the next few days Everson remained depressed, feeling as though he were sleepwalking through a new phase of his life. He took some solace in getting to know a few of his fellow COs, including Harold Hackett and Glen Coffield, both of whom became for a time good friends. Everson felt early on that Hackett had "the most penetrating mind, aesthetically," of the group. Younger than Everson, he too had an interest in both poetry and criticism, and more importantly was also a devotee of the poet's master, Robinson Jeffers.

It was Coffield, though, who was the most intriguing. He reminded Everson of "a bearded Poe, being high browed, wide-eyed, or rather wide-set eyed, with no cheek bones." Coffield was from Missouri, had gone to college, and wrote poetry. He "talked South, not rich drawling South or Oklahoma whang, but a kind of clipped utterance with a suggestion of nasal." And he was charismatic, as Everson related to Edwa on January 29:

In his absence the whole barracks got talking about him. Everyone stands in awe of him, and when his exploits are summed up it makes for something incredible. I admit this is largely fostered by his rank and uncombed beard, his shock of hair, and his incredibly ragged clothes. He has, I hear, a masters degree. He was a "little All-American" in football. He won second place in a national American Legion contest on Peace. He appeared on the radio program Hobby-Lobby with a home-made musical instrument. He walked 300 miles to his first CPS camp. He never complains, though he bears privations that would floor most men. He is also a basketball star, and the boys have organized a team on the spur of the moment and are, without practice, playing the Coast Guard at Waldport tonight. Coffield with his beard and head of hair is going to be a riot, especially if he's good.

The camp itself was situated just off Highway 1 between Waldport and Yachats. Surrounded by forest on three sides, it fronted a series of tourist cottages and a house which was rented in the summer by vacationers, and which in turn led down to a beach and the ocean. In the center of the camp was a large patch of ground that turned to mud in the winter. To the north stood four dormitory buildings, a laundry, and two garages; to the east, the mess hall, and to the west, a recreation hall; to the south, a combination chapel and music room, a supply building, the foreman's quarters, the infirmary, and the library. The dormitories themselves had 38 beds in groups of two along each extended wall, with a single locker allotted to each CO. Additionally, each dormitory had its own showers, dressing room, sinks, and toilets, which sat exposed, side by side.

The American Legion had brought pressure on the Selective Service Administration to ensure that no CO would "slouch." In devising the general daily camp schedule, the Administration used the army as a model, giving the CO six primary duties: he was required to remain in camp or with his unit at all times unless on authorized leave, he was required to accept transfer orders, he was required to perform his assigned tasks "promptly and efficiently," he was responsible for protecting the government property assigned to him, he was expected to keep both himself and his bed and clothing "neat and clean," and his behavior at all times was to be of a quality that would "bring no discredit to the individual or the organization." Further, the Administration required that all COs in CPS camps work at least as many hours as civilian government employees, a requirement that began at 40 in 1941 and increased to 54 by the end of 1943. Generally, Everson would rise at 6:30 a.m. to a "melodious chiming occasioned by the beating on some hanging rail-road irons," eat breakfast at 7, and be to his project of the day within an hour. The crew carried their lunches with them, returning to camp at about 5 p.m., with dinner at 6.

Evenings were usually free for letter writing, reading (though lighting in the dormitories was poor), conversation, and occasional social activities, like the monthly "birthday banquets" for everyone whose birthday fell within a particular month. At these events, a special dinner would be served, followed by speeches and sometimes a party for all the COs. At the first Everson attended, there were "dull group songs of the hail hail the gang's all here sort." But then the evening picked up as Coffield gave a dramatic reading of Vachel Lindsay's *The Congo*, followed by a scene out of Christopher Isherwood's Berlin, a dance by one of the camp's homosexuals dressed in drag. "For one in the know about these matters it was really a treat," Everson wrote Edwa after the gathering, "but to most of these boys who had no conception of the nature of such people it was merely a good impersonation. When the 'dancer' was announced, and the door swung open, and we beheld the beauty standing in the gloom of the entrance, I really thought the boys had brought in a woman. 'She' was perfectly made up, with a white satin gown, and showed a tantalizing bit of thigh—only a short-cropped head of hair, under a fake wig, gave 'her' away."

The daily project work load was taxing, and from his arrival Everson worked six days a week, "rain or shine." For the first few days he worked in the back hill country clearing trails; the land was in very poor shape due to earlier intensive logging. By the end of January, he was working on the "rock-crusher" crew, loading rocks on a cart which was then sent on rails to a pulverizing machine. Sledge hammering the rocks into manageable size was tiring, and the bad weather didn't help much—"a steady cold wind, with intermittent rains. My legs," he wrote Edwa, "got wet, my hands cold, my gloves soaked." Rain gear was sold at the camp, but pants and a hat cost $4, about two month's allowance. So he went without. On February 2, he sent Edwa the draft of a new poem called "The Internment (Rock Crusher)," which began

> To sunder the rock—that is our day.
> In the unstrong light,
> Under high fractured cliffs,
> We turn with our hands the raw granite.
> We break it with iron;
> Under that edge it suffers reduction.
> Harsh, dense and resistant,
> The obdurate portions flaw and divide.

The rock-crusher work was traditional prison employment, which must have pleased certain of the local American Legionnaires. Still, as Everson worked alongside both Hackett and Coffield, conversation was a balm.

By February, he had begun to adjust to CPS life. Edwa's letters came a bit more regularly (though both the slowness of the mails and her reluctance to write every day continued to plague him); there were new arrivals in camp; also, the poet was corresponding fairly often with both Powell and Henry Miller, who was a friend of Powell's. Besides the obvious sense of contact with a larger literary milieu that the letters from Powell and Miller must have engendered, both also kept Everson supplied with reading material. Powell provided him with a treasure, a paperbound, uncut edition of Baudelaire's poetry, while Miller sent in rapid order a rough draft of his first book review (of Walter Lowrie's *A Short Life of Kierkegaard*), a copy of Dane Rudhyar's *The Faith That Gives Meaning to Victory* (another of Rudhyar's books, *Astrology of Personality*, was included on his "The Hundred Books That Influenced Me Most" list), and most importantly, an issue of *View*, which "is now flabbergasting everyone in camp." *View* was a surrealist/anarchist literary journal edited by the poet Charles Henri Ford, publishing such writers as André Breton, Parker Tyler, and the fifteen-year-old Philip Lamantia. Obviously a magazine of weight and influence, *View* excited Coffield, Hackett, and others both because of its aesthetic and political stance and because of their own current publishing project.

Camp Waldport had an official newsletter, which was called the *Tide*. Appearing more or less monthly, it functioned as a low-budget, mimeographed *Stars and Stripes*, carrying whatever camp news could be presented in a non-controversial, inoffensive light. The February 1943 issue, for example, began with a brief article on "Religion in Camp," continued with reports of various activities, contained a generic "Dear Mom" letter ("A few weeks ago we had a swell snow. . . . Some of the fellows from California had never seen snow fall before"), a poem called "this death?" by Coffield, Everson's poem "Clouds," and notes on new internees, among other material. It was edited by C. R. Bunyan and E. Groff, with Kemper Nomland doing the composition. A year's subscription cost 75¢, and the *Tide* billed itself as "an unbiased, factual news organ, a bond between the various camps, and a source of information to constituents and friends of CPS."

Coffield, Hackett, and Larry Seimons (a sculptor) established a clandestine newsletter just before Everson's arrival to run counter to the *Tide*, with the motto "What is not *Tide* is *Untide*," and they soon courted Everson to contribute. In late January, their weekly mimeographed newsletter, *Untide*, ran the poet's "Coast Thought" from *San Joaquin*, and on February 2 he informed Edwa that they would print his "pacifist poems as a series, I think. At least Coffield sounds favorable." Between February 13 and March 27 the *Untide* published seven of Everson's "War Elegies" as loose, unpaginated inserts.

Although it was common knowledge in the camp who was working on the operation, no one knew who authored particular pieces and all were run without bylines (as opposed to the *Tide*, which required that all "opinionated articles" be signed). An issue would be written and assembled by various hands during the week, printed on the camp mimeograph machine late Saturday night, and distributed Sunday. Generally, Everson's role in the *Untide* was limited to his poetry contributions, a few drawings, and helping with the mimeographing. As he wrote Edwa, "Helped get the *Untide* out last night. Enclose a copy. I drew the picture of Seimons, goldbrick of the week. Also helped on some of the Alphabet, but not all. That's all I had my hand in this week." Then four days later he "drifted around to where the boys were meeting last night on the sheet. I have a pretty good relationship with them now. I'm not asked to meet with them, yet I always somehow help to get out each issue. A sort of casual interchange that I can fit to suit myself, and one that I like."

The publication of the *Untide*, Everson would recall in a 1977 interview, was "kind of a game. No one was hurt much by it; it was more entertainment than anything else. It wasn't as if it were really undermining anything. But the value it proved for us was that it got us working on our own and not through official camp channels like the *Tide*." Still, the game was not without its frictions. While at times Everson agreed with Edwa's assessment that the whole project was rather juvenile, he did feel that it filled an important need:

Here, where great tensions exist, the articles have a breathing and living quality because they epitomize very sore relations here between Forestry and CPS. The lead article is the counter-action against the current philosophy among some of the more sincere boys of actually trying to plant more trees for the good of the world. I'm not in sympathy with this aspect of *Untide*, but I love its unrelinquished grasp on its right to criticism, and I enjoy its cracks. The article on the editorial page hits harder. When *Trees, 4-F* came out last issue, Forestry really went up in the air. We had been planting trees that we knew would die and there was a hell of a stink among the fellows. *Trees, 4-F* was a joke, of course, but the forestry, stupid and a bit guilty, took it otherwise. It so happened that according to local repute the trees did not die of a disease but of natural conditions. The Forestry took this slight advantage to drag a herring across the trail, and over-emphasize the detail. The Forestry Director told the workers committee only a "diseased mind" could write such an article. Hence this editorial's very adroit way of correcting its mistake but glibly turning the point. Hackett did it.

And there were internal frictions as well. When Everson sauntered into one evening meeting of the staff in mid-March after working on a poem, he discovered Seimons harshly criticizing a number of Coffield's articles to the group in "the wrong tone, and Coffield blew up—his whiskers bristled all over the room!" On that occasion Hackett acted as peacemaker, and finally managed to defuse the argument. But over the next few months there were more agitated confrontations, especially between Coffield and Seimons. These episodes, however, can probably be attributed as much to a combination of overwork and close quarters as to any profound political or aesthetic disagreements. In any case, the *Untide* continued to appear, though at times irregularly, through the summer. And despite Edwa's misgivings, Everson thought enough of the newsletter to send copies to Powell, Miller, and other correspondents, as well as to continue to send a copy of each issue to his wife. When his friend Ham Tyler offered in a letter his opinion that the *Untide* "is certainly a superb little paper," adding that he thought Everson was "very fortunate in having your poetry in what is certainly the most 'advanced' periodical in the country," the poet forwarded Edwa the comment with the notation, "so there!"

Of more importance, however, was the publishing operation that emerged from the newsletter and in which Everson played a major role, the Untide Press. The *Untide*'s serial publication of Everson's "War Elegies" during March was well-received, stirring interest among COs at other camps, especially Cascade Locks, and thus Coffield, Everson, Nomland, and others decided to expand the newsletter's province into chapbook publication. Their first item was ready by April 1 and priced at only ten cents a copy; the Press already had orders for more than its first run of 100—Everson's *X War Elegies*, with illustrations by Nomland. The 20-page pamphlet was mimeographed and silk-screened by Everson and others, then stapled (publication was delayed over a week while the COs attempted to get hold of enough staples to complete the binding), and proved so popular that another 900 copies were produced and distributed by the end of the year. Everson attributed this reception to Nomland's rather avant-garde illustrations as much as to the poetry. The *X War Elegies*, he remembered, was not only the first Untide Press book but "the one that scored. I mean it went all through the camps. We sold hundreds and hundreds of copies. We got out a first edition . . . and then we began cranking out new editions. It began to go out and be reviewed in the secular milieu. And this is where the energy source began to pour out of Waldport, and not only the literary material, but the artistic material. Nomland's illustrations were better received than my poems were. So it was a kind of one-two thing." Certainly the Press drew attention to the literary and artistic energies of Waldport in a focused way.

The running of the Press, like the running of the *Untide* and a number of the camp's other CO projects, was essentially a group effort, fully democratic, with a symbolic leader. Coffield took a great interest in the enterprise, and in fact the Press's second book was his twelve-page *Ultimatum* (which he wrote, illustrated, designed, mimeographed, and stapled by himself for publication in July), while its third volume was again a Coffield item; both Everson and Charles Davis participated in the design and production of *The Horned Moon*, published in February 1944. With the reception of *X War Elegies* Everson certainly could have taken a very strong hand in shaping the direction of the Press, but he chose not to, preferring simply to have one voice among others in the spirit of cooperation. So the process was one of group agreement, with Coffield often holding center stage in the discussion. The project proved successful enough that the men purchased a larger press, paid for through working at various odd jobs on local farms during their free time. Everson, who had for a time installed septic tanks on the farms around Selma, was able to find that work nearby and contributed his pay to the general fund for the press. The whole process worked well for about three years, through the publication of eight volumes, until a serious quarrel erupted over the production of Kenneth Patchen's *An Astonished Eye Looks Out of the Air.*

During these months work on the production of *X War Elegies* preoccupied Everson, though he was involved in other concerns as well. He made plans, now realizing the essential impossibility of early release, to have Edwa travel up to visit him during the summer. He sent poems to a few magazines, though they summarily rejected his work. He began to give occasional readings of his poetry at camp gatherings, and led a few discussions with a small group composed primarily of the *Untide* staff on the state of modern poetry. Numerous speakers passed through the camp, and these also held his interest. For example, on March 20 Mary Fugurhason, a former Washington State Senator who resigned because she was a pacifist, addressed the group gathered for the monthly birthday celebration. As Everson wrote Edwa, "It was a discussion group, and we got into our problems. I should have said she was now a secretary for the FOR (Fellowship of Reconciliation), a pacifist organization. I think I told you how Selective Service had made vague provision for money earned by CPS men, and how FOR had delivered an ultimatum. . . . The speaker didn't know much but everyone blew off and got worked up." Further, there was the daily crew work, with thousands of trees to be planted by May; at times this produced a certain amount of tension, as in the April 2 incident Everson described to Edwa revolving around his friend Hackett: "Hackett and three others were planting far behind us—kind of lagged back—when Leper the forestry overseer went down and told them to go into camp, that as far as he was concerned they were R.T.W. (Refused to Work). Hackett, being what he is, took an obdurate stand." His point was that under an agreement between the Workers Committee and the Forestry Service, members of the Forestry Service could not involve themselves in matters of discipline. Hackett refused to go back to camp, and the whole question was sent to the Workers Committee, of which Everson was a member.

In the more democratic camps like Waldport, matters concerning overhead were resolved through group consensus. When conflicts over projects arose, however, the situation became more problematic as these matters involved the Forest Service. Earl Kosbab, who had come with one of the first groups of campers from Wahalla, Michigan, brought with him the idea of a Workers Committee to act as a liaison between the COs and the Forest Service supervisors. Kosbab asked Everson to draft a proposal for the committee to be presented to both Mills and other administrators, Everson's first real attempt at polemic. He argued in his document for the "principle of limitation"; that is, he admitted that the COs had absolutely no power over their own lives while in the camp, attempting to convince the supervisors that the imperative was not ethical, but rather practical. The pitch was simply that such a committee would reduce conflicts and thus raise morale, which would mean more output. Further, Everson argued that for the COs to handle their own discipline problems would simplify the administration's task, and have a greater measure of success in resolving problems as they were an elected body.

Matters were complicated further by the fact that Mills's original crew from Cascade Locks had taken all the overhead positions, which during the rainy winter were the optimum jobs. As the weather improved, the men asked Mills to assign them to project work so that they might enjoy the outdoors, with the promise of reassignment to overhead when the cold weather returned. These men and Mills were fairly close friends, which caused a certain resentment among the other COs, though they comprised a first-rate work crew. Neither Everson nor Kosbab wanted to challenge either Mills or his key men at the start, but rather through their Workers Committee plan hoped to open up a few of the lower-level overhead jobs, for Mills was a committed liberal and thus really couldn't stand in the way of such a committee, though he felt uneasy with the erosion of his control. Still, Everson's proposal so impressed him with its argument that he not only accepted the plan, but even sent copies of the document to other camps as a model for such action. For his part, Kosbab was not overjoyed at the implication that the CO community was in fact powerless on its own, but he accepted Everson's approach as tactically correct.

Aside from the excitement of the Press, Everson was also starting to cool a bit on the camp. Following a confrontation with a supervisor, Hackett was given a job in camp landscaping the grounds, and thus he and Everson began to see much less of each other. Everson allowed that this situation "was for the best. He has a stinging wit, and he pulls no punches, which is sometimes painful. Both of us have rather strong personalities, and they sometimes clash." Hackett seems to have toned down his once great admiration for Everson's poetry, perhaps because he wrote poetry himself and felt that Everson was getting too much attention. Yet at the same time, Everson retained his strong affection for the younger man. During these months members of an arts committee of COs from Cascade Locks spent time on a work exchange at

Waldport, and while they were there some put pressure on both Everson and Hackett to return with them. "There are some advantages," Everson outlined to his wife. "Proximity to Portland in case you get free (27 miles). A multigraph. Reputedly a good bunch of fellows. Hackett's against it, and I won't go unless he does. I mean I don't think I'd find anyone there that would be better than he." Still, Everson was attracted to the idea as he became progressively less stimulated by camp life, feeling "that the fellows are 'just folks,' and I'm retiring more and more into myself." When the Director informed him of the near impossibility of such a move, however, he gave up on the idea. In late April, when Cascade Locks' unofficial magazine, *The Illiterati*, appeared (and included poems by both Coffield and himself), Everson felt protective enough of his own group to write Edwa that the rival to the *Untide* was a "rather pretentious thing. . . . Personally, though I *may* be prejudiced, I think the Waldportites rather ran off with the honors. So much of the others are flashy, but thin." As an interesting footnote, this first issue of *The Illiterati*, which reprinted Everson's first two "War Elegies" from the *Untide*, was soon confiscated and destroyed by the United States Postal Service as a pornographic publication because of Kemper Nomland's sketch of a reclining female nude.

During these late spring months, Everson wrote little poetry, but he caught up on his reading, devouring books like Gide's *The Counterfeiters* (which he thought a completely realized, "fine piece of work"), Huxley's *Point Counter-Point* (which he felt was stolen from Gide), Eliot's *Four Quartets*, and Hawthorne's *The Scarlet Letter*. Of the last, almost prescient of his own looming fate, he wrote Edwa:

My biggest objection is that—however well the moral problem is handled, and surely the life of it depends on the ramifications of that morality, exhibited as they reflect and interact through every department of the people's lives—but biggest objection is to the fact that the sexual situation, and it is really upon this situation that the crux of the book is hinged, is never explored. The sin is remote and abstract. The interacting rhythm of affection and violation, attraction and revulsion, love and hate, tenderness and jealousy, never occur. There is only the concept of Sin, and the human problem turns only on that.

Wives were allowed to come to the camp for visitation, and during the summer of the first year Edwa traveled to Waldport and took one of the cabins just across the road. She was allowed to eat her meals, along with the other wives, in the common mess with the COs. Everson spent nights with her in the cabin, and she stayed most of the summer. Though continuing to work on various publishing projects, as well as his normal crew work and the Workers Committee, obviously Everson spent most of his free time during these weeks with his wife.

But the situation was not exactly an idyllic one. A few months earlier, Hackett had taken a furlough to Los Angeles, and Everson had suggested that he stop in Selma to see Edwa. When Edwa got wind of this plan, she fired back a letter asking where Hackett would sleep, as they had only one bed. Everson wrote that of course Hackett should sleep with her; he inexplicably explained that "Hackett is my friend. Take him into your bed." So when Hackett went down to Selma, and the inevitable occurred, she later blamed the whole incident on Everson. Thus, when she arrived at Waldport, she walked into a difficult scenario; her motivation for the trip seems to have been to pick up on this relationship with Hackett as much as anything else. For his part, Hackett was interested also in pursuing their affair, but he didn't want to get involved in a sticky situation. Obviously, this greatly widened the breach which was growing between Everson and Hackett, so the younger man backed off more or less completely, refusing to spend any time with Edwa at all. When the day came for her to return to Selma, as she and Everson sat alongside the road waiting for the bus, Hackett approached, but then stood for a time further down the highway. He waved at Edwa, but she wasn't looking and Everson waved back. His expression fell, and he sauntered back to camp. Not long after her return to Selma, Edwa attempted to rekindle the affair, writing Hackett that while she could "assimilate a surface stoicism," she wanted to spend time with him. "If, at Christmas, I came to camp and you should feel it necessary to leave during that time, I should feel foul, indeed. If this is so, I shall not come. Whatever I may have said on this, before, I retract. My purpose would be purely to overcome loneliness—the groceryman and the school children are no conversants and I have no friends." Hackett did not reply.

On September 21, Everson got his first furlough to go down and harvest his crop. This was not, however, his first leave, as earlier in May as a member of the Workers Committee he had been allowed to attend the Northwest CPS Conference in Portland for two days. He left for Selma at 5 p.m. on the second by bus with the poet Jim Harmon (later editor of the literary journal *Ark*), who had offered to go down with him and help pick the grapes. On the trip south the men met, as Everson related to David Meltzer, Theodore Dreiser on the bus:

Harmon and I got leave to go down to San Francisco. We took the coast stage south to Marshfield where we had to lay over in order to pick up the Portland bus southbound for San Francisco the next morning.

As we boarded the bus in Marshfield I noticed a man who seemed familiar. I said to myself, "That man looks like Theodore Dreiser." Harmon said it couldn't be, but Jeffers had spoken of Dreiser as a "tough old mastodon," and that's just the way this character looked. Hulking shoulders. Slack jaws. Strangely inattentive eyes that missed nothing. Even in his photographs his configuration was unmistakable.

During the war the bus travel was simply awful. In order to save rubber the law held their schedule down to thirty-five miles an hour, but the drivers went like hell between stops and waited at the next depot for time to catch up. So we had plenty of opportunity to look each other over.

At Gold Beach, Oregon, we pulled in for lunch. By this time I was sure it was Dreiser. As Harmon and I got ready to sit down Harmon forgot about lunch and followed the man into the lavatory. He came right out as if he'd really found gold on that beach. "It's him!" he exclaimed excitedly. "It's Dreiser, all right. Come on!"

Even as I got up I had my misgivings but curiosity got the better of judgment. Dreiser was standing at the urinal relieving himself, and not knowing what else to do I began to talk. I had never read any of his books, so I began with us. It was a fatal mistake.

"Mr. Dreiser," I began, "we're two poets on furlough from a camp in Waldport. We are going down to San Francisco. We hope to meet some of the other writers there and renew our acquaintance with the literary scene . . ."

Dreiser looked at me and I suddenly discovered I had nothing more to say. He slowly buttoned his fly, and as he turned to wash his hands, he said two words with extreme irony: "So what!"

Then he started in. Ripping a paper towel from the rack, he crumbled it in those fearsome hands and proceeded with contempt. "There are thousands of you. You crawl about the country from conference to literary conference. You claim to be writers, but what do you ever produce? Not one of you will amount to a goddamn. You have only the itch to write, nothing more . . . the insatiable itch to express yourself. Everywhere I go I run into you, and I'm sick of you. The world is being torn apart in agony, crying out for the truth, the terrible truth. And you . . ." He paused and his voice seemed to suddenly grow weary. "You have nothing to say."

I turned to go. Harmon was already gone. Opening the door into the restaurant, I looked back to let him know how sorry I was that I had accosted him, but I couldn't open my mouth. Then Dreiser stepped past me as if I had opened the door only for him. For a moment the contempt seemed to fade from his face and a kind of geniality gleamed there. "Well," he said, "take it easy. It lasts longer that way." Then he was gone.

Not really gone. His seat was ahead of ours, and we had already noticed that he was traveling with a young woman. After Gold Beach, aware of our presence behind him, he kept stiffly aloof, conversing with her circumspectly. But far down the coast, at the end of the long hot afternoon, when everyone was collapsed with fatigue, she could stand it no longer. Reaching out her hand she stroked with tender fondness the balding head. Dazed with exhaustion he accepted it gratefully until he remembered us. Suddenly thrashing his head like a mastodon caught redhanded in a pterodactyl's nest he flung the hand from him. She never tried that again.

Harmon stayed with the Eversons for about a week, then returned to San Francisco to continue his furlough. Both men were expected to report back to Waldport on September 22. During Everson's remaining days on the farm, little was said of the Hackett situation, and although the two of them seemed to get along fine, the poet sensed a certain distance in Edwa.

For the first weeks after his return to camp, Everson did not write Edwa quite so frequently, but moved back into his camp work routine, finding energy to get back to work on his poetry. For a time, he got interested in translation, especially from Rimbaud and Verlaine. He read no French, but had a friend named Bob Walker take the original poems and translate them into a very literal English, then working with a dictionary Everson worked on syntax and diction. On October 17, he sent Edwa his only translation that survives; never before published, it is of "Le Mal":

> While the red spewing of the shot
> Whistle all day through the infinity of the blue sky,
> While, scarlet or green, near to the king who rallies them,
> Flow the batallions en masse into the fire;
>
> While a terrible madness crushes
> And makes of a hundred thousand men a steaming pile;
> —Poor dead! in the summer, in the grass, in thy joy,
> Nature! O thou who made these men holy!—
>
> There is a God, who laughs at the damask cloths,
> At the altars, at the incense, at the great chalices of gold;
> Who in the lulling of hosannas falls asleep
> And wakes when the mothers, crouching
> In their agony, and weeping beneath their old black bonnet,
> Proffer him a fat penny tied up in their rag!

Everson called this the "most terrific anti-war poem I've ever seen."

Soon after Everson returned to camp, Edwa was in serious difficulty. Selma was a typically conservative Central Valley California town, and the owners of the ranch on which the two rented their house moved to evict her. The spring before, her job as a teacher had been in jeopardy because of Everson's internment, but teachers at that point were scarce and the school board realized the fact that his CO status was confirmed by the government. Now, however, as she faced eviction, she lost her teaching post. Edwa went into a grave depression, as she moved in first with her father-in-law. That lasted just two days. He had asked her how many War Bonds she had purchased, and when she replied none, true to form he told her to leave immediately. Next she went across town to a small rooming house, putting their belongings in storage. When she wrote Everson of these events, he assumed his CO stance was the cause, put in for emergency leave, and traveled again down to Fresno. When he arrived the truth of the situation came out.

Just six weeks after he originally left Selma in January, Edwa had begun an affair with a mutual friend, Kenneth Carothers. Within just a month after Everson's leaving the farm, Carothers had shown up on Edwa's doorstep. "Came home early and walked in to find Kenny," Edwa had written him in February. "I couldn't have asked for much better. A different Kenny, thin and pale and very nervous. The astounding news is that he's out of the Army for good!" It seems as if Carothers had some sort of mental breakdown and was sent to the psychiatric ward of the base hospital, spending three weeks in isolation. He was discharged, finally, as a homosexual, though he wasn't. "He is badly shattered," Edwa continued. "Anyway we talked until three this morning when he left taking your bicycle to use while here. Came out for dinner tonight. . . . In my selfish way I had hoped to see him frequently but his mother doesn't think it proper for him to visit me alone here." And as it turned out, Carother's mother's objection was well-founded, as was hinted in Edwa's letter two days later: "Had dinner with Carothers and Mrs. Moore at their place last night. Not planned—accidentally. Afterwards we headed for a show but Kenny can't sit still two minutes and we got up and left after 20 minutes or so. Came out here but he starts shaking, can't stand to be inside so we went walking. Miles of it. I feel so sorry for him for he's so obviously all mixed up. I guess our mutual lowness led us into frank discussions." Their talk, she concludes mysteriously, was "franker than it should have been. I should imagine he regrets his part too."

It is apparent through the year's correspondence that Everson sensed something was wrong, but first he thought it was simply the separation, then the brief affair with Hackett. During the summer the two spent together at the camp, Edwa hadn't let on anything about this situation; neither had she spoken about it while he was home on furlough. Now, just after his arrival, the two drove to see acquaintances in the evening in Sanger, a small farming town a few miles from Selma, and Everson talked animatedly about his friends to cheer her up. He asked, jokingly, if his old buddy Carothers was still a virgin. No, replied Edwa in a somber voice with her eyes down, and suddenly she began to cry. The whole story came flowing out—how she had been so lonely and depressed and overworked, and how she had turned, at first innocently, to Carothers for comfort—taking Everson, amazingly, completely by surprise.

He was the only one in the community who was surprised, however. It turned out that the affair was common knowledge, and in fact both the eviction and Edwa's loss of her job were not so much the result of Everson's internment, but rather the fact that she was being ostracized by the townspeople for her open relationship with Carothers. Obviously, Everson was shocked, but instead of leaving her, he set about helping her to prepare to leave Selma for Berkeley. Their first move was to sell most of their possessions, which proved a difficulty. Much of their furniture and many appliances had been purchased years before, and now with the war these items were very dear. The government, however, had put a ceiling on prices, allowing nothing to be sold above its prewar price. They ran an ad in the paper announcing items for sale, which was legal; Edwa talked Everson into charging the going price for goods, though, which was not. So for about a week they operated what was essentially a black market out of a second-floor room above a store.

The stand of the CO has never been popular, and understand-ably when Everson went down on his first furlough, he was so embarrassed by his situation that he more or less stayed on the farm all the time, refusing to risk a trip into town. Finally, Edwa had mentioned to the grocer they had traded with for years that Everson was home, and he insisted on seeing him, so the CO ven-tured in. The grocer, who had remained a friend, told Everson that the townspeople were in fact not very sympathetic, yet they had mellowed somewhat because when his father was running for re-election as district Justice of the Peace he had publicly disavowed his son due to his CO status, and though he had won the election many people thought this unseemly. Still, Everson generally thought it best to remain clear of the town. On this second trip, however, he went with a different purpose—the knight errant off to defend his lady. Even after the revelation about Carothers, he felt that if the townspeople could vilify Edwa to such a degree, they weren't worth worrying about. And thus to a certain extent this second trip was a kind of liberation from the culture and the land he had been tied to so closely for the first thirty years of his life. The two moved about openly, even brazenly, in town until their things were finally sold. It took about a week to tie up the loose ends, then the pair drove to Berkeley, where Everson left Edwa with Watkins, and he returned to Waldport. By this time, Carothers himself had moved to Berkeley. His main occupation was gambling, and there was a lot of loose money among the ship-yard workers in the Bay Area. Soon, Edwa gravitated into that life.

vvvvvvvvvv
THREE
vvvvvvvvvv

The
Fine
Arts
Project

One of the most successful features of the CPS camps was the special "schools," which were instituted to allow men of similar interests and talents to pursue them in a communal situation. The first
of these was started in Wellston, Michigan, as a School for Co-
operative Living, administered primarily by the Brethren Service
Committee. Other groups included the Mennonite Farm and
Community School in Maryland, and later in the war a School of
Race Relations, a Latin-American Study School, a Psychiatry and
Christian Service School, and an Education Workshop, situated at
various locations across the country. Because they were financing
CPS, the NCRO was able to persuade the Selective Service to
allow men to transfer to these specialty camps, and saw to it that
needed supplies were provided. One of the earliest of these groups
was the Fine Arts Project, located at Waldport.

Early in 1944, Everson and other COs involved in the Untide
venture began to discuss the possibility of forming a center for the
arts at Santa Barbara, and Everson was asked to approach Mills

with the plan. Mills agreed, perhaps hoping to have a number of his more radical campers transfer out, but precisely for that reason the Director of the Santa Barbara camp decided against the proposal. Soon after, Everson wrote Morris Keaton, a man known as the "intellectual" of the Brethren Service Committee at Elgin, about the idea, and Keaton made a trip to Waldport to investigate such a possibility. After Keaton spoke with a number of COs, he approached Everson, telling him that while there was a large group interested in the project, they would only participate if Everson himself directed it. The poet at first declined, arguing that he wasn't an administrator and had no interest in such a post. That evening, however, a group of his artist friends approached him with the case that they wanted the project but didn't want to take a chance on getting someone unfamiliar from outside the camp to act as a director. Everson was the only logical choice, especially as he had essentially initiated the idea, and they told him that if he wouldn't take the directorship there would be no fine arts program.

In the meantime, however, Mills had to be convinced, and this task was left to Keaton. Mills was very dubious about the project; like the Santa Barbara director, he was nervous about drawing artists from all over the country into his own camp. By this time, though, Mills's power and influence had eroded greatly. First, there was talk in camp about his habit of inviting COs to sunbathe nude with him out in the brush. At one point, Dick Brown, a good mechanic and carpenter who came with Mills's original group, decided to build a boat. The notion was that the craft would provide the camp with fresh fish, and on that basis Brown was allowed full overhead hours to work on its building. When the project was finished and the boat was taken down to the beach, Everson went along to help with the launch. As the men waded into the water, Mills stripped down to the nude, and several men followed. Three women walking along the beach happened upon this scene and reported it to the Coast Guard. The surf was too high to launch the boat, and the group pulled it back to shore. By the time the

Coast Guard arrived most of the men had dressed, but Mills had remained naked and thus was arrested with another CO.

It was primarily this penchant for nudism which began to strain Mills's credibility. Further, throughout the spring Mills had made a speech after dinner at least once a week to the assembled camp, warning them that the government was going to close the CPS program and ship everyone to mental hospitals. The upshot of this was that most of his original crew from Cascade Locks eventually put in for transfers and left. Thus, Mills was fairly isolated from the rest of the camp when the question of the Fine Arts Project was broached, and when Keaton presented the program to him as a way of infusing his administration with a new vitality, he agreed to the proposal.

The idea of the Fine Arts Project was simple. It was to be a school and performance center where artists with IV-E status could locate. The plan was that there would be both writing and arts workshops, as well as provisions for serious concerts and theater. Once approved, the plan took a few months to put into operation. Everson wrote the promotional material and sent it with letters to all the camps. By early summer of 1944, men began transferring into Waldport from across the country. Kermit Sheets and Kemper Nomland, for example, took up permanent residence from Cascade Locks, and a large group came out from the East. Some men who wanted to come had difficulty getting transfers, and had to have someone already stationed at Waldport agree to give up his slot. Both Hackett and Coffield agreed to do this.

While both men liked the idea of the group in theory, when it came close to being opened each became wary of the influx of a large number of strangers. Further, Hackett was still uncomfortable with the strain on his relationship with Everson following the affair with Edwa. For his part, Coffield had had another very serious blow-up with Siemons. Siemons had gone into the town of Waldport to try to cultivate a friendship with David Hall, editor of the city newspaper. He had hoped to get free publicity from Hall for the arts project and the press, as well as a bargain on paper. Coffield was opposed to this as Hall had been hostile to the COs in his newspaper, *The Lincoln County Times*, and in fact Hall used Siemons's overtures as an opportunity to attack the camp. When flyers for *X War Elegies* had gone out, orders came flooding in. Some, however, were misaddressed to the "United Press," and delivered to Hall by mistake. He asked Siemons to get him a copy of the pamphlet, which he readily did, hoping to strengthen their friendship. When Hall read the poems, and realized that some of them had gone out to soldiers, he went into a tirade, lambasting the COs in the city paper for being traitors. He sent a copy of his article to Walter Winchell, who was doing nightly news reports on the radio. About a week later, as Coffield, Everson, and others were listening to Winchell's broadcast, suddenly they heard in his distinctively hysterical voice, "Portland Editor's Alert! Contact Dave Hall of Waldport to get the facts on strange doings by conscientious objectors. . . ." It was a trivial incident, and nothing further came of it, but it was enough to finally sour Coffield on Siemons to the extent that he offered to give up his place at Waldport to an interested artist from the East, and left to serve as a participant in a series of medical experiments. Thus, by the summer of 1944, both Hackett and Coffield passed out of Everson's life.

About this time Everson received a furlough, and he went to Berkeley to stay with Lee and Milicent Watkins, hoping to spend time with Edwa. She was living with Carothers not far from the Watkins home, and after Everson had been in town for a couple days the two of them went out to dinner. That evening Edwa stressed that she still loved him, and that if given time perhaps she could work through her attraction to Carothers. So Everson tried to remain as patient and supportive as possible, hoping that in fact she would return to him. On another evening Everson, Edwa, and Watkins all traveled into San Francisco to listen to a jazz concert. Toward the end of his furlough, one afternoon Everson worked up courage to try to see Edwa at her house, and having been warned by Watkins of a latch-key problem with the front door, he went around to the back to knock. As he passed by a window, he saw Carothers and Edwa in bed together asleep. He left hurriedly, and made no attempt to see her again before returning to camp.

Earlier, COs who worked on the Untide Press were not able to get credit from the Forest Service for the hours they invested. With the coming of the Fine Arts Project, however, and the leaving of most of Mills's original crew, many artists were able to get soft jobs on overhead. This was resented by a number of the other COs, and one of Everson's most important early tasks as Director of the program was to find ways to mitigate this situation. Harold Row, the head of the Brethren Service Committee, paid a visit to the camp to examine the program's progress. Row had in fact been to the camp the earlier July, and Everson had met him, forming a very low opinion. "At present Harold Row is here," he had written Edwa, "(head of BSC)—a contemptible man, a mealy-mouthed, double-talking, two-faced, weasel-worded son of a bitch. A veritable shit-heel." The next evening, Row had insisted on eating dinner with Everson and Coffield and the conversation turned vaguely to the possibility of some kind of arts camp. Row's position was that if it somehow could be justified it might be a possibility. Now, with the Fine Arts Camp realized, he was very supportive, having been impressed with Everson's argument that if the camps were to mean anything historically, most likely it would be because of their art. This time, as Everson and Row talked, the poet took a second measure of the man and did a complete about-face, admitting that while Row had a reputation as an authoritarian, in fact once he lent his support to a cause he could—unlike Mills, the avowed liberal—be fully trusted. Everson explained to Row the morale problem concerning the work assignments, and the administrator was sympathetic. He told Everson that such a problem seemed endemic to the special programs, that at first the whole camp would be supportive but little by little resentment would set in, with the charge of special privilege. He tried to comfort Everson by telling him that the Waldport situation was actually quite mild compared to what had happened at the School for Co-operative Living, where the camp came close to being shut down.

The prime season of the Fine Arts Project was between the summer of 1944 and the spring of 1945. It was not long after that the war was over and the men began to pour out of the camp. But during these months, there was a flourishing artists community at Waldport. Besides Nomland and Sheets, William Eshelman, a young printer, arrived, as did the painter Clayton James, the printer/artist Adrian Wilson, actors David Jackson, Martin Ponch, and Joe Gisterak, and violinist Broadus Earl, who would later found the New Music String Quartet. Publication by the Untide Press continued, and two important journals, *The Illiterati* and *The Compass*, made their ways into the camp. Most of the music and art from this period hasn't survived, though the theater group that began there after the war moved down to San Francisco to become the Interplayers, one of the West Coast's most important postwar theater companies.

As far as the camp was concerned, the most interesting event during this first summer was the arrival of the visionary painter Morris Graves. Clayton James had seen his work in New York in 1942, and he was overwhelmed by its mystical qualities. When James arrived at Waldport, one of his first acts was to approach Everson about the possibility of bringing Graves to Oregon. Interestingly, Graves had already passed through Everson's life in another more or less synergistic fashion. Kenneth Carothers had been drafted before Everson, and had been sent to Camp Roberts, California, to work as a secretary to the commander there. It was there that he had learned to gamble, playing poker with other soldiers, becoming something of a night owl. Very early in the draft Graves himself had refused induction when he was called up, and the authorities didn't really know how to handle it so they put him in the brig at Camp Roberts. They began a long process of attrition to break his will, but Graves resisted. Carothers got to know Graves, acting as a liaison between the commander and the painter. Finally, as Carothers later told Everson, his commander realized the ineffectuality of the imprisonment and decided to reclassify Graves 4-F, claiming he was obviously mentally unbalanced. Graves was homosexual, and it is possible that the commander discovered this and decided to let him go. In any case, Graves was given a psychiatric discharge.

As Director of the Fine Arts Project, Everson looked for ways to promote the school. When James suggested bringing Graves in, Everson immediately sent an invitation to the artist, and he accepted. He arrived a few days before he was expected and built a lean-to studio for himself at the mouth of a river near the beach. Graves was thus introduced into the camp as a visiting artist under the auspices of the Fine Arts Project, receiving no pay save board. While Everson had little contact with Graves, in his *Imprint* interview he recalled an amusing anecdote involving the painter:

James and I were down there one evening talking with him, and here came a Jeep. It pulled up and this lieutenant got out. Two dog-faced GIs were with him, their eyes this big. We all had long hair back in the days when it just wasn't seen. I still remember the faces of those eighteen-year-olds. The crisp lieutenant stepped down and said, "Let's see your identification, please." Graves got up; he was soft, suave, and a gentleman. But that kind of strain . . . Not as if he were a smoothie in the way Mills was. Mills would have handled it an entirely different way. Graves got up very gently and said, "May I offer you some tea?"

"No."

"Would you like to have some tea?" (To the two GIs.)

"No."

The lieutenant interrupted, "Let's see your papers!"

And then Graves said, "This is Mr. Everson, and this is Mr. James, sir."

So finally he produced his papers, and the guy looked them over and saw that he held a medical release from the Army. Then he checked us. We didn't have any.

"What about your papers?"

And I said, "We don't have to have any. We're stationed over at the camp; we don't have to have any."

He didn't challenge; and then they went off. And then Graves just about collapsed. He just went "whewwwwwwww!" He'd just been through so much of that kind of harassment in the Army that he just said, "Issssss!" and sat down.

Because of these kinds of run-ins on the beach, and because James and Graves did not really get on well together, the painter ended up leaving after just a few weeks.

Shortly, though Everson now had experience both with the Workers Committee and as Director of the Fine Arts Project, he got bored with administration. Somehow, the headaches simply were not worth the slight rewards. As he remembered in a 1978 interview, besides this ongoing conflict about privilege, "there were a bunch of snobs in the Fine Arts movement. There were some real snobs, pains in the asses. There were some misanthropes. There were difficult people, temperamental, artistic, normal run-of-the-mill artistic, difficult people. The less talent they had, the more problematical they were. The ones who were really creative and productive created their way through and kept it together. But trouble was never very far away." Further, earlier that summer, a woman arrived at the camp and offered to help the Fine Arts Project in any way she could. She was a slim redhead, and very charismatic. Everson put her to work as a secretary, and she took a cabin across the road. She was helpful, but in time a complicating factor. A further rift was developing between the religious COs and the artists, and her presence only added fuel to that fire, as she was the first unmarried woman to live at the camp and rumor had it that she was sleeping with various campers. So at the end of the summer, Everson turned the Directorship over to Vladimir Dupre, a non-artist who had come on a transfer and had been responsible for the clerical work of the project.

While Everson was pleased with the arrival of both *The Illiterati* and *The Compass*, he was nervous about both the possibilities of tension developing among the rival publications and the idea of having the three most important journals of the CO movement (the *Untide* was still for a time in operation) located at one camp. Martin Ponch was the editor of *The Compass*, which had established itself as the primary CO organ on the east coast. Ponch's main interest in coming west was theater, but he was an amateur journalist, and he was able to bring *Compass* to Waldport simply because he held the subscription list. Actually, there was no real competition between *The Illiterati* and *The Compass* in that the first journal was devoted to art and literature. Its editors proposed on their title page "creation, experiment and revolution to build a warless, free society," rejecting "war and any other form of coercion by physical violence in human associations." They were wary of both "tradition as a standard and eclecticism as a technique," and besides poetry and graphics carried such pieces as "The Mikado in C.P.S." (a parody) and "The Metaphysical in Graphic Art." *The Compass*, on the other hand, cared about aesthetics only incidentally, focusing instead on social issues. Like the *Untide*, both were priced very low so that COs could afford to subscribe, and circulation was thus very good throughout the camps. The journals brought in enough money through a combination of subscriptions and donations that they were essentially self-supporting.

During the later summer, a pressman named Joe Kalal also transferred into the camp, from Wahalla. He was a friend of Larry Siemons, and like a number of men from Wahalla who moved into the camp after the initial rush, he didn't want to come, but rather was simply sent by his home camp. Kalal had settled himself in Wahalla, and was very angry about the move, generally letting anyone who crossed his path at Waldport know about it. But he was a first-rate pressman, and Larry Siemons talked him into doing work for the Untide Press. Everson set type before this for the Press, but he hadn't done too much presswork; years before, working in his father's shop, he had done paper feeding and other small tasks, but he had never made the press ready nor experimented with intricate forms. About this time, the Untide was preparing to print Everson's *Waldport Poems*, and thus Kalal arrived just in time; for this was to be a difficult job, given the subtlety of design, and especially Clayton James's four brown linoleum blocks in the text and on the cover. Kalal had been a journeyman printer at the *Christian Century* and was thoroughly professional.

The work on *War Elegies*, which even today remains a stunning example of letterpress printing, did not go smoothly, however. Kalal did not mellow as the days went by, and instead became a malingerer, going on sick-call as often as possible. Further, he wouldn't take his meals with the rest of the COs, but in the middle of the night would break into the kitchen to raid the refrigerator. Whenever a supervisor caught him, he'd simply demand to be sent back to Wahalla.

Everson's attitude to Kalal was one of guarded friendship. He respected his ability in running the press, though he soon realized that the two would never be close. During the days, he would assist Kalal in operating the press, learning from him all he could, then at night, after the operation had shut down, he would stay on to do all the clean up. He tried his best to placate him so that the presswork would move along on schedule. By August, they had finished *The Waldport Poems*, in 985 copies, all hand-sewn. By December, an even more sophisticated collection typographically, Everson's *War Elegies*, was ready in an edition of 982 copies; this item contained twelve large red linoleum blocks by Kemper Nomland, one heading each poem, along with sixteen zinc line cuts in black. Professional literary people outside the camp reacted very favorably to these chapbooks, both the poetry and the typography, with reviews of the latter appearing in *The Nation*, *Poetry*, *Circle*, and other important journals and newspapers. Unfortunately, at the start of the printing of the third pamphlet, Jacob Sloan's *Generation of Journey*, the following February, William Eshelman and Kalal had a falling out. That evening Everson was to go to a meeting and he asked Eshelman to fill in for him in helping Kalal; Eshelman agreed, but at one point vanished, and Kalal got so angry that he left the printshop and never worked again for the Press. Everson had to take over work on the Sloan project, and as this was his first experience with a complete job on letterpress, there was a noticeable falling off in quality from the previous two books.

By the end of 1944, Mills was finished. He had built an enviable reputation outside Waldport as one of the best and most liberal directors in the CPS system. Given all the problems concerning his sexual orientation, as well as his reticence about the Fine Arts Project, he had more or less managed to keep his poise throughout his directorship, even after his original crew had left, tending to handle all problems internally. Originally, Mills had been wary of Everson because of his relationship to both Hackett and Coffield, two men he thought of as being on the eccentric fringe, and Siemons, the camp goldbrick. But when Everson drafted his document arguing for the establishing of the Workers Committee, Mills was won over to the poet, sensing that his proposal had been a masterstroke in nipping in the bud the potential blossoming of a very serious problem. After that, as far as Mills was concerned, Everson could do no wrong, and in fact it was Everson's acceptance of the directorship of the Fine Arts Project which made the whole program at least palatable to him.

In his proposal for the Workers Committee, Everson had studiously guarded, against Kosbab's wishes, the usurping of any of Mills's power. This was a wise move politically, though on Everson's part it was probably motivated by his intimidation by authority which stemmed from his relationship with his father. The paternal authority figure was to him awesome, and he often had difficulty dealing with it in any other way than overreaction, which more than likely accounts for his need to cut his father off completely earlier on. Certainly it explained Everson's impulse to keep the peace between the various supervisory staffs and the other COs.

Yet after Mills's change in attitude toward him, Everson began to like and trust him, so much so that he even covered for him during a crucial camp meeting. In the early summer of 1943, Mills had met with Everson and the Workers Committee to select a new director for the education program. Three or four names were suggested, including that of a black man named Evans. At that time there were only a few blacks at Waldport, and Evans was an intellectual and a potter. Mills told the group that the man was not interested, so his name was dropped without further discussion. Later, at one of the after-dinner announcement periods after the appointment had been made, Evans stood up and asked Mills publicly to explain on what grounds he hadn't been considered. Mills was on the spot and Everson, trusting that somehow he simply had been misinformed about Evans's wishes, stood up and took the blame. He told Evans that his name was discussed but that the information the committee had was that he was not interested. Evans demanded to know who had told the group that, because he was in fact definitely interested, and Everson simply replied that he couldn't remember. Evans's response was an angry denunciation of the committee's technique of making appointments, and Everson stood and bore the brunt.

Mills had always hoped to have a social activist project, like Co-operative Living, at Waldport, figuring that such a program would certainly advance his career. When the Fine Arts Project was proposed, he hesitated for the reasons already mentioned. Actually, his fears were realized in that his serious problems with the camp began with the arrival of transfers into the project—they were generally, as he had anticipated, difficult individuals; further, while he was a master administrator and tactician, these men were better educated than he. Earlier, Kemper Nomland and Mills had quarreled perpetually; now, it was Mills and Jerry Rubin, the new head of the Workers Committee, who fought continuously. As the Fine Arts Project became more and more successful, his position was weakened because he had little control over the program. And unlike Everson, as head of the Workers Committee, Rubin, a Socialist who had worked as western publicity manager for Norman Thomas's presidential campaign, was not predisposed to negotiation.

Finally, one night in December, a fire broke out in the dining hall, and according to Everson, "There was a night watchman who'd been appointed by the Workers Committee whom Mills didn't think was responsible enough and he kept worrying about that. And one night a stove was overstoked in the kitchen and the place caught on fire, and he summarily dismissed the guy and the Workers Committee protested this dismissal without trial." Mills's reaction was to reach for Everson's proposal for the Committee, which began with the statement of the essential powerlessness of the COs, and turn this against the Committee and Rubin, disbanding the Committee and firing Rubin. The camp erupted in the controversy, and a massive meeting was held. There Mills again lost his temper and argued that he had been blocked "by the labor leader from New York" and had no choice, that morale had fallen so low he had to take action. Had he maintained his usual poise, the whole thing would have blown over; but the fact that he turned dictatorial and proceeded without a hearing, most probably because of his animosity to Jerry Rubin, brought about an intense reaction from the COs. Mills was legally within his rights as camp director, but it was winter and the men were tired and depressed, and the whole camp crystallized against him. As Everson remembered,

His whole thing broke down. The whole liberal facade went plooie at that time. So then he tendered his resignation and took off and wrote that summary in which he more or less attacked the Fine Arts movement and called into question our accomplishments and sent it around to every camp director in the system and saw that it got a good splash there. It was nasty all the way round.

But soon after Mills's resignation, it became apparent to the COs that the war was drawing to a close and thus their attention was drawn to making plans for resuming life after Waldport.

▼▼▼

At the beginning of 1945, camp morale was low, and a number

of COs simply walked out of Waldport and other Oregon camps without official release. Judges in Portland were beginning to fight the military, accepting the argument that if the Selective Service Act left the draft under civilian control, President Roosevelt had made an error in 1941 in appointing General Hershey to direct the program. Early in the war the courts had refused to pursue this interpretation on the grounds of national emergency; now, however, with the conflict winding down, the case was given a hearing. The controversy became such that if a CO walked out of camp and was later apprehended, and could show that somewhere along the line a member of the military had signed any document relating to his transfer (most of those to Waldport were signed by Colonel Kosh), judges turned him loose. Everson, unfortunately, had gone to Waldport directly from Selma, and thus his papers were binding, since he had been ordered there by the local civilian draft board. But the transfers into Waldport soon discovered that they could leave with impunity, as long as they were willing after being arrested by the FBI to go to jail for a few weeks before their release. Eventually Adrian Wilson, Clayton James, and many other members of the Fine Arts left the camp in this fashion.

In early summer, Everson got permission to go to Fresno for some emergency dental work, as that was the closest specialized unit for CPS men. When James discovered Everson was making this trip, he decided to join him, taking his wife along. They left Mrs. James with Watkins in Berkeley, and the men went to Fresno. The dental work took about a week, and at one point, while Everson was waiting for dentures to be made, he and James took a two-day pack trip into Yosemite. They returned to Berkeley, picked up James's wife, then traveled over to visit Ham and Mary Tyler at Pond Farm near Guerneville. Robert Duncan had been staying there and Everson hoped to see him, but when they arrived he had already left for a brief trip into San Francisco. Leaving Everson after a few hours, the Jameses decided to hitch-hike back north.

Everson chose to stay a few days, as he had a little time left before he was to report back to Waldport. The Tylers were getting ready to leave Pond Farm for Treesbank, near Sebastopol, and were making daily trips to the new house to work on it; Everson went along to help out. One afternoon Edwa, who had been alerted that he was there, arrived, and she and Everson spent a day going to wineries in the Napa Valley. Edwa bought a number of good wines, including a special, very expensive bottle for Carothers. Getting out of the car at Pond Farm, Everson accidentally knocked that particular bottle off the seat, and it broke in the driveway. Ham Tyler, who watched this happen, laughed hysterically, mumbling over and over, "Freud would *love* this." The next day Edwa returned to Berkeley and Everson caught a bus to Waldport.

Everson's own disillusionment with the Untide Press came not long after this, with the decision to publish Kenneth Patchen's *An Astonished Eye Looks Out of the Air*. In August, the Press had published Eversons' *poems:mcmxlii*, a chapbook of 40 pages which the poet had actually begun to print in late 1944, but had no real interest in until Kalal quit his post. Now there was a move among members of the Press to take on a Patchen manuscript. A young man who was from New York, but now involved in the Arts Project, knew Patchen, and on a furlough he returned to New York where the poet was living at the time. He took with him the various Untide publications, and seeing them Patchen took a strong interest in the Press. On the basis of this encounter, Patchen wrote immediately to Everson proposing that Untide do an edition of his collected antiwar poetry. There was an urgency, however, as Patchen wanted to ensure that the book would appear while the war was still on. Everson at first balked at the project; he was again haunted by the memory of Edwa and was considering divorce.

Up until this time, she had continued to correspond with him fairly regularly, arguing again and again that she only needed time and would eventually return to him. In a series of letters written in late summer this continued as her constant theme. She was attracted to Carothers sexually, she wrote in August, and his companionship was important to her, but at times she felt "hatred toward him—a rather unintelligible hatred, I suppose, for what he has done to my life and our life. . . . I long for creative encouragement which you can so well give. Kenny reacts upon me in the opposite direction." It wasn't just Carothers, she continued, in any case that commanded her attention, but the "life of the city. . . . Take this week for instance: Monday—saw 'The Maltese Falcon'; Tuesday—Heard the Budapest String Quartet; Wednesday— Heard Louis Armstrong; Thursday—London Quartet and saw 'Long Voyage Home'." Then, a month later, she told him again that while it would be difficult for her to make a break from Carothers, "I don't entirely respect or love him. . . . I have felt for you and still do feel as strongly as I am capable. . . . I intend to fight with all I have for what I want and what I want is you. I do want you but you alone. I don't want the camp and I don't want a 'you' who is involved in camp life. I want a security, a home, a life involving just the two of us. . . . The feeling of a common purpose and an equality in that purpose." Still, on occasion he became disgusted with the whole situation; as he wrote her in late 1944,

It seems impossible to go on. We are so utterly different people than we were when we parted. If it were separation only—but it's *alteration*. Why should we presume that what we once were we yet are? My dear—you are a stranger—you are a name only. My wife. Utterly meaningless relationship! Why this pretense, this old dragging on, this preposterous subterfuge? Good God, let us be done, be finished. We are chains on each other's necks. We're living in an extension of the past, without meaning, without sense. And the formality is choking us. Let us say once and for all that it's over, and go on, and try to find something nearer our needs. Please see it this way. It's like living in a tomb. And I don't think it's something reunion can heal.

Generally, like the proverbial spurned lover, he clung to the hope that somehow she would return to him after the war, that they would move back down to Selma and pick up the life that had been so forcibly interrupted. Lee Watkins, however, saw Edwa almost every day in Berkeley and wrote Everson that such hope was fantasy, that regardless of what Edwa told him in her letters, it was apparent to everyone that she would not leave Carothers. Finally, as Watkins was one of his oldest and closest friends, he began to accept the truth of his analysis.

William Eshelman and Vladimir Dupre continued to put pressure on him to take on the Patchen project, and eventually between them they talked him into it. A number of other problems arose immediately. First, it was the Press's longest book, which meant that many hours would have to be devoted to the printing. Further, while Patchen wanted Nomland to design it, he insisted on having input into the design and typography. Also, while Patchen was a pacifist, like Kenneth Rexroth he was classified medically disabled, and thus this would be the Untide's first publication by a non-CO. Finally, earlier Robert Duncan had told Everson that Patchen was the one poet "small presses fold on," that he put so much pressure on them that they tended to give up and go out of business rather than cope with his interference. Still, Everson started the project in good faith, working closely with Kemper Nomland. Nomland ran into difficulty immediately with Patchen, who it turned out wanted to have complete control over design. More important, however, at one point Everson ran out of paper and traveled to Portland to get more. The paper company was out of stock of that particular type, and Everson didn't want to proceed until the exact paper was reordered. When Patchen heard this, he insisted that the printing continue with a substitute paper, as it appeared the war would be ending any day. Everson stood firm, refusing to compromise; he then turned the correspondence over to Eshelman, not wanting to carry the argument further. After some weeks, the paper company informed Everson that the line had been dropped altogether, and thus he was forced to proceed with the paper they offered as a replacement. Patchen was vindicated in the sense that readers seemed not to notice the difference, though forty years later Everson, a perfectionist in his printing, would still wince whenever he ran across a copy of the book. At the end of 1945, Waldport was closed, and the COs along with the Fine Arts Project were transferred to Cascade Locks. Everson and others put their press and supplies on a trailer and took it along. As Nomland and James had by this time walked out of camp, Everson and Eshelman were left alone at Cascade Locks to finish the Patchen project, which finally was offered for sale in May of 1946.

Needless to say, as the COs waited at Cascade Locks for demobilization, morale hit a new low. They were told at first that the CCC camps had been closed in a month and that it wouldn't take any longer to close CPS as there were far fewer men involved, but that wasn't the case. The Army stepped in and refused to demobilize the COs any faster than soldiers with similar entry dates, and there were about 13 million men under arms. As early as October 15, 1945, the Families and Friends of Imprisoned Conscientious Objectors picketed at the White House demanding amnesty for all COs, and by December 1945, a Committee for Amnesty had been officially established. On Christmas Eve of that year, President Truman issued a blanket amnesty for all ex-prisoners who had served in the Armed Forces for at least a year, proclaiming that "such convicted persons ought to have restored to them the political, civil, and other rights of which they were deprived by reason of such conviction and which may not be restored to them unless they are pardoned." This edict said nothing, however, of COs. Some COs were getting official discharges, tied to stringent requirements that jobs would be waiting for them, but generally demobilization crawled along at a snail's pace. On Japan's surrender in mid-1945 there were still 3,000 COs left in the camps, and on July 1, nearly a year later, that figure had dropped by only a third.

Everson's projected date of release was May 1, 1946. By this time, as men transferred from camps that were closing to others, no sensible work plan could be undertaken and the Forest Service began giving the men simply make-work projects. In response, the Glendora, California camp went on a work strike, and some other camps followed. A representative was sent to Cascade Locks to attempt to convince them to join, but Everson drew back, not wanting to jeopardize his May release. Earlier at Waldport, when James walked out, Everson had refused to work for three months as an expression of solidarity for James's position. According to camp regulations, any man designated RTW would have that time tacked on to his wait for demobilization; because Everson had put so much effort into the Workers Committee and the Fine Arts Project, his supervisor covered for him during this period, and thus when he returned to work he narrowly escaped penalty. But he simply did not want to chance the situation again. He still seemed to have a sort of power among the COs, especially among the more radical Fine Arts men. They were willing to strike because most of them didn't have that much to lose, generally having entered CPS much later than the poet. With the problems with Edwa, the *Untide*, and delayed demobilization weighing on him, Everson became so demoralized that he dropped out of all camp activity, save finishing the Patchen and taking a night watchman's job (though he did at this time discover Wilhelm Reich's *The Function of the Orgasm* in the camp library, a work which would later be important to him). On the night of the announced country-wide CPS strike,

I was going around stoking fires. There was a guy named Danzeisan, a Brethren, a real sterling character. He wasn't into the Arts Group, but sympathetic. He was one of those Thoreau types. He didn't care if anybody else was going to strike or not. It didn't matter to him; he was going to strike. He made his posters up and placed them around, and got ready to strike. One man in the whole camp.

Then Hildegard Erle, the wife of Broadeus Erle, the violinist, began talking to me about why I didn't strike, and I said, "Because I don't want to jeopardize my release." And she said, "But your release is already in the mail. Those things are always given out on the first." And I said to myself, "Wait a minute." And the devil of expediency began to gnaw at

me. Before the morning dawned, she'd talked me into it. I went on strike
and the group followed. Wham! As soon as it broke on the news, the
Portland *Oregonian* had a flash headline: "COs strike Cascade Locks."
The next thing you know, police were out there. And the next thing you
know, Washington was pulling our releases out of the file. Just stashing
them away at the back of the cabinet, and I was there three months
longer than I was supposed to be.

vvv

When the strike began, Jerry Rubin knew just what to do. He
alerted the wire services, and orchestrated all the publicity. Earlier
at Waldport, when the Brethren Service Committee was casually
reassigning men with families to camps without consideration of
their wishes, Rubin had organized a hunger strike, which proved,
after just a week, very successful, and the BSC rescinded a number
of papers. This was one of the causes of Mills's hostility toward
him. The second strike in 1946 proved a failure, however, due primarily to the confusion that attended the whole demobilization
program, and the generally negative public opinion it aroused. In
any case, Everson's papers were not forthcoming as the government was closing down Cascade Locks, and he and Eshelman were
sent to Minersville, California, to await final release.

Minersville was rumored to be the Siberia of the CPS program,
and Everson and Eshelman were sent there because they had participated in the general strike. It was located in the far northern
end of California near Trinity River, and was opened very late by
the government and not administered by the NCRO. Every CPS
camp had some COs who were rather rebellious, generally not
intellectuals but rather people with emotional problems. If these
men refused to work, the government could attempt to prosecute
and send them to prison with stiff sentences. This was difficult to
do, however, as any CO who refused to work could always come
up with a minimal excuse which was almost impossible to dis-

prove. This wasn't too much of a problem until the government began to establish its own camps in 1943, as they simply left these problem cases up to the NCRO. But after a few years' experience with men subverting the system at every opportunity, they picked up an old CCC camp at Minersville, just about the most isolated place they could find, to act as the repository for recalcitrant COs. There, the discipline was tough. At one point, for example, twelve COs refused to dismantle the partitions they had erected around their beds, and they were arrested and brought before a grand jury for insubordination. Everson and Eshelman were in fact the first two NCRO men who were transferred to the camp.

While Everson awaited his release, he worked on various projects—fighting three forest fires, digging pipelines, clearing brush. He made friends quickly there, as it turned out the men were not pathological but rather anarchists who simply despised the government's assumed authority. Eshelman had shipped all the Untide Press materials, including remaining copies of all the books, to Kemper Nomland in Los Angeles. Everson had no plans to continue as a member of that operation, though Eshelman and Nomland would publish one more book in 1947 under the imprint, George Woodcock's *Imagine the South*, as well as a few more issues of *The Illiterati*. The weather was lovely and warm, and during the evenings Everson and Eshelman could go down to the river and sit talking about their postwar plans, occasionally building a fire and roasting hot dogs.

On July 23, a particularly hot day, Everson was sent with a small crew to a mop-up operation after a spot fire. The men had to take water from the river in buckets and climb up a series of ridges about a mile and a half away and dump it on stumps which were still smoldering. When he returned to camp that evening, exhausted from what was he remembers the hardest day of work in his life, his demobilization order was waiting on his bunk.

FOUR

Berkeley

When Everson left Minersville, he was demoralized—his marriage was on the rocks, his CO friends were going their own ways, and he was broke. When he had helped Edwa move up to Berkeley, they had left the farm with a real estate agent who had managed to sell it for $2,500, making a substantial profit for them. But Everson and Edwa deposited the money in a special savings account and agreed not to touch it. He took a bus down to Berkeley and stayed a few days with the Watkinses, sleeping in their living room, then made his way to Treesbank, where the Tylers were now living. He saw nothing of Edwa during these first few weeks.

Everson had thought long about what he might do after the war. He hoped to make a name for himself as a poet, but beyond that he had considered very seriously continuing his work on the hand press. While Eshelman and Nomland had hoped he would continue with them in work with the Untide Press, they were inclined toward journalism, and Everson felt himself drawn to fine press work. In February of 1946 he had been given a short furlough and he had taken a trip to the Bay Area. While in San Francisco he saw a Washington hand press in the window of Ed Ottsman's shop on Sansome Street on sale for $175, and he immediately knew he had to have it. Though the price was very low, it was still far beyond his means. His parents, however, years before had purchased a Metropolitan Life Insurance policy for him and he went to the branch office of the insurance company and startled the agent by cashing it at a loss, for exactly the amount of the press. Ottsman agreed to hold the press for him for three months, as Everson was sure he would be demobilized in May, though as the deadline passed, the poet Kenneth Rexroth had to intercede for him with the owner to keep it until he was released.

Treesbank was a farm of about eighty acres, a third of which was apple orchard, located a few miles from Sebastopol. The Tylers had hoped it would thrive as a kind of artists commune, and Everson had been invited to move there after his release to begin his printing venture. Hamilton Tyler had grown up in Fresno, and Everson had met him before the war. While the poet was essentially apolitical, Tyler, a little younger, was consumed with politics. He had joined the Communist Party in the thirties and in 1936 traveled to Spain to fight with the republicans against the fascists. On the battlefield, seeing the atrocities by both sides, he became a pacifist, deserted, and made his way home; had he been captured at that point by either side he would have been executed. He ended up in Berkeley, married a woman named Mary Hamilton, worked as a welder in the shipyards, and took courses at the university. Through Lee and Milicent Watkins, he learned of Everson's poetry and pacifism, and during the Christmas holidays of 1941-42, he drove to Selma to meet him. The two men hit it off immediately, and continued to see each other and correspond through the next few years. Tyler had gotten a medical exemption from the draft, and he and Mary soon after set up a farm in Lincoln, in the foothills of the Sierra Nevada, financed by Mary's father. At the time of his first furlough in the summer of

1943, Everson visited them there for an evening on his way to Selma, keeping them laughing all night with stories of Waldport eccentrics. Two men, he told them, were arguing about the relative merits of eating meat; one was a vegetarian, the other not. The non-vegetarian had pointed out to the other man that he was wearing a leather belt, whereupon the vegetarian whipped it off, threw it to the ground, and in a rage hacked it to bits with a hoe.

In July of 1945, the Tylers moved to Pond Farm, a retreat, they remember in their memoir of Robert Duncan, that was brought to their notice by Everson. It was a low-key version of a "cooperative for artistic people," owned by a woman named Jane Herr, "who sincerely espoused Lawrencian views of no certain shape." According to the Tylers, "Pond Farm was perched on a hilltop which was more suitable for crafts students who summered there than for our herd of cows, but the fragile arrangement was that we would feed these artisans in summer, then sell cream to the buttermaker and eggs to the co-op for the remainder of the year." Robert Duncan arrived the following summer, and for a time the three of them lived "in a converted chicken house which made one side of a corral where the cattle came up to await feeding and milking." Many artists and writers from the Bay Area visited both the Tylers and Duncan there. At the end of the war especially, the Tylers remember,

Many unknown visitors called or were paraded through our quarters, but old friends also showed up after the long wartime drought. One memorable evening Rexroth and others arrived for a poetry session which began with Kenneth reading a new play by lamp light—the electric generator having broken. Then the younger poets had their turn with Kenneth playing the schoolmaster. Finally, Robert read, concluding with Sitwell's "Serenade: Any Man to Any Woman." That really marked the end of the war for all of us; we were free again, writers were writing and we could be together once more.

But they had numerous quarrels with both their landlady and various neighbors, and on January 7 the following year made their move to Treesbank.

Everson spent a few days at Treesbank making the apple-dryer shed ready for his press, then he picked up the Washington from San Francisco with a trailer a CO friend had brought down from Cascade Locks and had given him, and took it to the farm. As Mary Tyler recalled,

Bill had most of his meals with us. I think he planned on baking his own bread because he brought a sack of whole wheat and a grinder. He was a wonderful help to me in the kitchen. I still picture him in the backyard peeling apples and singing in his great crackling voice, "As I went out one morning to take the pleasant air, I chanced upon a mother a' scolding her daughter fair . . ." Also I can vividly see him preparing breakfast and breaking eggs into an iron skillet. He carefully broke the shell and carefully dropped the egg in the skillet and the shell in the firebox. He became rather mesmerized and equally carefully broke the shell and dropped the egg in the firebox and the shell in the skillet. Ham and I ever after referred to that kind of mistake as "doing an Everson." Our evenings were spent reading poetry. Bill also read from *Tropic of Cancer* while we listened and laughed.

By this time, Duncan had left the Tylers to live in Berkeley, though an ex-soldier name Hal Lubin who had separated from his wife was staying with them. It was late August and the apple crop had to be harvested—the plan was that eventually the apples would support the farm—so Everson spent most of his days with the Tylers and Lubin picking apples; there was an ample harvest, though unfortunately the market was bad that year and they made no profit. Everson slept out in the apple-dryer, next to his press.

In a memoir, the poet and Berkeley professor Thomas Parkinson, who later would become a strong supporter of Everson's work, recalled meeting the poet at the Tylers for the first time:

Everson was a modest, retiring, and quiet man, and when I first met him at Treesbank, I had a sense of fellow-feeling, of comradeship, of being at home in natural surroundings with him. He had a printing press in the barn, and I walked out with him to inspect it. We were both poets, although he was eight years older and had published and written much more than I had. We did not have much to say to each other, but I did not feel awkward or uncomfortable, any more than I should have felt with the bears that sometimes emerged from the woods when I was logging in the Siskiyous. Everson was a great deal like the people I had worked with at Pondosa, and I am not trying to romanticize him as a primitive indigene. To put the matter simply, Everson was a working man. His work was his center.

During these weeks, he continued to brood on his loss of Edwa; the Tylers were well aware of the situation, and had hopes that he might seriously begin a new relationship. Acting as matchmakers, not long after Everson's arrival the Tylers invited a female friend up to Treesbank for a small party. That evening, Ham Tyler put on a jazz record and everyone danced. As Mary Tyler remembered, "We were particularly fond of doing our version of Flamenco dance which was largely a matter of stamping our feet and shouting Olé. Bill did a very imaginative dance which called for his wriggling across the floor on his belly." Everson and the Tylers' friend seemed to hit it off, and though she returned to the Bay Area later that night, Everson imagined himself to be in love. Within a few days he set to work on the eight-part sequence, "The Blowing of the Seed," which he completed in just a week. The poem is a lyrical hymn to the poet's recovery of woman:

> Under my hand your heart hits like a bird's,
> Hushed in the palms, a muffled flutter,
> And all the instinct of its flight
> Shut in its wings . . .
> I have been fulfilled in a winter season,
> Wakened under a rain;
> Like the seed of the mustard,

Like the seed of the vetch that is harrowed into the hill,
Rolled in the mulch of the lifeless slope,
In the leafless orchard.

I move to meet you now in a greening time.
I come with wind and with wet
In a soft season.
I bring you my hand.
I bring you the flesh of those fallow, fallen years,
And my manifest reasons.

It was his first major piece of writing after demobilization, and finishing he closed down his press, packed his few belongings, and
headed for Berkeley.

vvv

Moving into a house on Ashby owned by a friend, Everson set out
to find a job. A number of ex-COs were employed at a co-
operative food warehouse in Oakland working as laborers and
truckers. It was hard work, but no more difficult than the various
projects in the CPS, and with this job Everson was paid a reasonable salary. Unfortunately, however, after two weeks the warehouse ran out of work and he was laid off. Soon after, Milicent
Watkins told him the University of California had staff openings
on occasion, so Everson went to their employment office. There
was an opening for a janitor in the main library, but as it turned
out, there was also a long waiting list. When the poet told the
interviewer of both his experience doing janitorial work years
before at Fresno State College, as well as his CPS experience, he
was hired immediately.

Everson's primary assignments were to clean offices in the basement and on the second and third floors of the building, as well
as the main reading room. He worked with a partner, though the
reading room was massive, filled with large oak tables and heavy
chairs, and it was again taxing. His shift lasted from 4 p.m. to mid-

night, and he made just over $200 a month. In the meantime, Lawrence Clark Powell had written to a friend who ran the University bindery, telling him that Everson was a first-rate craftsman, and suggesting that he give him a job. The friend approached Everson and offered him a place at the bindery with a raise in salary, and thus the poet gave the janitorial service notice. The bindery was in the same building, but in the basement, and Powell's friend had neglected to tell his manager that Everson would be hired. When he went down to begin work, the secretary in the office had no information about this move, and checking into the situation discovered that he had been quoted the wrong salary—that in fact his pay would be reduced. He talked this over with a friend and decided that it would be a mistake to take the job.

He was thus in something of a fix, but in the long run the mix-up was fortunate. When Everson told his former supervisor, who had already hired another man to take his place in the library, he offered him another janitorial job, this time at the University of California Press. He was to receive the same pay as he had been getting, and work the same hours, sweeping the offices and cleaning the third-floor bindery, but the work was not as hard. He could finish each evening by about ten o'clock, then spend his last two hours reading in the Press's extensive library books on printing. As he remembered in his essay "The Latter-Day Handpress," written in 1949 for *The California Book Club Quarterly*:

There were many tasks to do at the University Press, but none in which I could learn as much as I could at the task of janitor. For my work took me into all places, where I could watch all phases of bookmaking, and gave me good friendships with many fine craftsmen who were eager and pleased to share their knowledge. Also my work took me into the Press library where the late Mr. Samuel T. Farquhar, Director of the Press, housed his splendid collection of books on printing. And it was there, in the back issues of *The Fleuron*, *The Dolphin*, of *Signature* and *Print*, and dozens of books of ancient lore and craft, that I began slowly to acquire the rudiments of typographical taste.

It was now April of 1947, and Everson remained working at the Press until June of 1949, when he received a Guggenheim Fellowship.

For the remainder of the year, he worked at breaking back into civilian life. He found the Press hours to be conducive to his writing in that he could spend his mornings working on his poetry and printing rather than going off to a job. Beyond that it gave him an excuse to stand back from the flourishing night life of the period, as he was constantly invited to events arranged by Duncan, Jack Spicer, and Robin Blaser in Berkeley, and Kenneth Rexroth and Philip Lamantia in San Francisco.

During this time, Everson's two primary literary projects were putting the final touches on his selected poetry, which would be published by New Directions the following year, and writing another long love-poem sequence, "The Springing of the Blade." His obsession, however, was to get his own printing venture underway. In the early fall, Richard Brown drove him up to Treesbank and they dismantled the press and hauled it back to the Ashby house on the trailer. Brown had been at Waldport, and now moved in the Duncan circle. (In fact, Duncan's "Ode for Dick Brown. Upon the Termination of His Parole: March 17, 1947" marks, according to Ekbert Faas, the poet's "new start towards a political poetry different from the kind he had written in early student days.") Brown and Everson thus had much in common, and through the spring and summer he helped him convert a woodshed at the back of the house into a pressroom; they poured a cement floor and strengthened the walls. Such work was not easy, and after a time Brown became impatient with Everson's equivocations, as he changed plans for the design three or four times during their work. He was supposed to arrange for some friends to help them unload the castiron Washington when they arrived, but the poet had neglected to do it, and thus the two of them had to set the thing up alone. As far as Brown was concerned this was the last straw, and when they finished he simply left and never offered to work on any facet of the project again.

Up to this point, Everson's press experience was still fairly limited; he had assisted his father as a boy, he had worked with the
Untide, he had assisted Kalal, and he had closed the war by finishing, with Eshelman, the Patchen book. On one of his later furloughs, he had tracked down the printer Wilder Bentley, who
gave him a lecture on the operation of the handpress, how to make
it ready and print with it, though he did not give him a demonstration. Later, when he was first released from Minersville and
had stayed with the Watkinses in Berkeley, he had been introduced to James D. Hart, and spent many hours watching Hart
print a chapbook, *Ode to the Virginian Voyage*, on his handpress.
Interestingly, this was the first time he had ever seen such a press
in operation. While he worked at the U.C. Press, experienced
printers like Ted Freeman and Joe Baxley gave him general advice,
while an old binder named Vic George talked of the craft of binding. But both Freeman and Baxley worked Linotype, and thus
while their input was to some extent useful, Everson learned to
run his press by reading and through trial and error.

During their discussion, Bentley had advised Everson not to purchase a large press, telling him that "they tend to kill one off." But
when the poet had discovered the massive Washington in San
Francisco, he "knew there would be times when I would not
regret that extra leverage, that spacious bed, and that stalwart
frame."

Carefully fitted, its parts exactly gauged one against another, it has never
once given me to think it either cumbersome or slow. Its great bed,
26x39 inches, alone weighing several hundred pounds, slides in its track
at virtually finger-pressure ease. And the powerful bar, carefully set for
maximum purchase, has a fine snap in its retrograde action. There is,
among handpressman, an attitude of condescension toward the
Washington. This is natural for, in England, which is the cradle of the
fine handpress tradition, it is the Albion, of British manufacture, which
carried the honors . . . But, once it is properly made ready, the right
impression achieved, and the bearing-off points placed on the bed; once
printing is begun and the run fairly underway, it moves into the work

with a wonderful dispatch, its very sparseness stands it in stead; and so perfectly gauged are its meeting parts that I do not see how, impression for impression, any handpress could print better.

Further, as Everson outlines in his handpress essay, while "all printing is complex, the handpress is its simplest implement." It costs little to operate, is easy to learn, and it can produce first-class work. With only taste and patience—two qualities that he perhaps mistakenly feels endemic to all men—"the amateur comes into his own . . . it matches your most breathless dream."

Everson decided to name his press Equinox, both because the equinox fell in the month of his birth and because of its implication of balance, and set out to print as his first project a prospectus for the enterprise. Bentley had advised him, "Don't get the idea that handpress skill is something you can pick up in a couple of months," but having made his way through books by such masters as Moxon, Johnson, McKellar, Timperley, Ringwalt, and Gill, he approached his first press run with a great confidence in his own untested abilities. Bentley, he soon discovered, was right as he seemed to get further and further away from the result he had hoped for. "For one thing," he later admitted, "my sights were too high. Not only did I have to learn the handpress technique, from damping paper to stretching friskets, but I also tried to revolutionize the ancient process, and, at the same time, achieve the most beautiful broadside ever printed." He found the damping of paper to be the most difficult task of all, for having never seen the operation he had to experiment endlessly. But after four months of intense work, the prospectus, with a blockprint of a griffin, was issued in an edition of 500 copies.

Soon after the release of the prospectus, he sold the trailer that had come down from Waldport to buy an expensive, handmade English Tovil paper for his first Equinox Press book, *A Privacy of Speech*. He had written this ten-part sequence while at Cascade Locks awaiting demobilization, a rather dark and mysterious meditation on act and motivation, sexuality, and freedom:

Cried out all night,
What the wind cried,
What the wave
Cried to the rock,
What the nightbird said in the crumbled gully,
Spoken purely of self,
What the leaf said.

A privacy of speech—
And the noun quickens.
Vibrant between the breathing verbs
It gains its dimension.

And the anxious hand
Gropes again toward its dense future.

Loose in the grass
The feather lifts and settles,
Lifts and settles.

The bird begins.

Everson set about the very long process of printing. "There were many runs, for I used red and black throughout and made separate runs for the cuts." The actual presswork for the 29 pages of text took over a year, and was finally completed on Candlemas Day, February 2, 1949. Then Everson began the binding. "To this also," he remembered,

went many months, for I determined not to compromise at any phase of the labor: The sheets sewn on vellum strips and stitched to the boards, the headband worked on with the sewing as in the incunabula—surely a unique thing in modern editions—vellum spine and corners, parchment hinges under the endsheets fore and aft, and gold-stamping on the spine, laid on with the old, slow, vinegar and egg-white size, and hot-stamped on the handpress itself (another technique virtually to invent and perfect). And, as I say, many mistakes, for one learns in binding, as in printing—

and in printing, as in life—that for every perfection there is an imperfection, and he may no more attain the one than he may escape the other.

A Privacy of Speech, which would be the only issue besides the prospectus of the Press, was finally offered for sale in an edition of 100 copies in mid-summer. As often happens with fine press printing, the artifact of the book drew far more attention that the poem itself, winning for its design and execution "highest honors" in the Rounce & Coffin Club "Western Books" selection.

vvv

On an afternoon in January 1947, Everson received a telephone call from Kenneth Rexroth asking him to his Potrero Hill apartment in San Francisco. The British writer, critic, and editor Cyril Connolly was in town for a brief visit and Rexroth wanted to introduce him to a few members of his circle. Philip Lamantia and Hillary Belloc (son of the novelist) were also invited and arrived early. The elder poet was still getting on with Duncan at this time, and wanted to invite him, but he could not be reached. As Everson crossed the Bay Bridge, Rexroth was baiting Connolly, an elitist intellectual of the kind Rexroth scorned as "Mandarin." This was the period in which Rexroth was working on his *New British Poets* anthology for New Directions—why didn't Connolly print any of the new, vital, younger poets in his magazine *Horizon*, he wanted to know; a whole new wave of postwar creativity was emerging and *Horizon* seemed oblivious to it. Further, Rexroth had just received the latest issue of *Now*, a London anarchist journal, which carried a scathing review of Connolly's latest book, *The Condemned Playground*, something he had not yet seen and which Rexroth was only too pleased to place before him. The same issue happened to contain two poems by Everson ("The Revolutionist" and "The Outlaw"), as well as Rexroth's "Lyell's Hypothesis Again." Needless to say, when Everson arrived, Connolly was resentful and defensive.

Rexroth hadn't seen Everson since a previous November's party for Lamantia. At that time, Everson, still fresh from the CPS, was the image of Rexroth's "autochthon"—long hair, large Whitmanesque hat, forest service clothing, and boots. Now, when Rexroth opened the door he saw, as he later complained, a "typical square." Everson's hair was short, his hat was gone, he was wearing slacks and a sports coat, and his shoes were shined. Rexroth was not pleased by the change in persona, especially with Connolly in the room.

After a little strained conversation, someone suggested that Everson and Lamantia read from their poems, but before they started Rexroth addressed Connolly directly: "You and I and Philip here are Modernists," he began. "We have inherited its legacy and live by its lights; but this man is something else. Everson is truly autochthonous. You won't find in him the Modernist touchstones by which we others go about what we do. He doesn't need our sophistication because he possesses a primal innocence; he doesn't need our ideas because he thinks through his skin and suffers through his thought." It was Rexroth's opening stroke in the creation of an autochthon, though the whole speech certainly would have carried more weight had Everson retained his earlier manner of dress.

When the poets had read Connolly was polite but noncommittal, remarking that nothing much could be told about a poem from a single hearing, but if they wanted to send him some manuscripts he would be glad to consider them for *Horizon*. Thus encouraged, Everson responded, "I already have, but your printer refused to touch them, so you sent them back." Connolly pricked up his ears. Turning to Everson he said, "Are you the poet who sent us those wonderful poems we were forced to return?" Springing from his chair he seized Everson's hand. "How good it is to meet you! As you must recall we responded warmly, praised what you sent, regretted we couldn't use it, and asked for more, but we heard nothing more from you." Everson explained that Connolly's letter had arrived just before he had left Selma for Waldport, and there was much confusion at the time. He himself had simply forgotten to follow the matter up with another submission. Connolly took a sheaf of poems from Everson and began to leaf through it. Suddenly he exclaimed, "Here it is!" Turning to Rexroth, "You call this unsophisticated? No technique?" And he launched out into a reading of "The Stranger," which just happened to be the one poem Rexroth had repeatedly urged Everson to discard. As Connolly began it, Rexroth swore, clapped his hands over his ears, and rushed off into another room. Connolly, delighted with his find, read fervently:

> Pity this girl.
> At callow sixteen,
> Glib in the press of rapt companions,
> She bruits her smatter,
> Her bedlore brag.
> She prattles the lip-learned, light-love list.
> In the new itch and squirm of sex
> How can she foresee?
> How can she foresee the thick stranger,
> Over the hills from Omaha
> Who will break her over a hired bed,
> Open the loins,
> Rive the breach,
> And set the foetus wailing within the womb,
> To hunch toward the knowledge of its disease,
> And shamble down time to doomsday?

Rexroth was also upset at the Tylers' occasional match-making, as he wanted Everson and Edwa to reconcile. Now that seemed an impossibility. In fact, not long after Everson had spoken with Rexroth about his problems with his first wife, during his furlough, the elder man had been introduced to Edwa and Carothers at a party by mutual friends. It was, Everson later remembered, "an archetypal encounter." Rexroth was quite taken with Edwa—while Everson was an autochthon, she was a sophisticate. He had made a few passes at her, which had angered Carothers. Carothers was a slightly built man, and Rexroth related that he "could have taken him to pieces," had he wanted to. Instead, he had written Everson at Waldport the glowing details.

vvv

When Everson arrived in the Bay Area after demobilization, there was a flourishing literary culture, presided over by Rexroth in San Francisco, Robert Duncan in Berkeley. "In San Francisco," he recalled, "Rexroth was our group's *paterfamilias*, but on the Berkeley side Duncan was its energy. He was indefatigable in his arrangement of poetry readings as our key creative outlet, since the dominant centers of publication were largely closed to us." Duncan had organized weekly discussion groups on the work of a particular poet (in June of 1947, for example, Rexroth made the trip across the Bay to speak to them about Lawrence). Such a group, however, already had been meeting for a few months in San Francisco, organized by Rexroth, Duncan, and Lamantia. The group met once a week in Rexroth's apartment, then later rented the top floor of a hall on Steiner Street, for discussions of anarchist politics. In the second volume of his autobiography, *Excerpts from a Life*, Rexroth remembered that this group "had by far the largest meetings of any radical or pseudo-radical group in San Francisco. The place was always crowded and when the topic for the evening was Sex and Anarchy you couldn't get in the doors. People were standing on one another's shoulders, and we had to have two meetings, one upstairs, the overflow in the downstairs meeting hall."

The group, which eventually came to call itself "The Libertarian Circle," introduced a Poetry Forum to the agenda each Wednesday. Two Wednesdays a month discussion would center on the work of a writer in the circle—Duncan, Parkinson, Rexroth, Muriel Rukeyser, Sanders Russell, Jack Spicer, Everson, and others—led by the writer himself. Alternate Wednesdays, Rexroth led classes in poetry and criticism. This Poetry Forum soon evolved into the Poetry Guild of San Francisco, whose founding members included Rukeyser, Rexroth, Everson, Edith Henrich, and William Justema, and whose directors were Duncan, Madeline Gleason, and James Broughton. Aside from regular meetings, discussions, and readings, the Guild co-sponsored four "Festivals of Modern Poetry" with the San Francisco Museum of Art. Participants at these events included, in 1949 for example, Duncan reading his "An African Elegy," Spicer his "Second Elegy" and "Psychoanalysis," Rukeyser her "Orpheus," Gleason her "The Drudge and the Doppelganger," and Everson his "At the Edge," "In the Dream's Recess," and "Triptych." Further, in early 1947 Rexroth had also organized a weekly seminar for ten members, "preferably those who have written verse of some merit," for discussion of his "A Selected Bibliography of Poetics, Modern Period," which included studies by Aiken, Empson, Eliot, Lawrence, Pound, Spender, Riding, Yeats, and others, charging each member a dollar a week tuition. Everson attended just two of these sessions; with his university night job he found it impossible to be a regular participant.

While Duncan was an important force in this flurry of literary activity in the Bay Area, for Everson Rexroth was, finally, the presiding figure, taking on for a time at least the role of both father and mentor. As he would remember in his brief memoir of the elder poet, "Shaker and Maker," Rexroth

quarrels with his friends as readily as he clobbers his enemies. He demands unwavering loyalty and, poets being what they are, that is not always forthcoming. He tends to drop the movement he has fostered . . . Rexroth touched the nerve of the future and more than any other voice in the movement called it into being. Though others picked up his mantle and received the plaudits, it remains true that today we enjoy the freedom of expression and lifestyle we actually possess largely because he convinced us that it was not only desirable but possible, and inspired us to make it be.

When the two poets first met on Everson's furlough, Rexroth was, of course, already a brilliant and established man of letters. Since

1927, he had been living in San Francisco, first with his wife Andree then, after her death, with his second wife Marie, writing, painting, and thoroughly involving himself in Anarchist politics. In 1941, he had declared himself a conscientious objector (though he was more or less past the draft age), and in 1944 his long philosophical poem, *The Phoenix and the Tortoise*, had outlined his anarcho-pacifist beliefs, winning the California Literature Silver Medal. Though the city had a literary tradition running through Samuel Clemens and Edwin Markham, when he had arrived in San Francisco, it had become, in his estimation, "a backwater town where there just wasn't anything happening." But through his own extended efforts as much as anything else, by the time Everson arrived that had changed. Rexroth acted, according to the poet, as a general heading "the long honorable San Francisco tradition of Bohemian-Buddhist-Wobbly-mystical-anarchist social involvement" in its decade-long storming of the New Critical fortress (represented by critics like John Crowe Ransom and Cleanth Brooks, and journals like *Sewanee Review*), culminating in his editing of the special "San Francisco Scene" issue of *Evergreen Review* in 1957.

A few months after the incident with Connolly, New Directions published D.H. Lawrence's *Selected Poems* with Rexroth's inflammatory introduction: "Any bright young man can be artful," he wrote. "It is always the lesser artists who are artful, they must learn their trade by rote." And again, "I suppose it is the absolutism which has swept over popular taste in the wake of Cubism which has encouraged the ignorant to expect a canzone of Dante's in every issue of their favorite little magazine, a School of Athens in every WPA mural." Although Rexroth supported numerous younger writers in the Bay Area after the war, Duncan, Lamantia, and Everson were singled out by the elder poet as his crack troops. Everson recalled that "During the war, Rexroth brooded deeply, wrote his best poetry, and began to put it all together":

Looking back on it, it seems to me that the only mistake he made was his rejection of Jeffers. Other than that, he saw the gleam of the future in the combination of Lawrentian passionate eroticism, populist-anarchist-collective surge and American precisionist adhesion through Bill Williams. I was to be his Lincolnesque populist pacifist—the "pome splitter," Duncan a celebrative Dionysian aesthete with formalist adhesions to the precisionists, Lamantia a Dionysian surrealist.

"It would have worked," Everson concluded, "if we could have held it together, but the personality problems and the women blew it up. Thus San Francisco." The "personality problems" were as real as with any group of artists working in highly charged and competitive circumstances, leading to various fallings-out. One of the more indicative in terms of internecine warfare within Rexroth's ranks involved George Leite and Duncan.

The most important literary journal to appear in the Bay Area during this period was *Circle*, edited by George Leite and Bern Porter, published in Berkeley. *Circle*'s first issue appeared in 1944, and ran for ten issues, the last appearing after a two-year hiatus in 1948. Its focus was literary, though it was both pacifist and anarchist as well; its credo: "When a technique becomes a school, death of creation is the result. Eclecticism is the only approach to Art in which there is no death. *Circle* is completely eclectic." Contributors included Everson, Rexroth, Duncan, Henry Miller, Anaïs Nin, Josephine Miles, Kenneth Patchen, William Carlos Williams, Thomas Parkinson, Harold Norse, Glen Coffield, and many others. Rexroth was particularly helpful in the early stages, writing short pieces on Robert McAlmon and Mina Loy under the title "Les Lauriers Sont Coupe"; further, he designed the cover for issue 3. And for a time, the journal was a focus of the Bay Area literary scene.

Everson first met Leite through Lee Watkins. The Watkinses had been living in Berkeley since 1940, and that year they met the editor. Like Ham Tyler, on Watkins's advice Leite traveled down to Selma to meet Everson because of his interest in the poet's pac-

ifism and his literary work. Everson got along with him, though
certainly not as well as with Tyler, yet he remained wary. Still,
while a CO the poet contributed poems to two issues of the journal. But by the time Everson had moved to Berkeley, Leite's connections with the Bay Area literary group were strained. During
the last year of the war, he was working as a taxi driver in the East
Bay. One night he allegedly took a drunk to a bar, followed him
into the men's room, and came running out fast. The drunk came
lurching out, muttering that Leite had taken his wallet. A few days
later the police arrested him and he was brought to trial for assault
and robbery. He asked a number of his friends, including Lee
Watkins, to act as character witnesses for him, but he refused to
take them into his confidence as to what he was charged with or
as to his guilt or innocence. According to Everson, it wasn't until
they were all actually in the courtroom that they realized what
was going on. The prosecution didn't have, finally, enough evidence for conviction, but Watkins didn't appreciate being manip-
ulated in that way and after the trial he wrote Leite a letter telling
him he wanted nothing more to do with him. Rexroth and his
friends had been giving him much support, but because of incidents like this drew back from him. When Everson, not long out
of CPS, spoke to Rexroth of Leite, the elder poet said simply, "I
belong among the Watkins friends of George Leite."

Duncan had his own problems with the editor. His poem "An
African Elegy" had been accepted by John Crowe Ransom for
publication in *Kenyon Review*. When the poet's essay "The
Homosexual in Society" appeared in Dwight Macdonald's *Politics*,
Ransom, in what has become an infamous incident, returned the
poem with a letter telling the poet that he felt all homosexuals
should "be castrated." Leite had published Duncan's "The Year
As Catches" in May of 1946, and now Duncan approached him
with the "Elegy." Leite agreed to publish the poem, but wanted
to run along with it materials relating to Ransom's rejection.
Duncan at this time was trying to downplay the incident, and the
two men wrangled over the sensationalizing of the poem.

Although it eventually appeared in the last number of *Circle* without any apparatus as "Towards An African Elegy," this run-in marked the end of Leite's relationship with Duncan. Thirty years later, Leite, who in the fifties gravitated to the Henry Miller group in Big Sur, told one of Everson's publishers that the only member of the Bay Area group he had any respect for was Everson, that both Rexroth and Duncan had betrayed him.

From the start there were other strains as well. Thomas Parkinson and Josephine Miles, poets and Professors of English at Berkeley, had serious quarrels with both Duncan and Jack Spicer centering on the Berkeley Writers' Conference, which Parkinson and Miles, along with Leonard Wolf, had started with university funding soon after the war. Parkinson and Miles had invited both Duncan and Spicer to participate, and by 1948 they were each conducting their own workshops under the aegis of the Conference, as well as inviting speakers like Rexroth to lecture on occasion. There were widespread rumors that Duncan and Spicer were simply using their positions to monopolize the project, and that the whole thing was turning into a kind of "homosexual conspiracy." The group's regular publication, *Literary Behavior*, which was funded by the university's Department of English, ceased publication when Duncan, Spicer, and their poet friend Robin Blaser (who had been elected chairman of the Conference) tried to print a story by Richard Montague with homosexual overtones. After a serious confrontation between Mark Schorer, also a Professor in the department, and Duncan at a meeting to discuss these matters, the whole project was disbanded. Obviously after this, battle lines were drawn, with Miles and Parkinson on one side, Duncan and Spicer on the other.

Further, Duncan and Spicer themselves were moving more and more apart in their conceptions of the poet's vocation, with Spicer accusing Duncan of self-aggrandizement and criticizing his "Venice Poem" as "untrue"; Spicer would soon leave Berkeley for Minneapolis. Another of Duncan's close friends, Sanders Russell, had arrived from New York after the war. Like Duncan, he was strong-minded, and he immediately ran into conflict with both Rexroth and members of his group. In his arguments for the essentially ritualistic nature of true poetry, Duncan had also chosen to attack Rexroth's sense of poetry as communication, and thus a breach was widening between them.

vvv

Perhaps because of his temperament, or perhaps more simply because of his forty-hour a week job, Everson managed to remain more or less outside these quarrels, though eventually he would have a serious run-in with Rexroth, and after his conversion to Catholicism Duncan would simply drift away. His major literary project during these Berkeley years was the completion and compilation of his selected poems, *The Residual Years*. By the time he was demobilized, he had published eight short collections of verse. Through the years Kenneth Rexroth was instrumental in bringing a number of west coast writers to the attention of James Laughlin (Gary Snyder, for example, attributes the favorable response to his work by New Directions to Rexroth's "kindness"), though Everson was the first, as in early 1945 the poet approached Laughlin about the possibility of publishing Everson's collected poems. Before committing himself to such a project, Laughlin asked to publish a selection of Everson's most recent work in one of the New Directions Annual volumes, and thus *The Waldport Poems* was reprinted in volume 9 in 1945. Laughlin later told Everson that his poems were "better received" than any others in the book, and it was because of this that New Directions yielded to Rexroth's prodding and agreed to publish a selected poems the following year.

Everson worked on the compilation of *The Residual Years* during his few weeks at Treesbank in the fall of 1946. He asked Rexroth to write an introduction, but the elder poet refused, saying that the poems could stand on their own; as for the selections, Everson pleaded that he simply could not choose among his poems, and Rexroth agreed to do it. In his later introduction to Everson's collected pre-Catholic poetry, the 1968 *The Residual Years* (not to be confused with the earlier volume), Rexroth notes that he first read the younger poet's work in his short collection, *These Are the Ravens*, the self-published pamphlet which had appeared in 1935. Everson thinks Rexroth's memory is faulty in this instance, that in fact he first read his 1944 collection *War Elegies*, and this is probably not only correct but of some importance. About this time, Rexroth wrote Everson that he had met C.F. MacIntyre (the poet and translator whom Everson knew through their mutual friend, Lawrence Clark Powell), and during their meeting talk had turned to the CO's poetry. MacIntyre said he felt Everson's work was too derivative of Robinson Jeffers. Rexroth, who apparently had seen only the post-*Masculine Dead* verse, was astounded, unable to comprehend what MacIntyre was talking about. Rexroth was, it must be remembered, a bitter foe of Jeffers, an animosity brought about most probably by a profound reaction to Jeffers' philosophy of "inhumanism," and his imputed fascism. Everson then sent him *San Joaquin* and *These Are the Ravens*. Rexroth couldn't believe his eyes:

> Cry *peace* if you will.
> There is in the plasm the mood that denys it.
> There is in the fist the love of the striking.
> And out of the heart the savage inviolate flame.
> Life comes to it shining: grass choking, the wolves slashing.
> Napoleon, nor Ceasar, nor Genghis could have led the hordes,
> Unwilling, into the jaws. They ran down singing.

The Jeffersian stance and rhetoric are apparent, and Rexroth was not about to let this mar the image of the autochthon he was presenting to the world.

Later, in the *Evergreen Review* San Francisco issue, Rexroth would sum it up, writing of Everson that:

Like so many young poets he was naively accessible to influences his maturity would find dubious. In his case this was Jeffers, but he was, even then, able to transform Jeffers' noisy rhetoric into genuinely impassioned utterance, his absurd self-dramatization into real struggle in the depths of the self. Everson is still wrestling with his angel, still given to the long oratorical line with vague echoes of classical quantitative meters, but there is no apparent resemblance left to Jeffers.

But in 1947, with his poetic revolution at stake, Rexroth was taking no chances, and in editing *The Residual Years* he very consciously muted, if not completely expunged, the influence of Jeffers. He decided against Everson's original chronological arrangement, preferring to begin the volume with the six later pacifist collections, printing them entire. Rexroth then rather grudgingly selected a number of poems from the sixty-four printed in the first three volumes, and included them at the end of the manuscript. In 1946 he wrote Everson a letter on the subject:

Dear Bill,
    The honor is all mine, but let's not start Alphonsing and Gasconing about this.
    I have been reading over the poems in the first 3 books—there are not as many pages as I thought, but I do think there should be some pruning. Here is a first list of suggestions, see what you think of it.
    From THESE ARE THE RAVENS
Winter Plowing
First Winter Storm ("as I lay *there*" is more idiomatic)
Who Lives Here Harbors Sorrow?? The line used for the title is not idiomatic—"Those who live here harbor . . . sorrow . . . And *hold.*"

He goes on in this vein, listing twenty-eight more poems with comments from *San Joaquin* and *The Masculine Dead.* "These are just suggestions," Rexroth continues,

please don't think I am trying to be bossy. I have omitted poems that I thought were too obviously influenced, and, otherwise, those that suffer from the principle fault of your early verse—self-conscious Poetry. I would advise you to go through them all and catch any nonidiomatic, Poetic, language, and put it in normal speech—e.g. inversions, "not . . .

nor," "folk," "what of," "it is for us," etc. and cut out lines that over-explain the poem.

However, these are all just blemishes. It is an impressive performance for a young feller from the farm, better than most of the tradition in which you write—than any of Masters, than much of Sandburg, especially his late stuff, I think it compares very favorably with the few very best poems of Wallace Gould, whom you resemble most. The greatest blemish is the persistent echo of Jeffers in many of the poems in San Joaquin especially. After all—there is no resemblance whatsoever between the demons that possess you and Jeffers. Of course it is hard to write about the overwhelming and dehumanizing California landscape without sounding a little like Jeffers. Even I do—and I dislike him intensely, or anyway, did—I mellow.

The other books are a different kettle of fish. I don't think there is much to change or omit in them.

This gives about 25 pages set up like my book, maybe a little less, including only the poems about which I have no doubts, but including the M Dead as it is. Which should make maybe 70–75 pages altogether, and the rest to fill up with the Chronicle of Division.

The stress in this letter is obviously on ridding Everson of any semblance of "self-conscious Poetry," and in general the younger poet took the elder's advice. (He did not always agree, however; where Rexroth suggested, for example, that Everson change the line in "First Winter Storm" to better capture the idiomatic, the younger poet declined, feeling that the revision did not suit his ear.) Further, Rexroth's ordering of the poems proved effective—no reviewers mentioned the Jeffers influence. As Everson later recalled,

What makes this more remarkable is that Jeffers, having enjoyed the heights of celebrity following the Broadway success of his play *Medea* was just then being attacked coast to coast for *The Double Axe*, his protest poetry against World War II. The point is that Jeffers was very much in the foreground, and any derivation from the older poet would have been seized on and censured. As it turned out, not once did this happen.

"The entire episode," he continued, "is a remarkable testimonial to Rexroth's political acumen." The book was, on the whole, successful in establishing Everson as an autochthonic voice. James Dickey, in a later disparaging review of Everson's Catholic poetry, would recall that *The Residual Years* was "full of the hatred and necessity of sex, and of a very convincing and powerful from-the-inside-the-thing feeling about California farmers and farming"; that the poems collected there were "unforced and open."

A problem of a different nature arose, however, one that centered on the book's promotion rather than its poetry. Earlier I quoted passages from Rexroth's introduction to Lawrence's *Selected Poems*, an introduction that was as much a manifesto for a new poetry as an explanatory preface. Taking such occasions to throw down the gauntlet to the Literary Establishment was, of course, typical of Rexroth—his introduction to his *New British Poets* anthology is another well-known example. While he decided not to write any kind of preface to *The Residual Years*, he did write an extended anonymous blurb for the dustjacket:

A great deal of modern poetry has been complicated, intellectual, and unmotivated, and people weren't reading it any longer. William Everson's poetry is simple, sensuous, and passionate, as Milton said great poetry should be.

These poems are not abstract "aesthetic objects," but the utterances of a living man to other living men and women. As such, they are of the finest expressions of the new poetry of the post-war years, the best of which is characterized by its strong personal contact, lucid and direct presentation.

This kind of poetry may outrage academic circles where an emasculated and hallucinated imitation of John Donne is still considered chic; but others, who have been waiting for modern poetry to stop clearing its throat and stammering, should be delighted. The best poetry is not "public speech" as Auden would have it, or private speech to oneself as the surrealists and metaphysicals say, but intimate speech, from one to another, and it is this kind of poetry William Everson writes. He belongs in the tradition of D. H. Lawrence, a poet unfashionable recently, but now returning to influence. Everson's kin amongst contemporaries include Patchen and Rexroth, who share with him his intense personalism, his religious anarchism, and his rejection of war . . .

When Everson protested the jacket blurb Rexroth attributed it to himself, Laughlin, and another New Directions editor. He did say that he was surprised to find his name on the book three times, once in the acknowledgments and twice on the jacket. In any case, the blurb certainly carries the stamp of Rexroth's polemic.

And Leslie Fiedler, in a discussion of the book (along with new work by Randall Jarrell, John Berryman, and William Carlos Williams) for *Partisan Review*, rose to the well-cast bait. Interestingly, though not unexpectedly, Fiedler didn't deal with Everson's poetry much at all (quoting not a single line), but rather focused his attack on the blurb:

The jacket blurb on William Everson's book . . . is a kind of manifesto: poems are no longer to be "abstract aesthetic objects," but intimate speech, sensuous and passionate. The paired adjectives suggest, of course, Milton, but it is D.H. Lawrence via Rexroth and Patchen, who is actually invoked, and we should perhaps read for the most conventional pair—phallic and sentimental. . . . For Everson, at least, Lawrence serves primarily as a guarantor for the transference of bad writing, that is to say, flagrant sentimentalizing about copulation from prose to what is, presumably, verse. . . . In the end, his poems are *parasitic*; they define themselves negatively against the convention of the last generation, what he, or his publisher, chooses to call "emasculated imitations of John Donne . . ."

I'm not sure at all that this last statement is true, and in any case if it were it would qualify Everson for inclusion in the ranks of Harold Bloom's company of stronger poets. But in 1948, Everson was once again caught in the cross-fire of a raging literary civil war.

Everson from the start had been unhappy with the blurb, feeling that it would draw comment which would be more a rebuttal of Rexroth than a consideration of his own work, and when he read Fiedler's review the tension that had been developing between the two men reached the point of strain. They had already had a number of extra-aesthetic disagreements. Rexroth had been trying to publish a journal he wanted to edit, and he asked Everson to print it. When James Laughlin made a trip to San Francisco the three men discussed the project. Rexroth made his proposal, but, once he left the room, Laughlin told Everson, "Kenneth doesn't understand these things; of course we can't go ahead with it." Everson's handpress printing restricted his capabilities to fine printing and limited editions—he certainly would not have been able to undertake the large-scale, on-going job Rexroth envisioned. When he was at last convinced that Everson could not print his journal, Rexroth declared they should go to Grabhorn Press, a respected San Francisco printer. Laughlin demurred, saying that they were too expensive. "Too expensive?" Rexroth replied. "The Grabhorns can sell everything they print! Why, they could print clap medicine stickers for public toilets and sell them to collectors for five dollars apiece!" The journal never got off the ground and Rexroth soon accused Everson, unfairly, of subverting the project.

To make matters worse, Everson was disappointed with the typography of *The Residual Years*, printed by Peter Beilenson, one of the best printers in the country, and he angered Rexroth with his objections. Further, Rexroth wanted to throw a publication party for the book, but Everson equivocated. Rexroth was stung by the rebuff, and the idea was dropped. Which of these trifling incidents proved to be the last straw is not clear, but when it came it was vicious. "You son of a bitch," Rexroth wrote. "You're the most evasive man I have ever known. When we meet again, come in swinging!"

But the deepest irony lay in the fact that the review that most furthered the reception of *The Residual Years* was not written by one of the San Francisco writers but by a New Critic. Writing in *The Saturday Review*, Dudley Fitts, after noting many faults, concluded,

Despite of which lapses and California extravagances, *The Residual Years* makes its point and makes it powerfully. The opening sequence, as marital narrative, may not be more than ordinary; but there is something more than the ordinary in the assurance of its psychological probing, and entire sections of it—especially the first, a sharp and unforgettable treatment of a camp for conscientious objectors—are completely integrated and achieved poems. "March"—a poem about love though scarcely a love poem—is an example of how economy and sheer control can prepare for and make plausible a conclusion whose sexual violence would otherwise blow the poem apart. There are small but perfect jewels of symbolic landscape, such as "The Approach" and "A Winter Ascent," and so on. "Flesh violent with love, / Brain coiling and breeding these germinal poems"; the description is just. *The Residual Years* is germinal, and its proliferation haunts the mind.

It was this review that brought Everson to the notice of poets like James Dickey, Robert Lowell, and Richard Eberhart. What Rexroth thought of it Everson would never know; by the time it arrived the elder poet had left for Europe on a Guggenheim, and the two men were, temporarily, not speaking to one another. Rexroth's revolution was for the moment put on the back burner, but in the fifties it would flare again with the emergence of the Beat Generation. The rift with Rexroth would heal and as Brother Antoninus Everson would once again be his autochthon, only no longer billed as the Lincolnesque farmer but another John the Baptist in a Dominican habit.

▼▼▼

It was the publication and reception of *The Residual Years* that led Everson to apply in 1948 for a Guggenheim Fellowship himself. His letters of support came from Lawrence Clark Powell, Josephine Miles, Ruth Stephan (whom he didn't know, but who had given *The Residual Years* a positive notice in her journal *Tiger's Eye*), and Robert Duncan. Duncan wrote in November an especially extended statement for the Foundation, arguing that *The Residual Years* marked Everson as a signal poet, one whose "widest concept" was "the poetic synthesis in which one heartbeat may be realized poetically for man and nature."

This concept is not for Everson—as it was for Blake—to project a mythic synthesis; but it is—as it was for Whitman or Melville, for Thoreau or for Emerson—an effort of the imagination to relate all of the world experienced to a whole of dignity and meaning. Thus, Everson has had little interest in developing verbal elaborations or metaphysical overtones. What we witness is the successful emergence from the pen of a poet sophisticated to and learned in all the major developments of modern poetry of a personal idiom without diversion from the singleness of its task.

Picking up on Rexroth's image of the autochthon, Duncan dismisses, like the book's jacket-blurb, the "major devices of modern poetry"—wit, irony, metaphysical conceit—insisting that Everson's interests, like Whitman's, lie elsewhere: "What we find is—at its worse, a tortuous uprooting of the barest emotions, a painful utterance, a barbaric earnestness; at its best, a subtly varied consonantal alliterative Gothic structure allowing for the most rooted dignity."

Duncan goes on to single out Everson's sequence tracing his life in the CPS and his separation from Edwa, "The Chronicle of Division." No poet in the west, he argues, including Jeffers and Rexroth, "has surpassed the vision and eloquence of the passages of this poem which form a refrain evocative of the sea."

Here is in poetry an art which reaches in achievement toward the great and devout monuments of Japanese painters of the Pacific; and there is recall to our minds of those earliest Saxon poets, men of the sea, or of passages of Eliot's meditations upon the sea in "Dry Salvages" . . .

Part of all this picture is the integrity of all efforts which this poetic life has demanded. At the present time, working 8 hours a day as a janitor, Everson at once maintains his life as a poet corresponding with other poets, reading at public meetings, not only continuing to write, slowly—reworking and discarding—but at the same time seeks to realize a synthesis further between his writing and its presentation. Like William Morris—who also devoted his life to realize thru art the natural dignity of man—Mr. Everson has worked to produce his work from a handpress—a process as slow, as beautiful, as effortful and exacting as the demands which he has placed initially upon his writing.

"The Medieval Christian world," Duncan concludes, "had a concept of Grace and of Work done in the sight of God. It is something of this concept of work which has been realized both in Everson's printing and in his writing."

It is unfortunate commentary on literary politics in America that west coast writers have traditionally been slighted in terms of major awards. Almost unbelievably, when Gary Snyder won the Pulitzer Prize for Poetry in 1975 for his collection *Turtle Island*, he became the first California poet to ever win the honor—Jeffers did not, nor Rexroth, nor of course Duncan. Thus, the fact that when on April 11, 1949, the year's Guggenheim Fellowship recipients were announced Californians, for the second year in a row, led the list of artists, writers, and scientists with 27 out of 144 nationwide winners is rather astonishing. Receiving average stipends of $3,000, California Fellows included Wallace E. Stegner, photographer Homer Gordon Page, composer Leon Kirchner, and classicist Maria-Rosa Lida Malkiel. Rexroth received a year's extension of his 1948 award, while Everson was given a grant of $2400 (his salary at the university) to free him for a year to write poetry and continue his printing.

In their reporting of the awards, the Bay Area newspapers latched on to Everson's janitorial job, and for a few days his Fellowship received the most attention, with articles and photographs running under such headlines as "Berkeley Janitor Wins Famed Prize As Poet" (*The Oakland Post Examiner*) and "Janitor

Who Got to Parnassus On a Mop Will Take Time Out" (*The San Francisco Examiner*). The story in the *SF Examiner* was particularly amusing, opening with "Rarely in these days does a poet ride to fame on anything so utilitarian as a dirty mop." According to the reporter, Everson believed that the best way for an artist to make a living was through manual labor—"You can get a much better perspective of human beings from the lower levels," the poet is quoted as saying; "if you're too far above them, the picture is distorted." Further, he is portrayed as the stereotypic, care-free amateur poet, "I've never made much money, but it has been enough. I'm still writing and I'm still happy." There is no mention of his CPS experience, his pacifism, his anarchism. "The mop and pail," the reporter assured his down-to-earth readers who might be put off by the poet's university affiliation, "are Everson's only connection with the university. He never went to college, is uninterested in anything about the school except its press." In the margin of his clipping of this article, Everson wrote on April 13, "A Tissue of Lies. The reporter talked to me about 15 or 20 minutes. I never said nor implied these statements. It is a piece of unforgivable snobbery served up for 'the man in the street.'" Regardless of the paper's distortions, however, the award was real, and in June of 1949 he took a year's leave from his job at the U.C. Press.

William Everson
at age one

Everson family: William, Louis, Lloyd, Vera, Francelia, 1920

William Everson,
high school yearbook,
1929
*(Courtesy of the Bancroft Library,
University of California, Berkeley)*

Everson family: Lloyd, William, Vera, Louis, Francelia, Christmas 1934
(Courtesy of the Bancroft Library, University of California, Berkeley)

Everson reading in Edwa Poulson's backyard, Selma, 1937

At Treesbank: Hal Lubin, William Everson, Mary and Ham Tyler, 1946
(Courtesy of Mary Tyler)

Treesbank,
the apple-
dryer, 1946

Kenneth Rexroth

*(Courtesy of
James Laughlin)*

FIVE

Conversion
and The
Catholic
Worker

In 1932 Carl Jung wrote that "among my patients in the second half of life—that is to say, over thirty five—there has not been one whose problem in the last resort was not that of finding a religious outlook on life." In 1948 Everson was a year beyond Jung's climacteric. He had undergone the traumas of his internment and his divorce from Edwa, and his pantheism, as he explained in a 1965 interview, was failing: "My pantheism had suffered a stunning blow at the collapse of the first marriage because that pantheism was based on a kind of religious sexuality which was really brought up short in the breakdown of that relationship. In a way the whole strength of my pantheist adhesion had been shocked by the human failure. It was as if my intent to make a religiousness out of sex alone had come a cropper on the bare human personal relationship. The fact of the personal relationship disrupting in the middle of this transcending mysticism, sexual mysticism, it was like one part of my nature saying, 'Hold on a minute!'"

Perhaps because he had embarked on Jung's quest, or perhaps

more simply because he wanted to please a Catholic woman he was seeing regularly, Everson had started occasionally attending Sunday mass. In either case, however, his interest soon became more than academic as he found himself drawn to the personal element in Catholicism. He felt his marriage was flawed by his inability to form a close enough bond with Edwa. But now his relationship with this Catholic woman "broke both my Jeffersian pantheism and my Lawrentian erotic mysticism. She personalized this, her whole touch was to personalize, to humanize; she had that laughing sensibility of the personal dimension in the human physical and natural context . . . It was this that was my stepping stone to my conversion to Catholicism." In October, he came across a copy of St. Augustine's *Confessions*, which Everson lost himself in thoroughly, responding to Augustine's intense conversion experience, his obsession with women, and his sense of a highly personal God. "The candor is wholly winning," he wrote later, "so frank, so *manly*, that I found myself melting . . . Augustine is a great psychologist, one of the very greatest. The confidence through which he exposed the weaknesses of his humanity by addressing himself to his creator, is most edifying. He taught me how to confess, and what to confess. This insight into confession gave me an insight into my excessive self-denigration, one of the more crippling facets of my nature, and showed me the possibility of reprieve, through the objectivity of the sacrament."

The Christmas of 1948 was the first after the disorder of the war years that midnight mass was reinstituted in San Francisco. On Christmas Eve, Everson went to midnight mass at St. Mary's Cathedral, which has since been destroyed by fire, where "the nuns had prepared the Crib to one side of the sanctuary, with fir trees banked about a minature stable." There, suddenly, as he

crouched out there on the sheepflats of man's terrestrial ambiguity, with nothing but the rags of pitiful pride between me and that death something was spoken into my soul, and hearing I followed. When the fir-smell reached me across the closed interior air of the Cathedral, binding as it did the best of my past and the best of my future, shaping for the first time that synthesis of spirit and sense I had needed and never found, I was drawn across, and in the smell of the fir saw it for the first time, not merely as an existent thing, but as a *created* thing, witness of the Word, the divine Logos, who made all earth, and me, a soul in his own image, out of very love. And I saw in the fact of Creation the end of Creation; and in the end of Creation saw indeed the unspeakable Lover who draws the loved one out of the web of affliction, remakes him as His own. It was then that I could rise from the pew, and, following like a hound the trace on the air, go where the little images lay, in the Crib there, so tiny, among the simple beasts, watched over by the cleanly woman and the decent man, and these humble ones, my good friends the sheepherders, who in that instant outleaped the philosophers. That was the night I entered into the family and fellowship of Christ—made my assent, such as it was—one more poor wretch, who had nothing to bring but his iniquities.

By early April Everson had begun taking instruction as a catechumen at St. Augustine's Church in Oakland. After the conversion experience he had begun attending mass almost every day, though he could not receive communion as he was not yet baptized. There were thirteen other students in the class, which met once a week for three months. Between his years in the CPS camp and his friendships with other writers, he had covered often in late-night argument most of the basic religious questions that served as subjects for discussion, and thus found himself acting as much as self-appointed assistant to the priest as a student. On one occasion, a middle-aged woman who was taking the course because, like most of the others, she was going to marry a Catholic, insisted on knowing why Catholics had saints dedicated to every conceivable trivial concern. As the priest tried patiently to explain, using Saint Anthony as an example, Everson suddenly shot out from the back of the room, "Only fools would ask that kind of question. Nothing's trivial. Pray for every single breath you take!" with the enthusiasm of the newly converted. At another instance, a student accused the priest of cannibalism when he brought up the subject of the Eucharist. He stumbled for a reply, and again Everson broke in. "Of course it's cannibalism. The body and the blood of Christ! And that's why it's so wonderful—it satisfies one of man's strongest instincts, to eat his kind!" Needless to say, at times the priest could only shake his head in bewilderment.

On July 23, the poet was baptized at St. Augustine's. Madeline Gleason came from San Francisco to act as his godmother in a private ceremony attended by only the two of them and the priest. Through the remainder of the year, Everson attended daily mass, receiving communion, and going to confession. His reading during this period was fairly exclusively in theology, more Augustine and Aquinas, and especially in the lives of the saints. He was struck particularly by a biography of St. Francis, the figure he felt most drawn to at the time. He did manage, however, to read through Eric Gill's autobiography, finding interest in Gill's sense of the printer's craft.

Before receiving instruction Everson had written "Triptych for the Living," his opening salvo as a Catholic poet:

> As if the great device of the flesh,
> The need of the flesh
> Made flesh, the flesh
> Founded forever upon the flesh,
> Blood on the blood—
> As if, on the instant, the stroke were checked,
> And the same flame sprang through,
> Purely, between the forces of the pang,
> Hued with the flush of Godhead,
> Sets round with the tongues of angels,
> Burning and flashing
> In the strewn litter
> On the somber floor.

The three-part poem was completed within a week of the conversion experience, and a number of religious poems followed in rapid order. Everson's usual output was about a dozen poems a year; now, between "Triptych" and November 22, he wrote 28 poems, including "The Making of the Cross," "The Wise," "The

Massacre of the Holy Innocents," and the poems that comprise the "Falling of the Grain," a major sequence of eight parts tracing his life since the war.

During these months, Everson began to think seriously of entering a religious Order, as he felt in danger of entering into another sexual relationship. Further, in his convert's fervor, he wanted to get to the core of Catholicism as fast as possible, and this seemed to him located in the hermetic traditions of the Orders. Thomas Merton had continued his vocation as a poet and essayist after becoming a Trappist, and Everson hoped that membership in an Order would both allow him to more fully embrace his Catholicism while at the same time support his poetry and printing. His first thought was to apply to the Benedictines because he was particularly interested in continuing his printing and the Order had a tradition of handcrafts. In the late summer he had an interview with the Novice Master, but it did not go well. When he asked about the possibility of his continuing to write and print, he was told that he couldn't lay personal claim to such talents, that if the Benedictines saw a use for them in their general plan, then he would be encouraged; otherwise, he would not. When a month later he traveled by bus to Santa Barbara for a similar interview with the Franciscan Novice Master, he was told the same thing. Thus while he did not give up the idea of entering an Order, for a time he pursued it no further.

▼▼▼

By April 1950, Everson had to vacate the Ashby house. During the late summer he had sent his "Triptych for the Living" to the *Catholic Worker*, edited by Dorothy Day, and it was accepted for publication. "Dear Mr. Everson," Dorothy Day had written him in November accepting the poem, "It is inexcusable of us not to have written you sooner. We were overwhelmed by your poem. It is beautiful . . . Do look up Fr. Duggan at St. Mary's in Oakland. We hope to start a house near there. I'll be out in

January some time and hope to see you." And thus he packed his things and headed for Maurin House in Oakland.

Dorothy Day, whom at her death in 1980 David O'Brien in an article in *Commonweal* called "the most significant, interesting, and influential person in the history of American Catholicism," was like Everson a convert, and like him had been greatly influenced by Augustine. Coming from a background of radical thought (early in her life she had worked for the Anti-Conscription League and *The Masses*), she founded The Catholic Worker organization in 1933, with a Frenchman named Peter Maurin. Their program was simple, "to realize in the individual and society the expressed and implied teachings of Christ," and frankly socialist. Two important aspects of their mission were first the founding of various forums for dialogue to present the message of Catholic socialism (which included the establishment of a newspaper) and second to create Houses of Hospitality in every parish in the country to deal with the homeless and unemployed. On May 1, 1933, the first issue of the *Catholic Worker* appeared and was distributed at a Communist rally in Union Square in New York, and within just two years the circulation grew to 150,000. The paper described the establishment of the Houses of Hospitality, though none existed at first; derelicts, reading the announcements, began to show up at Day's apartment for food and lodging. Soon, the Catholic Worker took a building of its own, both for the paper and to feed the homeless, and the idea eventually spread throughout the East Coast; by 1943, there were thirty such houses, each founded according to the principles of the Catholic Worker, yet each independent and responsible for its own maintenance. According to the paper's first editorial, the *raison d'etre* for both the publication and the Houses was to address "those who think there is no hope for the future, no recognition of their plight":

It's time there was a Catholic paper printed for the unemployed. The fundamental aim of most radical sheets is the conversion of the readers to Radicalism and Atheism.

Is it not possible to protest, to expose, to complain, to point out abuses and demand reforms without desiring the overthrow of religion?

In an attempt to popularize and make known the encyclicals of the Popes in regard to social justice and the program put forth by the Church for the "reconstruction of the social order," this news sheet, *The Catholic Worker*, is started.

Everson had been raised to believe that the Catholic Church was a rigid, authoritarian organization, but reading issues of *The Catholic Worker* at Waldport earlier had shown him that there was a strain of the Church that was both anarchist and pacifist. Now it was to this Catholic social activism that he found himself drawn.

Maurin House, one of Day's first west coast Houses of Hospitality, was located at 5th and Washington Streets, just off Broadway on Skid Row in Oakland (the building has since been razed for construction of a freeway). Everson had immediately taken Day's advice and introduced himself to Fr. Duggan, who was in fact at that very time in the process of making final arrangements for the opening of the house. He explained his situation to the priest—that he felt called to an Order but couldn't give up his writing, that his Guggenheim was almost finished, and that he simply needed a place to live—and Duggan insisted that he gather his belongings and move into Maurin House, working at odd jobs for his keep, and spending as much time as possible in prayer. When Everson had received his fellowship he had taken a leave of absence from his university job; now he told the Press that he would not return and instead decided to accept Duggan's offer.

In the spring of 1950, Everson moved into the house, which was being administrated by Charles Gahegen, a Catholic Worker layman from New York whom Dorothy Day had sent out to open the facility a few months before. He had been introduced to Gahegen in January by Fr. Duggan, and though he had misgivings about Gahegen's obvious homosexuality, he soon saw that Day had chosen the right man for the job. Generally, the Catholic Worker did not meet with great public approval, so at times soliciting operating funds was a difficulty. But as Everson remembers, "Gahegen could be ruthless when he saw an opening he needed to exploit. He began to cultivate income from some of the Catholic Irish office holders around the city, and soon he had community support. He was a fine propagandist." He immediately got a soup line going, getting the parish to set up a store-front kitchen, then a few doors away he got hold of a dilapidated rooming house for a very small rental.

Gahegen had worked for Day at various Houses of Hospitality on the east coast, and although she knew he was homosexual there had never been any complaint about his personal life. When he showed enthusiasm to go to Oakland to establish the house, she sent him without hesitation. Unfortunately, however, within short order, before Everson's arrival, Gahegen's homosexuality did become a problem. The strain of working day and night essentially by himself to set up the facility took its toll very quickly. The rooming house could sleep forty men, and the beds would fill rapidly; Gahegen would allow additional men to sleep on the floor. In part, this was to protect them from the cold. However, because of the crowding he could conveniently let a young man sleep with him in his office just off the main room without, he thought, much notice. At one point, Gahegen had an altercation with one of the transients, and he was forced to kick the man out of the house. The transient immediately went to complain to Fr. Duggan of Gahegen's homosexuality. At first Duggan dismissed this information as being simply the fantasy of a man who wanted revenge. Not long after Everson arrived, however, there was another complaint to Duggan, who this time confronted Gahegen with the charge, which he admitted to, and Duggan was forced to ask Gahegen to resign. Thus the running of the house, within a matter of just two or three weeks, fell to Everson and Carroll McCool.

▼▼▼

One of the primary reasons Duggan suggested to Everson that he go to Maurin house was the presence of Carroll McCool, an ex-

Trappist monk. He had been at the Utah Trappist monastery for about eight months, then gravitated to Oakland to begin work with Gahegen. Now suddenly he was director of the house, with Everson acting as his assistant, and though while neither man was particularly prepared for such responsibility, they managed to work together and keep the house operating for the next fourteen months. Duggan had hoped that McCool's rather naive Catholicism would have a good effect on Everson's need for prayer and reflection, and it did. Within days of meeting each other, before Gahegen's leaving, McCool suddenly turned to Everson and told him that he wasn't praying enough. Everson was rather astonished at this, considering he was going to mass and saying a rosary a day, but McCool told him that such an effort was painless. He had been a G.I. during the war, had gone through the entire European campaign, fighting in both Africa and Italy, as well as Germany, and he carried into his religion simplicity but extreme concentration garnered from his wartime experiences. "You follow me on a regimen for ten days," he told Everson, "and I'll *guarantee* results. Say ten rosaries a day with me and it'll change your life." Everson accepted his challenge:

I started with him on it. We were going around the streets saying the rosary, really pouring it on . . . *Hail Mary full of grace, the Lord is with Thee.* Parishioners at St. Mary's began to protest to Duggan—'these nuts are making a travesty of our religion, walking around the public streets together mumbling their prayers.' The priest came to us and asked us to cool it, to confine it to the house and the church. So after that we spent our days after our house work in either of those places. Soon we began upping the ante, so that we are saying 30 rosaries every day. It was grueling work, utterly grueling.

On the tenth day of this intense prayer (which included besides the rosaries, up to four masses a day and the reading together of St. Teresa's *Way of Perfection*), Everson was utterly exhausted. At six a.m. on the morning of the Feast of St. Joseph he knelt down at mass at St. Mary's, fearful that he would not be able to continue with McCool's program, when suddenly, as he recorded in a note-book from the period,

I was seized with a feeling so intense as to exceed anything I had previously experienced. It was a feeling of extreme anguish and joy, of transcendent spirituality and of a great, thrilling, physical character. I knelt in the pew, twisted to one side, the rosary wound in my hands, the tears streaming down my face. From the tabernacle had issued to me something like an intense invisible ray, a dark ray, like a ray of light seen in the mind only. I saw nothing with my eyes but I felt it very powerfully in my soul. I knew instantly that this ray came from our Divine Lord, and further I knew that it was the character of the Sacred Heart. It was utter concentration, the quintessence of love. It was as if all aspects of human love I had ever known, both spiritual and physical, were suddenly brought forward a thousandfold and thrust against my heart. It was as if His very lips, as if His mouth wonderfully sweet, were pressed to my heart.

This invasion of light is common in such accounts, occurring even in Augustine's *Confessions*, wherein in his apostrophe to God Augustine exclaims, "You shone upon me; your radiance enveloped me; you put my blindness to flight." The event proved to be the outstanding mystical experience of Everson's life. It was as if the Christmas conversion had merely pointed him towards the door of the Church; now, "I realized that although I had wanted to believe in Christ before, and had sworn I did, I was believing in an abstraction, something I had in no way experienced. But now for the first time I had the powerful and overwhelming experience of the unmitigated love of Christ and for the first time I truly believed."

Not long after his vision, Everson related the experience to Fr. Duggan, who immediately suggested he explain the episode to a friend of his who was a mystical theologian named Fr. Leo Osborn, a Dominican at St. Albert's College in Oakland. Everson went to see the man one afternoon and over coffee described his daily regime and the experience itself to him in great detail. As he spoke, the priest lowered his eyes and began nodding in recognition. "Yes," he told the poet, "this is authentic. But you must modify your intense prayer life. Ease off a bit; it has served a real purpose, but you'll destroy your health." At that moment he became Everson's spiritual advisor, though for the next two weeks McCool and Everson more or less kept up their pace. On June first, he wrote in his notebook,

My second conference with Father Osborn yesterday. I told him that after our first conference two weeks ago I had let down from the six to eight hours of prayer per day, probably by virtue of what I took to be his implication that this was extreme; that the two weeks interim was full of difficulties and distractions and seeming remoteness from God . . . I told him of my need to get out in the country and be a solitary, my great desire to take up my printing and writing, and my need for mortifications and my inability to exact them here.

Life at the house itself was not particularly physically taxing for Everson. Whenever McCool was away, he would be in charge of organizing the meals and the sleeping quarters; otherwise, aside from a few odd chores he was free to spend his time as he wished. For breakfast the shelter provided day-old pastries from a local bakery and coffee for the work crew; for lunch, up to a thousand men a day received soup; for supper, the crew and the forty men who were lucky enough to get beds would have their one good meal of the day of meat, vegetables, and potatoes. "What surprised me," Everson later remembered, "was that the whole thing worked the way Dorothy Day said it would—each day people would bring produce to us, so all we ever had to buy for the soup was the stock, and even that was often donated by butchers. Gahegen early on had a great gift for getting that stuff, but once he left both McCool and I were too bashful. Once a woman asked me if I'd go out to her apostolic women's group in the suburbs to talk about our work, with the proviso that I could make a pitch for money. I got out there, was eloquent on the work, but when it came to asking for money, I couldn't do it. Finally, a lady came over and gave me a dollar, then the rest followed. The things we needed just seemed to show up." Although St. Mary's sponsored the house, the men who were served were not required to take part in any type of religious activity; there was one group rosary after supper, but no one was forced to participate, and there was no chapel in the House. Beyond management, Everson was responsible for little other work. He would go to six o'clock mass each morning, receiving daily communion and confession once a week.

Yet living on Skid Row was dispiriting, and looking back at his fourteen months there he sees it as "the dark night of the soul, being in the whale's belly. I would have died had I stayed there permanently, gone through a real crisis. My sensibility was in a state of revolt and I was getting thinner and weaker each day." He told Fr. Osborn of his "disgust with West Oakland, the squalor, filth, and sin, and the assailing and deliberate temptations the region breeds." And as he noted in his journal,

Yesterday God made a great Wound in my heart, and made me wretched. It is better to be wretched. In my wretchedness one sees what the self is. It is best to be wounded, to suffer. When we suffer the Wound of God's love we live in that suffering—we are from that time cut away from our pride . . . It would be better for one if he could live with that Wound always. These must be the saints. For while the Wound is with you everything you are is known as the truth—pure debasement, pure fallenness.

And again,

I am exhausted. I crave rest, surcease. My soul is dry, arid, speechless, mum. I love God with my whole will but my will only, and I am being shown how weak I am and how easily I may be deflected. I do not know if I will ever be taken back into his graces.

At first, Osborn advised Everson not to take up his writing and printing for a time, as each would prove a distraction to his prayer life, "that God had brought me to West Oakland, perhaps for purification, and that Christ uses us to continue his own work of purification in the area." But as the meetings continued, apparently in an attempt to offset his depression, he soon suggested that it was time for the poet to return to his craft. The advice proved very apt, as some of Everson's most powerful early religious writing comes directly out of this period. The first poem he wrote once given Osborn's permission, and arguably still his most compelling, was "The Canticle to The Waterbirds," which he completed on August 5 (though later he would date the poem October 4 in honor of the Feast of Saint Francis). In a preface to the poem he explained,

In the long summer dusks we used to walk to the Oakland estuary among the deserted factories and warehouses, and out along the silent piers. Where all day long an inferno of deafening racket enveloped the machines, now lay a most blessed peace. In these moments of solitude we thought of the men back at the hospice, broken, shabby, wine-sotted, hopeless. Out there on the estuary, over the water, the gulls lifted their wings in a gesture of pure felicity. Something hidden and conclusive broke bondage within me, something born of the nights and the weeks and the months. My mind shot north up the long coast of deliverance, encompassing all the areas of my ancient quest, that ineluctable instinct for the divine—the rivermouths and the sand-skirted beaches, sea-granite capes and bastions and basalt-founded cliffs—where despite all man's meanness a presence remains unspoiled, the sacred zone between earth and sea, and pure.

Then came shortly after "The Encounter," followed rapidly by the first section of the two-part "Hospice Of The Word," which describes his disgust at life at the house:

> In the ventless room,
> Over the beds at the hour of rising,

Hangs now the smother and stench of the crude flesh;
And at the grimed sink
We fill the basin of our mutual use,
Where our forty faces, rinsed daily,
Leaves each its common trace . . .

Further, also on Osborn's advice he moved his press from Ashby
to Maurin House, setting it up in a small shed in the back of the
rooming house. There he began work printing *Triptych for the
Living*. Although publishing only an announcement and *A Privacy
of Speech*, the Equinox Press had established a reputation; still,
wanting a more specifically religious connotation, he decided to
change his press name to The Seraphim. Interestingly, though by
this point Everson was seriously interested in the Dominicans, he
chose the Franciscan model over the Dominican.

The Seraphim is one of the orders of angels. It is the order that of all
angels is the highest. I think the two highest orders of the angels are the
Seraphim and the Cherubim. The Franciscans have adopted the
Seraphim as their "mascot." The Dominicans have adopted the
Cherubim. The Cherubim were supposed to move more by knowledge
and the Seraphim moved more by love. My instincts at that time were
very much more Franciscan than Dominican. I was a natural born beatnik type of Franciscan. The Dominicans, with their real structured intel-
lectuality and what not, were too Apollonian for me.

The shed which housed the press was far smaller than either the
room at the Ashby house or the apple-dryer at Treesbank, and
Everson could barely make his way around the massive
Washington. Within a few months, however, he managed to print
200 copies of the book, though he destroyed about half the sheets
because he felt they were flawed, and didn't get around to binding
the edition until the following year.

The Bay Area literary scene of the late forties had temporarily
cooled, as Rexroth remained in Europe and Duncan headed to St.
Elizabeths to visit Ezra Pound. Soon, under the influence of

Osborn's counseling, Everson began to read books by English and French Dominicans, who at the time were more intellectually sophisticated in matters of theology than their American counterparts. Eventually, Everson suggested to Osborn that perhaps he had been directed in a very roundabout way to the Dominicans for a purpose. As he wrote him in early 1951,

He will not let me be. What is He goading me on to? What is this hunger for the habit, for a life wholly involved in religion? This perplexes me. In the world I have everything I need for my fulfillment: two careers budding, and they are certainly more advantageously pursued where I am than in an order. I have no responsibilities or attachments, familial or institutional. Furthermore, I am now living a life of poverty, celibacy and performing the works of mercy. Yet I am constantly drawn on. I hunger for the habit, for the vows, for the obedience. And I hunger for the life. I hunger for the knowledge—the soul and the knowledge of the religious life, for the amplification of the mind in the things of God, and for the total commitment. And here, I think, is the center of my search: I have the persistent feeling that everything I am will remain at a lesser stage of realization until I make this step—even my art, which is far more fully practiced here than there. For the art springs from the life, is rooted in it, it cannot advance beyond the soul.

He felt that any sort of religious life outside an Order was doomed to failure, as in the case of two of his own heroes, Eric Gill and D. H. Lawrence: "The other day a friend told me: You are just a misplaced priest trying to cram the values of the religious down the throats of the laity. Sometimes I think that that is a secret flaw in the whole branch of the lay apostolate. Then again maybe we are merely God's irritants, cinders in the smarting eye of the world, that it may not become too complacent. Surely this is the secret of the frustration of Eric Gill, married before his entry into the Church, yet a born priest; and poor D. H. Lawrence, that noble soul who never found the faith, made sex a God, and died miserable. God gives vocations where He chooses, among the heathen as well as the children of Israel. It is our own torture to find where he wants us."

And through his sessions with Osborn, his reading, and his contemplation, Everson continued to the priest, he thought he had finally found his own direction:

Now I will say what I have been almost afraid to broach, that the time has come on. I have been wondering whether or not I should become a Dominican Lay brother. When I went out to see the Capuchins a few months earlier I knew I was not going to go with them: the whole temper of my mind had been swung a different way by the preceding crisis, for through my efforts at trying to find a way through my problem I had come to a fuller realization of the Dominican mind, and seen what there was in myself that could share in that and partake of it. As I considered myself I had come to understand that my religious irresolution sprang from the fact that I was no pure contemplative, but rather was divided. And that this division in me might be understood in the following way: the contemplative side, which is yet only partially formed and strengthened, we could call the Carthusian; but the active side is itself divided into pairs, which once more deepens the irresolution. They are the inclination to spontaneous action and spontaneous expression, which we could call Franciscan; and the inclination to perfectionism, to find the *whole* truth, which we could call Dominican. For instance, in my writing my first draughts are very Franciscan, a kind of loose soaring uninhibited light of utterance. But that never contents me. I must work it and work it. Sometimes the draughts go over the hundred mark, perfecting and refining. But never just to be refining—refinement is the death of art—but to absolutely establish the veracity of the original impulse in the art-form. And that only the mind can do.

And it is this aspect that I have come to think of as Dominican, and I hope I have not done all of you a violence. But it seems to me the highest uses of the thinking man . . . A wonderful compassionate generosity of soul, which will not rest until the whole truth emerges; the whole truth, which is the aesthetic synthesis, the full sympathy of an art. I guess it is the knowledge of how much I need all that in my own soul that draws me there.

Osborn's response to this rather lyrical outpouring was sympathetic, but measured. As he later told Duggan, at the time he didn't think Everson was suited to the highly organized life of the monastery. He explained to the poet that as his counsel he was far too close to both him and the Order to help him make such a decision, so he sent him to speak to Fr. Meagher, who was St. Albert's Master of Theology. As before, in the progress of their interview, Everson asked the fatal question—what about his talents as a poet and a printer? The old priest

never batted an eye. 'Of course you will develop your faculties,' he said. 'St. Thomas insists that the talents are God-given. I once had a superior who claimed that if the order accepted a man with a fine tenor voice it was obligated to develop it, even if it had to build a soundproof room!' I stared at him in disbelief and exclaimed, 'Let me in!'

SIX

Brother
Antoninus

During his last few months at Maurin House, Everson went to Sunday mass each week with a Catholic lady friend; afterwards, the two of them would join Ruth Hallisey and various other Catholic women for breakfast at a nearby restaurant. Ruth Hallisey was a teacher and apostolic, and it was she who had aided the anthropologist, linguist, and writer Jaime de Angulo in his conversion to Catholicism on his deathbed in 1950. Everson had immediately been accepted by the Provincial of the Order, Fr. Blank, as a novice Dominican lay brother, as Blank was both impressed by his enthusiasm and in need of another lay brother to do menial chores at St. Albert's. Generally, there was no particular ceremony surrounding the acceptance of a novice lay brother into the Order, though at these women's insistence, Osborn allowed a short ritual marking the donning of the habit to be performed for Everson with the women in attendance just after dinner on the evening of his arrival at the college. Today, many members of religious orders are allowed to choose their saints names, but in 1951 that was not the case, and Blank chose for Everson Brother Antoninus. As Everson remembers, "The talk was that there had been three Antoninuses before me which he named, and all three had left the Order. He'd be damned if he wasn't going to get one to stick. So the choice was, in a sense, whim."

St. Albert's is a Dominican House of Studies in which the majority of members train for eventual ordination into the priesthood. Usually, men enter the Order as postulants (a status that lasts six months), then spend a year as novices; at the end of that time they take first vows. After three years they repeat the vows, then at the conclusion of their seventh year, take final vows, which means that they remain members of the Order until death. At the time of his entry, however, Antoninus had no intention of studying to be a priest, but rather was content to begin the life of a *donatus*, a lay brother who is not under any particular vow (and who may be asked to leave, or choose to leave, at any time); he is little more, from a theological standpoint, than a worker wearing a habit. He knew when he entered that the situation might well be temporary, but he hoped it would be permanent, that he and the other members of the house would get on well together.

Antoninus worked hard to adapt to the schedule and keep up with his work (at first, mainly washing dishes three times a day) during his first weeks at St. Albert's. Very shortly the extended depression that had hung over him through most of his fourteen months on Skid Row lifted; he began to put on weight and his color returned. The change was so dramatic that Fr. Osborn, who as soon as Antoninus was installed had had to leave to go east for six weeks, couldn't believe the difference when he saw him again. Regardless of whether or not his misgivings about the poet's suitability for long-term life with the Dominicans were proven out, it was obvious to him from simply the point of view of mental and physical health that the move to St. Albert's was a positive step for Antoninus.

The Dominicans are essentially an apostolic Order, officially known as the Order of Preachers. The group's first monastery (which traditionally they called convents) was founded in Toulouse in 1215, and soon the Order grew into its mission to "deliberate on the improvement of morals, the extinction of heresy, and the strengthening of the faith." From the start, the Preachers adopted the three traditional monastic vows of obedience, poverty, and chastity, adding to them an ascetic element known as "monastic observances"—rigorous fasting and abstinence, using only wool for clothing, adopting a hard bed and a common dormitory, and fairly perpetual silence in their houses. Through the centuries, however, many of these later practices were dropped so that when Antoninus entered St. Albert's, he was given a room of his own and an ordinary bed with a mattress. The habit of the Dominicans has remained distinctive from the start, consisting of a white tunic and a black cloak (though for a lay brother, like Antoninus, the scapula and the capuce were also black). Traditionally, study, commentary, and teaching of the Bible was their primary task, with Albertus Magnus and St. Thomas Aquinas being probably the most celebrated intellectuals of their ranks. In addition, though, Antoninus was aware of their contributions to the arts, which included examples of fine printing, church painting and architecture, and sculpture.

St. Albert's itself was founded in 1850 in Monterey by the Order; four years later it was moved to Benicia, then in 1931 to North Oakland, presumably to provide easier access to the university. The five-acre estate was built by Raymond Perry, the East Bay's only dredging contractor, in 1908 and formally opened after the Dominicans' acquisition on February 5, 1932. Prior to the arrival of Antoninus, the original mansion underwent a number of modifications and transformations, including the construction of dormitory wings, St. Albert's chapel, and a marvelous garden.

Because the whole Province was undermanned, the west coast lay brothers were given little religious instruction formally; any energy and time the teaching priests at St. Albert's had left after providing for the seminarians had to go into parish work, and this disappointed Antoninus, who had hoped to make rapid progress in his education in theology. Yet, he was kept busy enough. Life at St. Albert's was, he wrote, "a context intense but simple, a life concentrated but serene." Typically, Antoninus would rise at 5 a.m.

and go down as Sacristan to make the final preparations for the great devotional activity which opens our day. The night before I laid out all the vestments in the color of the Feast, for there are many priests, and each will say Mass, which means many altars to be prepared. The high altar is flanked by several side altars, and there are various others at convenient places about the monastery. Going down early, I set out the great gold chalices, placing the unconsecrated hosts upon the patens, and arrange them each under the burse and chalice veil. There is then the wine to be poured into the cruets and placed beside the altars, and when this is done, a few minutes of meditation in the quietude of the chapel, before the community, which rises at five-thirty, descends to begin the Great Devotion.

The service itself would last about an hour and a half, beginning with the chanting of the Hours ("the contemplative's great conditioning element, the thing he breathes, the deep, fulfilled, very basic, very intense masculine intonation, the up-pouring of the whole aspiration in the need of God"), divided by a half hour of silent meditation and concluding with the Mass.

The whole group would go single file into the Refectory for breakfast, then Antoninus would spend another hour back in the sacristy returning the vestments to their drawers. Afterwards he would return to his room to make his bed, shower and shave, then until 11:30 he would wash dishes, stopping when it came time to return to the chapel for the offices of Sext and None. Following lunch, there would be chanting of Vespers, then a short recreation period. At 1:30 he would return to dishes for a time, then spend the rest of the afternoon reading until about 5:30, when he would go back into the chapel to participate in the chanting of the Compline (though actually, because he knew no Latin, he usually sat or kneeled silently through the offices, saying his rosary).

Dinner would follow, and according to Fr. Finnbar Hayes, who arrived at St. Albert's as a student-brother studying for the priest-hood not long after Antoninus,

Meals were eaten in silence with hoods up, with a reader who read what-ever book was assigned by the superior. The reading was done as a form of training in public speaking. Twice a year each one of the clerical broth-ers would be required to preach a sermon. The refectory was very large, with the pulpit area at the far end. There were speakers attached to the walls, looking for all the world like ceramic chamber pots. The longest collection of books that I can remember being read was *The Lives of the Popes*, a very painstaking treatment. Another was *No Man Knows My History* by Fawn Brody, a story of the Mormons. A lot of history was read, some literature, a little current events.

Next was the reciting of the rosary and a one hour recreation period, during which Antoninus did more dishes, or sometimes acted as porter, answering the door and the telephone. At 7:30, he would return to the sacristy to lay out the next day's vestments, and at 9:15 go with the community back into chapel for Matins and Lauds before retiring.

"So much then for the basic schedule," Antoninus wrote during these years.

Against it fluxes the ceaseless onslaught of The Unexpected: program changes, sick lay brothers whose work must be assumed, errands to be run for the needs of the house, minor operational emergencies, sudden visitors or telephone calls, moments of inexplicable exhaustion in which one can do nothing but collapse upon a bench: all the consequences inex-tricably involved in community life, which is simply family life, as com-mon, as demanding, and as happy. And you learn to live expecting noth-ing, surprised at nothing. To fight fiercely to maintain one's own inviolate schedule is, in monastic life as in family life everywhere, even-tually to go mad.

▼▼▼

Although he had spent a great deal of time printing the *Triptych* and was fairly pleased with the result, Antoninus hoped to discover a major handpress project. He had arrived at St. Albert's in May, and after just four months hit upon the *Psalter*. "It was a mistake for me to attempt that project so early," he later admitted. "Breaking into the Order was quite enough in itself. But my confessor told me right away that I should not let my press sit idle, that it was a vocation for me. So I thought I'd try for a major work. He said that even if I fail, the fragments will have value, they'll show off everything God has inspired you to do. He was right. And I almost made it."

In July he moved the Washington from Maurin House to St. Albert's, once again disassembling it and carting the pieces by pickup truck the few miles between the two places. At first he took the press into the attic of the college, three stories up. He discovered, however, that the room was far too hot during the summer months; also, he was getting complaints from the seminarians about the noisy operation, especially at night. Thus, he again dismantled the entire device and the whole thing was moved down into the basement. According to Fr. Hayes, who watched the scene with horror,

The rumble of the thing could be heard far and wide. When he decided to move it, he and one or two others were damn near killed. The bed was enormous; it must weigh several hundred pounds. I remember people trying to bring it down the stairs. There was one guy who was pretty tough, John Victor Kane, a red-cheeked, gum-chewing, cussing Boston Irishman. He was not the kind of person who would otherwise be around Antoninus, but he was helping haul the press because he was husky. He came awfully close to being pinned against the wall and crippled.

But they finally managed to get the press into the basement,

which, while poorly lit, offered enough space and seemed to solve
the noise problem.

Even before bringing his Washington from Skid Row,
Antoninus was so excited about his project that he had already set
a page in type. Once the press was operational, he went to work
in earnest. Fortunately, his superiors supported his scheme, and he
was relieved of his dishwashing chores so that he might use those
hours to print. "As I look back on it from a psychological point
of view," he explained in 1965,

I can see that what had happened was that I was captured by the great
work archetype. I was filled with this terrific idealism in my work, and
I wanted to do some great work to contribute in some great way to the
life of the Church both as a writer and a craftsman. Being in the Order
and in my monastic phase, it was that monastic side rather than my literary side, my charismatic side that was winning out. It was more of a
complement to my monastic psychology than the writing of poetry. So
I conceived this plan. In 1945 Pius the Twelfth had approved a new
Latin translation of the Psalms. There had not been an improved translation since the Vulgate, which was almost 1500 years before. I saw this
as a great moment for a printer. I also saw that the Mainz *Psalter* was
coming up; the quinticentennial of the Mainz *Psalter* would be coming
up in 1957. This was 1951. I thought that in six, actually five—I could
not hope to begin before 1952—years I could produce my book in time
for the quinticentenary of the Mainz *Psalter*.

This was, obviously, a major undertaking for a single individual,
especially a printer whose longest work until this time had run 26
pages.

There were myriad problems with such a project. First, there
was the fact that Antoninus would be working in Latin, a language
he did not know. Such a situation is not really unusual for professional typesetters, but certainly a difficulty for a novice. Next, he
planned an edition of 50 copies at about 300 pages, folio size. As
he remembered, "I had never worked with folio size before. By
working on quarto size, you could work and turn the sheets. You

would damp once, print from head to head, turn the sheet over and print the other side, then dry. This way I had to work at one side and then work the other side. It required a totally different method of handling the paper and keeping the moisture constant." Then there was the whole problem of purchasing the paper itself. Because the Order would not underwrite the project, Antoninus had to buy his supplies himself. The paper he chose was handmade Tovil, which was produced in England and sold through a dealer in New York; it was fairly expensive, so that he could only afford to buy part of what he needed at first. Such handmade papers vary considerably from batch to batch, and when the time came for a second purchase he ran into the same problem that had plagued him on the Patchen book at Waldport—his second shipment did not match his first. He finally solved this problem by getting a special making from England, but this set him back almost six months. He had decided to use Goudy New Style type, which he felt to be "the greatest roman type yet achieved in America." But again this caused a whole series of problems, both in design and access. It is available only in one size, eighteen point, and thus, as he explained in his preface to the edition, "It is this that determined the particular character of the title page and other preliminaries, as well as the essential simplicity of the entire book. The occasion demanded a more ostentatious display; the limitations of the type forbade it." Then too Goudy New Style offers no italics. Further, while Antoninus had a good quantity of the type of his own, there was not enough to set a folio signature, twelve full pages. Fortunately, he was able finally to borrow fonts from both the Grabhorns in San Francisco and the University of California Press. As he concluded in his preface,

Such was the manner in which the *Novum Psalterium Pii XII* was conceived, and found its early formulation. It began as a dream, a valid dream, certainly, but one not without a large admixture of self-consciousness and pride. It took the first two-and-a-half years to reduce that pride from my heart, and this was done by the onslaught of a series of reversals that seemed intent on my annihilation. I discovered that great endeavors are not achieved by great dreams only. To print a crown folio of three hundred pages is quite another thing than the thin quartos I had done before. Each sheet goes through the press twice as many times; no job, I found, for one man, but having found it out I could not turn back. Problem after problem arose to confront me. The extremes of temperature in the monastery. Also, the technique of damping paper which I had developed for the quartos proved enigmatically insufficient when applied to the folio: it took me that year as well to discover that the slightest over-damping made the sheet just limp enough so that it would not lie out true from the points on the tympan, resulting in variations of register; and then when damped subtly enough for constant register, would not hold its moisture over the final runs.

Finally, Antoninus had carried with him his intense need for perfection in his printing that had caused him endless anxiety at Waldport, and at every turn as the project progressed he felt gravely disappointed with his results.

While the *Psalter* was essentially a one-man project, Antoninus had occasional help from Finnbar Hayes, who came to look upon the poet as a kind of father-figure, and became his closest friend at St. Albert's. They entered the House of Studies at almost the same time; Antoninus was thirty-nine, Hayes just nineteen. Hayes had been born in Ireland, and had attended a Dominican boarding school in County Kildare (his experiences there, he remembers, were similar to those James Joyce recounts in *A Portrait of the Artist as a Young Man*, which took place at the Jesuit school just five miles away). In the summer of 1949, his father decided to emigrate to San Francisco, and soon as the family arrived he took a job as a busboy in order to help support them. He quickly re-established contact with the Dominicans and within just a few months joined the Order, spending his first year at the novitiate house in Kentfield, just north of San Francisco. In the spring of 1951, he was transferred to St. Albert's to begin his studies for the priesthood, and it was there he first met Antoninus.

Antoninus was at that time just making his first presence in the Dominicans. I don't think he was even wearing a habit yet; he was wearing Big Ben black jeans and a torn t-shirt, working in a room in the basement binding books. I was a newly professed clerical brother, and because the academic course didn't begin until September I was loose and free. I remember poking around in this basement and I saw a crack of light through the door. I moved towards it and saw that there was a seventeenth-century folio book holding the door open, with a brick on the other side of it, and inside was this gaunt figure bent over a wooden press running a bone up and down the spine of a book. He saw me and invited me in, and I just sat and watched him for awhile. That room eventually became the home of the handpress.

Hayes became a kind of apprentice, in the fashion of Eshelman at Waldport, though unlike Eshelman he did little actual printing. He ran errands for Antoninus, helped dampen paper, and did some proofreading.

Following the advice of his confessor, Antoninus presented the idea for the *Psalter* to the brother-master, Fr. Albert Wall, who in turn took the proposal to their superiors where it was approved, though without any financial assistance. So from late 1951 until the spring of 1954, with occasional help from Hayes, Antoninus was preoccupied with this project, printing at every free moment. Time became a problem, both because of the difficulty in obtaining the proper paper and because a shortage of lay brothers meant that for an extended period of time he had to do extra work at the house. He had planned to have his 300-page edition completed by August 15, 1957, the five hundredth anniversary of the publication of the first *Psalter*; in the spring of 1954, after two and a half years of intensive work, only a quarter of the book was complete, just 72 pages. It became clear to him that the project would never be finished:

The whole thing blew sky high. I just reached the terminus point and could not sustain it up to completion. I can look back now, and knowing what I know now, I can say that I should have finished it; I should have gone forward and I'd have done it. The monastic psychology, which was the dominant impress when I began it, began to break down after several years because it was an artificial thing, an imposed thing. Monasticism, as I was trying to lead it, cannot be reimposed on the modern sensibility. I am a man of my own time, and my own self began to break through. The false projection on a merely attributed monasticism could not sustain that work. I should not have tried such a big one.

Word of this enterprise had gotten around to various book dealers on the West Coast, as well as other printers. When he decided to abandon the project, Antoninus wrote to Muir Dawson, a Los Angeles rare book dealer, and asked if he would be interested in marketing the uncompleted book as a fragment. "The material I have," he wrote him on Easter Sunday, "consists of the following: There are 48 copies of five signatures each, pages 17 to 76. . . . To this can be added another earlier rejected signature, pages 1 to 8. . . . Besides this there are some 16 complete 12 page signatures which may be sold separately, and some 95 single sheets of four pages which may also be sold separately." He further suggested his essay "The Printer as Contemplative," which was forthcoming in the *Book Club Quarterly*, as a preface to the book. Dawson's response was immediate and positive; he proposed that Antoninus write, however, a special introduction to the volume which would be printed by a commercial press, then with the extant leaves it would be bound and sold in an edition of 48 copies. According to this scheme, the book would be sold at minimal cost, enough to pay the printer and the binder, with Dawson and Antoninus each getting ten dollars per copy. So the poet sent all his sheets off to Los Angeles.

Within a few weeks, however, the whole situation grew more complicated, as Countess Doheney entered the picture. Mrs. Doheney was a wealthy Catholic laywoman living in Los Angeles who had been made a Papal Countess, an honorary title often bestowed on benefactors. She was a rare book collector who amassed a large library, which she then gave to the archdiocese of

Los Angeles. When Antoninus first started printing the *Psalter*, he began to write letters asking for subscriptions to the volume in advance in order to raise funds for supplies. Lawrence Clark Powell contacted Mrs. Doheney and tried to solicit money from her for the project. "Her secretary at her library told me later," Antoninus recalled, "that the Countess got miffed at his pressure, that he queered the deal. He asked her to support the whole project, but he put a little too much pressure on her and she backed out." She did agree, however, to buy a few copies in advance and sent Antoninus a check for a considerable sum.

When Mrs. Doheney discovered the entire edition was sitting in an office at Dawson's, she immediately made an offer to the bookdealer to buy all the sheets, and Dawson, without Antoninus's consent, accepted. "I certainly did not know what was going on," Antoninus told Ruth Teiser,

I might have been informed, but not in any way that I could have grasped it. It was something that was done. I think it was done that way because their dependency on her was so great. They were her bookseller and they had done thousands and thousands of dollars of business for her. When she began to move into that context, there was very little resistance possible there. I was really distressed by the way the whole thing turned out.

One thing that was particularly galling to Antoninus was that in the check Dawson sent him for his percentage of the sale, the money Mrs. Doheney had given him as an advance had been deducted.

Once she purchased the sheets, Mrs. Doheney contacted R. R. Donalley & Sons rare book bindery in Chicago (Saul and Lillian Marks' Plantin Press in Los Angeles had done the preliminary pages) and made arrangements to have the book bound in full Morocco. It took almost a year to find the right leather, but the edition was finally ready for the Christmas of 1955. The Countess then distributed most of the copies, with her hand inscription, to institutions, with copy number one going to Pope Pius XII, number two to Antoninus, and number three to Cardinal McIntyre. Today the *Psalter* is regarded as one of the two or three finest examples of handpress printing in America, though from the poet's point of view, "I see it in terms of my vision and I realize that it is not mine."

▼▼▼

Without being aware of it, the residents of St. Albert's were living the last decade of fifteen hundred years of traditional Western monasticism. While it was not as rigorous as that of the Trappists, it was authentic and reasonably austere. As Hayes relates, "There were very strict divisions in terms of categorization. Lay brothers were not supposed to mix with student brothers, student brothers could not contact priests, and so forth. We were supposedly sealed off and cross pollination between us of ideas could occur only in unusual circumstances, and Antoninus' printing shop was one of those." Spurred on by his example, Hayes and another student-brother, Leo Thomas, set up a second press in an anteroom a door away from the Washington, where they set to work doing job printing for the house of announcements, letterhead, and so forth. Antoninus gave them continual instruction and advice. In time, they came to call their operation the Albertus Magnus Press, and Hayes and Antoninus developed a logo, which the poet then cut. As Hayes recalled,

There was a little pamphlet that came out annually called the *Directory of the Western Dominicans*, filled with addresses, birth dates, and so on. As a project for the press I got approval to print it; for anyone else this was immaterial, but for me it became a big production. I was determined to produce the most error-free directory in any Dominican province. It was done in two colors and typographically designed by a major typographer, Antoninus. He didn't participate in production, but he did design the thing. He would do all kinds of chores in our printing office—feed the press, print envelopes for the house, stationery, whatever. He wasn't at all snooty about doing just his own work.

Thus Thomas and Antoninus soon got to know one another fairly well. Although like Hayes he was younger than the poet, Antoninus greatly respected his intelligence, finding him especially adept in Thomistic thought. The two men often spent hours discussing theology in the pressroom. Antoninus, for example, had written "The Massacre of the Holy Innocents" before he entered the Order, and one afternoon he showed the second part of the poem to Thomas. The young theologian told Antoninus that it was flawed from a doctrinal point of view, and the poet had so much faith in his judgment that he didn't attempt to republish the poem. Further, as Hayes remembers, "Thomas especially was very much respected among other students, and he was very quiet. While I could go around yapping to everyone about this tremendous Brother Antoninus because of my youth, Leo could be quiet but by his very presence with Antoninus he could create an atmosphere among the students of acceptance for someone as unusual as Antoninus."

And he was unusual. About 1953 St. Albert's saw an influx of a number of student-brothers from the Midwest who were waiting for their own house in the Chicago province to be built. According to Hayes, "They were a different breed altogether. Most of them were combat veterans of World War II, infantry men, bomber pilots, etc., and they were very middle-west: square-shouldered, clear-eyed." These men were astonished to discover, as just one example, Antoninus's rather bizarre late-night vigils in the chapel, occurrences that had early on become commonplace. "There are men my age living who can still imitate Antoninus in the chapel," explains Hayes. "He would be in there in the middle of the night, presumably alone, or not caring whether he was alone or not. And the fact of the matter is that he was just going through agonies of soul—and you heard it! One of his wonderful ones, a great cry, was 'Rectify, Lord, Rectifffyyy!' You'd hear this echoing from the rafters of the chapel. Another was 'After 'em, aaafter 'emmmm!' As far as we knew this could be a struggle with demons or whatever, and it was graphic." It was out of the experience of these nocturnal vigils that Antoninus wrote "A Frost Lay White on California":

> God. Spell dawns
> Drained of all light.
> Spell the masterhood of the means,
> The flanges of extinction.
> Spell the impotence of the numbed mouth,
> Hurt, clenched on the bone of repudiation,
> Spurning.
>
> I grind it down. I grind on it.
> I have yet to eat it up.
>
> Crouched in my choir stall,
> My heart fisted on stubborn revolt,
> My two arms crossed on my chest,
> Braced there, the cloak
> Swaddling me round.
>
> It is night.
> I bore the darkness with my eyes . . .

"That was part of the real delight in being with him," Hayes continues; "things were never overly subdued with Antoninus around." "I was unlike anything they had ever had before," the poet later admitted. "I was older than the students, which has a great deal to do with it. I threw myself into prayer, into the monastic life, in a way that no one ever had there before. I practiced instant obedience. And then gradually my reputation as a poet began to seep in, my Guggenheim, my publications, and so forth. This meant that all those who had any aesthetic sensibilities at all came within range of me, which is the way I met Blaise."

Blaise Schauer, close to both Hayes and Thomas, was the third of Antoninus's closest friends at St. Albert's. While he was a member of Hayes's entering class, like the poet he was older when he entered the Order; at thirty, he was midway between the two men. He had been born in Gallup, New Mexico, where his father served as justice of the peace (years before his birth his father, an immigrant from Austria, had run a small cafe in Bisbee, Arizona, frequented by Pancho Villa and his men). Schauer received an undergraduate degree in musicology from Berkeley and did a year's graduate work there, before spending a few years in New York. In his late twenties, he found himself drawn to the life of the French Dominicans—the "worker priests"—and decided to enter the American branch of the Order. Like Hayes, he spent his first year at the novitiate house at Kentfield in Marin, then arrived at St. Albert's just a few months after Antoninus.

Unlike either Hayes or Thomas, Schauer had little interest in printing per se, though he was very interested in the arts and thus discovered an immediate affinity with the elder brother. Very soon he found himself attempting to infuse life at St. Albert's with an interest in music and art beyond the simply canonical, and pushed hard for the establishing of a music library there which would also serve as an art gallery. Antoninus was sympathetic and supported him in this project against the more conservative faction of the student-brothers and priests. Further, while Schauer had done a year's stint in the Army-Air Corps during the war (before getting a medical discharge he was one of the members of the first clerical crew to work at the newly constructed Pentagon), he was a CO at heart but didn't have the courage to opt for that status when he was drafted. He knew of Antoninus's Waldport experiences and greatly respected him for his position.

The two men quickly became confidants; like Thomas, because of his range of experience and his age, he was on a more equal footing with Antoninus than Hayes. Often they would spend their recreation time in discussion of literature and art, and eventually depth psychology, which interested them both intensely. According to Schauer, "Antoninus always had what I consider to be the most profound evaluation of what he would experience. He was endlessly discovering new dimensions of whatever he happened to be into. We just seemed to enjoy talking to each other.

. . . I was interested in art and beauty and obviously Antoninus penetrated these things. Beauty was for him as valuable as it was for me. I always went to talk to him about anything that was of real consequence for me, but I think it was a very reciprocal kind of relationship. He had his own problems too, and we could bounce them off each other."

vvv

One of the problems confronting him was the paucity of his writing during these first years at St. Albert's. Where before he had been writing a dozen poems a year, now in the Order he was writing just one or two a year. Following his attempt at a second section to the "Holy Innocents," the first poem he wrote after moving to the house was "A Jubilee for St. Peter Martyr." As he recounts in the epigraph, St. Peter Martyr was one of the first Dominicans, murdered by a rival sect in 1262. "Struck down, he dipped his finger in his blood, and wrote upon the ground the words: *Credo in Unum Deum* (a last slap at the Manichaean who killed him)":

> He lived the long gestation of the Word,
> That was the birth that drove him.
> His death approaching out his earliest years
> Grew in him toward an ultimate emergence
> His every act must verify, his whole speech affirm:
> City to city the stamp of recognition
> Struck on the consciousness of men . . .

Like the "Holy Innocents" the poem highlights what seems to have been one of the central theological questions for Antoninus during his first years in the Order, the problem of martyrdom. And little wonder: the estrangement from his father, the internment during the war, the betrayal by his wife with a close friend. Life in the monastery punctuated by his nocturnal "dark nights of the soul" certainly would have engendered a martyr complex in even the most stable psyche. He had broached the subject with Thomas over the first poem, then followed with "A Frost"; now, just a few months later he gave a two-page typed outline of his assessment of the problem to Fr. Meagher, one of the teaching priests, with this cover note:

Ever since I entered the Faith I have been troubled by the problem of the Terrible Meek, the innumerable souls, innocent of crimes worthy of death, who have yet been victim in the massacres of all times. I have been told that there is nothing in this manner of death that intrinsically merits salvation, that to these souls apply only the conditions afforded any other soul dying outside sanctifying grace. The unique character of such a death has always made it difficult for me to accept such an explanation.

Apologizing for appearing an "amateur theologian," Antoninus then went on to argue that while according to Catholic dogma the victim lacks "sufficient volition" in the matter of his death and thus cannot be assured salvation, in fact because at the moment of his death he corresponds to "Christ as Victim," he must "by participating in the eminent dignity of Christ's death" be considered saved. The autobiographical pleading here is all too evident.

"A Jubilee" was followed the next year with "A Savagery of Love" (a canticle of the feast of St. Mary Magdalene, protectress of the Dominicans), then in 1953 with "A Canticle to the Christ in the Holy Eucharist" (for the Feast of the Most Precious Blood). All of these poems are occasional, frankly religious (though with more than a trace of eroticism in their imagery), and a strong autobiographical strain runs throughout, as like St. Peter Antoninus seeks his "source." These are extended and well-crafted poems, though obviously Antoninus could not devote much time to his writing of verse during these years (besides these occasional poems there were only a few additional short lyrics).

This is not to say that his interest in poetics waned during this period; in fact, the situation was quite the contrary as he worked hard to reorientate his verse into the monastic context. In an April 1954 letter to Lewis Hill, he attempted to explain in detail his sense of the movement of his own new work, using "A Jubilee" as a bearing-off point. While other poets were interested in either the Christian culture or the Christian ethic, and made use of the supernatural merely to enhance this interest, he maintained, his approach was different:

The Thomistic view is quite different, and the Peter Martyr poem is a demonstration of it—the actual, real, and realizable mesh of the natural and supernatural orders, with the hierarchical view of reality as the great groundwork in which the action is cast. My relation to this is precisely the same as Dante's: the rendering of the supernatural with the positive actuality of the natural, and to see them both with the clarity of true existence.

He felt that his relationship to Dante was unlike T. S. Eliot's, "a link to the cultural continuum," but rather that because of their religion both have the same world view. While he admitted that his early Catholic poems used symbol in "the straight orthodox Christian sense," he dissociated himself from Thomas Merton whose "more static method works up the paraphernalia of religion in an effort to realize the supernatural by association." Echoing Coleridge, he explained that

I don't generally think of a poem as a construction—more as a process, like a current you turn upon a conceptual area and use to expose the reality that lies there. The poem picks up its ingredients as it proceeds, and lays bare the area by the assimilation of the matter which the creative intuition acknowledges and seizes upon. All the material of the poem: images, metaphors, figures, tropes, etc. are as pieces of evidence the intuition sweeps up and correlates together, working rapidly upon everything it can lay hold of to expose and give-glimpse of the conceptual reality it seeks to appropriate. Thomistically speaking, this is the beatitude that obtains in all created things—the trace of the Creator left in them because they are His and of Him.

Antoninus concluded by reminding Hill that the "true line of American poetry ran from Whitman to Jeffers," that there are in essence three true American spiritual types: "the sensual, affective type of Whitman, the remote, ascetic type of Jeffers and Thoreau, and between them the integrated, whole-man, and indeed noble type of Lincoln." Other attitudes (including those of Eliot and Henry James) are "Europeanisms," and it is only the American sythesis, "when strengthened and resolved by a true religious invigoration," that can withstand "the influence of the French, an influence which blights English poetry wherever it touches it . . . With French culture we Americans are like savages with whiskey." It is not a matter of ideas, philosophies, or form, but rather "interior disposition, a matter of heart." He concluded this exposition with the rather surprising surmise that "due, doubtless to the ordered life of the monastery and a resolved and comprehensive view of reality, I suspect that I will soon write only in traditional forms." Save for an occasional poem, however, this did not prove to be the case over the next decades.

Throughout this period, though, his poetry didn't receive his primary attention; as Antoninus he was consumed with his *Psalter*. Further, as he remembers, during these first three years at St. Albert's he "clung to the solid program of prayer and work. We had an afternoon each week off, but I never even went out of the house." Finally, almost simultaneously with his scheme to print the *Psalter* Antoninus decided to write, with the enthusiastic support of his fellow brothers, a spiritual autobiography on the model of Augustine's *Confessions*. Augustine's work is an extended apostrophe to God, and when Antoninus reread it now at St. Albert's he realized that "the form fit me like a glove. I could work readily within that structure." In later years he would come to dislike large sections of the book—"especially the 'holier than thou' attitude of much of it, the piety and the inflation, the shock and gasping at the sins of the world"—but between 1952 and 1954 his primary writing energies went into this 500-page manuscript, "Prodigious Thrust."

Kentfield, Breakthrough, and "Prodigious Thrust"

In the late spring of 1954, after over three years as a donatus, Antoninus decided to apply for entrance into the novitiate to study for the priesthood. According to his request, he had come to the understanding that he had "gifts of eloquence that could not be utilized as a lay brother," and that a desire to reach the core of Catholicism had its fulfillment in ordination. Certainly both of these reasons were valid, but the poet confessed to additional motivation. As it became evident that he would not have the stamina to finish printing the *Psalter*,

I thought I would abandon my press for a greater vocation. This is one of the subtle ways by which you can get out from something. You can find something greater. Then everyone will be compelled to say that you did not fail, that you advanced to something nobler. That is what I cooked up in my own unconscious. I cooked up this higher state which would deliver me from this terrible burden and also from the fear of failure, the fear to admit to the world . . . Already this book was becoming celebrated among printers. The fear of failure was very great although I did not understand it at the time. I conceived this higher vocation then which no one could impugn me for. I asked my superiors and they said yes. They were not really convinced by it, but I kept the heat on until I talked them into it. Finally, they said I could try it. So I abandoned my *Psalter*.

Making the move was not automatic. Antoninus had to get a dispensation from his marriage to Edwa, which was the reason that he couldn't take formal vows when he entered St. Albert's to begin with. Such a dispensation was simply canonical; it could be effected easily by the authorities in Rome. Yet once a year after he arrived he had petitioned his Provincial to submit such a request so that he might take formal vows, and each time the Provincial had rejected Antoninus's plea because, like Osborn, he was not yet sure that the monastery was the proper place for him. However, the Dominicans are a democratic Order, and they elect a new Provincial every four years. In early 1954, Fr. Joseph Fulton was elected to the office; he and Antoninus had gotten to be friends at St. Albert's, where Fulton had been student-master for a time. Thus, when Antoninus approached him to enter the clerical novitiate in Kentfield priory, although he was skeptical, Fulton told him that he would support him.

Academic life had never been the poet's strong suit, and now suddenly he closed his press, stopped writing, and plunged into the study of Latin in an attempt to rectify his deficient background, as Latin was the universal language of the Church. Antoninus enlisted Hayes's help as a tutor in this project. As Hayes recalls,

It was a typical Bay Area summer—fog, fog, fog. I remember sitting in a little classroom at St. Albert's going through fundamental Latin grammar with him. Of course he had a very quick ear for words, and the advantage of having someone doing grammar with him who knew him was that instead of just taking Latin from the ground up the way a kid would do it, I would simply work from the words he knew. In the course of one of our conversations I used the word "ambit"; he had never heard the word and he stopped like a connoisseur at a wine tasting, rolling it on his tongue, toying with it, then smiling a great big smile, saying "That's a wonderful word. But what does it mean?"

Through the summer, the two men devoted every free moment to this study.

The dispensation had not yet arrived, Antoninus was told, when the classes at Kentfield began in September, but Fulton allowed him to move to the priory anyway to start his course work. Kentfield Priory was in Marin County, just north of San Francisco. The house was more secluded than St. Albert's, with far fewer residents, and as in the house of studies Antoninus was given a room of his own. Classes were very small, with only four or five students in each, centering primarily on theology and Latin. Because the focus of the house was study, Antoninus had few other duties. Unfortunately, however, the other novices were far younger than the poet, and he developed no close friendships there.

During his last year at St. Albert's, Antoninus had worked out a very severe regimen, which included fasting and abstinence from meat. When he entered Kentfield, his superior Fr. Aquinas Duffner insisted that he abandon these practices, as well as the long hours he spent in chapel during the night. This was obviously for his own good; his superior realized that such private devotions would ennervate him, making successful study impossible, but Antoninus saw it as an attempt to make him conform for the sake of conformity and remained unhappy about it. He still feels that if he could have maintained his night-vigils at Kentfield he could have made it through the novitiate at least, but the novice-master was adamant. Nor was this all. As the autumn wore on, Antoninus came more and more into conflict with his co-religionists. Soon came a crisis.

After I had been there a couple months, during the Christmas season, they took us into San Francisco to see a film of Shakespeare's *Romeo and Juliet*. It was a fine film, but it was too much of the world for me. This was a break-over point. I set my heart against it and just crouched there in my seat. It had the sensuousness of the Renaissance, with the lovely ladies in their rich brocaded gowns, and it bothered me deeply. I was spitting blue fire, distracting the other brothers throughout the show, gasping and moaning.

The next day Fr. Duffner called him in to explain his behavior, and Antoninus told him that he felt he had made a mistake in coming to the priory. His studies were not going well, he felt he had no kindred spirits there, and the life at Kentfield was just not ascetic enough for him.

In fact, shortly before this event Antoninus had already revised his decision. As early as October he had written Fr. Fulton,

Now, as time goes on, I gain nothing in the way of positive conviction as to why I am here, and am sustained in my interior conviction that another way of life is actually meant for me. . . . I have for some years felt that I might be called to the life of the religious solitary. . . . It is probably possible only as a Third Order Member, but so long as I could wear the habit in the cell I would not object to that. Both St. Catherine and St. Rose were Third Order solitaries. The tradition is unquestionably valid.

He went on to explain that he hadn't made such a proposal formally before attempting the priesthood for a number of reasons: first, he had tried to make such a case earlier but his spiritual director regarded "the solitary life as a temporal idiosyncrasy, not particularly difficult, and not worthy of serious consideration"; next, although he considered the offering of the Mass "the crown of the solitary's life," he no longer believed "in the *active* side of the Dominican priesthood for me, and I can't presume on the Order to spend years training a solitary who happens to want to say Mass"; third, he was constitutionally unable to sustain long periods of study; further, he felt that the entry into Kentfield was necessary both to point toward alternatives and to allow him to become "detached from involvements at St. Albert's."

In a second letter, written to Fr. Duffner after the film incident on January 9, Antoninus again made the argument that his problem at Kentfield came down to his inability to reconcile "the relationship between religious life and the world." In fact, *Romeo and Juliet* had taken

us back to Fourteenth Century Italy, but yet it was but the same world I had known—the world of vanity, cupidity, vainglory, lust, sex, murder, violence, fear, spiritual and psychological anguish. These are not all it was, indeed, but its problems were worked out in that essential context. When I could no longer look and lowered my eyes, after you would not permit me to leave the theater, it was because I had to close out of my consciousness a world I could no longer acquiesce in, no longer accede to, no longer participate in, at least, not on the level of interest and curiosity and indulgence. To go into it for the salvation of souls would be one thing. To go into it for entertainment and diversion is another. . . .

Nor do I believe that my reaction is either neurotic or unnatural or the result of some psychological blockage or the residue of my pre-Catholic past. . . . There was a time when contempt for the world and the things of the world was a manifest sign of the religious state, and when it was commonly expected that it should extend to his basic attitudes and behavior. That a religious should repudiate the world and the things of the world was not considered an oddity.

Sensing Antoninus's disposition, Fulton had in fact never applied to Rome for his dispensation, and thus by early spring of 1955 the poet was once again granted his wish, and he returned to residency at St. Albert's.

vvv

For the next year, Antoninus went about his tasks in a black depression, not unlike the feeling of desolation he had suffered through while at Maurin House. He continued to be stung by the failure of the *Psalter* project, he had abandoned all hope of the priesthood, and again the poetry had dried up. One bright spot, however, was the presence of Fr. Victor White, who spent the term at St. Albert's as a visiting lecturer. The Order at St. Albert's was very much under the influence of the English Dominicans during the fifties. *Blackfriars* magazine, published by Dominicans at Oxford was very popular, and such eminent British Dominican scholars as Gerald Vann and Sebastian Bullough spent time in Oakland. White was Reader in Theology at Blackfriars College at Oxford, a foundation member and lecturer at the Jung Institute of Analytical Psychology, and he knew C.G. Jung as both a teacher and a friend. For many years White had planned to write an extended historical, psychoanalytical, and theological treatise on the relationship between God and the unconscious, and though this project remained unfinished, twelve related papers were collected in 1952 in his *God and the Unconscious*.

Antoninus came to depth psychology and Jung through White, though he did not read *God and the Unconscious* until later, and even then, as he explains in his introduction to the volume's recent reissue, he was "suspicious of depth psychology's pertinence to the spiritual life, preferring to suffer it out with St. John of the Cross." While White was at St. Albert's the two men did not grow particularly close, but the priest and the brother occasionally spent afternoons together, discussing such subjects as "the doctrine of the non-essentiality of evil as seen in the abiding tradition of the Church since Augustine, which Jung opposed." And when White left for London at the conclusion of the spring term in 1956, he gave Antoninus a number of books he had been sent for review, including Herbert Marcuse's *Eros and Civilization*. Antoninus had never read Freud, but during his months at Cascade Locks had encountered him through his reading of Wilhelm Reich. In Berkeley, however, he had let this interest lapse in favor of religious speculation. Now, lost in his depression and following White's example, Antoninus returned to the psychological.

Not long after White's departure, Antoninus got a phone call from a woman named Jane Hartman, whose husband he had known in the CPS, the first pro-Catholic intellectual he had ever met. The couple was having some difficulty, and she asked Antoninus to try to help. The brother had Thursday afternoons free, and soon he found himself going regularly to the Hartmans in East Oakland to speak to them, along with an attractive woman named Mickey LaPlaca and their children, on Catholicism, an activity he kept up for more than a year. "This going out into the world again," the poet recalled,

meant that I had to meet women again, and thus that I was once more exposed to my unconscious. It was at this point that I began to feel myself falling in love with Mickey LaPlaca. It was partly a maternal thing. I didn't say anything about this, then eventually her husband began coming around, and I got to know him. But all this just sent me further into my deep depression.

Antoninus turned to Blaise Schauer at this point, and Schauer suggested that he enter into some form of psychotherapy. At first, Antoninus dismissed the suggestion, thinking that his depression was caused simply by events beyond his control. But as he read the Marcuse, with its explicit recounting of Freudian theory, he began to see a pattern in his behavior—that from childhood on, whenever he suffered some real or imagined slight, he would go into a similar depression. In this case, his "plunge," as he called it, was brought on simply by an offhand expression of disinterest in his poetry one evening by Hartman, who had become jealous of Antoninus's influence on his wife. Further, at this time he got a request from a scholar for comment on his early poem "The Raid," based on the attack on Pearl Harbor. At first the poet thought to answer that the poem was based on a simple truth, that "those who live by the sword, die by the sword." But now, suddenly, he began to see the flyers as the sons, and the poem from an Oedipal perspective.

That night he had a dream in which these various strands seemed to come together, a dream which began the breakthrough out of his psychological morass. According to his journal account the next morning,

Very generalized beginning. I and an associate are in the presence of a woman. She is not distinct, just the presence of a woman. The associate too is not distinct, just another presence, but we are equal, whereas the woman is superior to us both. . . . It develops from this, however, that we seek information about the way to a destination. We turn to the woman presence which is our polarity here, and the communication given us is that Eric Gill could show us how to get out, but Eric Gill is not here. . . .

The woman presence beside us is manifesting herself, communicating. We turn our attention to her and see that she knows something; she is smiling, but looking down. The quality is that she is not intruding herself but rather suggesting, hinting, as a mother will hint to a child to enable it to find out for itself the thing it wants to know. Then she says, as we examine her for more signs, our attention quite fixed on her, "Well, what are we waiting for?"

Our attention is now strongly upon her as we search her for signs and we say, "What do you mean?"

She gestures with a kind of fleeting wave of the hand toward the religious, who in this exchange had quite lapsed from our attention. We stare at the religious and then back at her, in wonderment.

"Is *that* Eric Gill?"

She smiles . . . her enigmatic smile of assent. We wheel from her and start for the religious . . . As we come up to him and open our mouths to ask him the direction to the destination . . . The way lies east towards the rising sun. It was at this point in the dream that the alarm clock had gone off. Now as I come out of my dozing I realize that today is the seventh anniversary of my baptism.

At this point in his commentary, Antoninus saw the dream, which on the face of it was rather mundane, as "obviously relating to my recent indecisions about my vocation," but soon he focused on the figure of the mother: "Edwa, strong maternal type, full-bodied, a woman before her time. On her I could pour out my libidinous maternal attraction, seduce her. Her own mother was dead so she was the 'mother' of her house." And of another woman, "After first meeting . . . I said to myself: 'She was too much like my mother. I could never fall in love with her . . . ' She was the Wise One, the Mother, the Anima, the spiritual one. Whereas my seduction of Edwa had been conquest, rape, she freely invited me to her bed . . . She opened her door with her key and gave me a key. Then when she turned on me in the impotence scene, it was terrible. It was as if she had lured me into her trap and now was murdering me. She relates to mother, who gave me her breast and dandled me, yet punished me for my incestuous desires of her."

This last realization set the poet off on a three-day pouring forth of his repressed eroticism, writing madly, sometimes almost incoherently, a progressively more vivid, obscene account of a sexual confrontation with his mother. According to the third-person commentary which is included in this unpublished record, Antoninus overcome, left his cell and

stumbled down the hall to the cell of his confessor, and there made confession . . . He explained how all his life he had been tormented by the sexually obscene, and how depth psychology had at last given him a glimpse of something of the nature of these compulsions, and of determining to discover the forces that had wracked him for so long. He had determined, with the help of God, to go down into himself, and unmask the devil that drove him; and that taking pen and pencil as his weapons . . . he had made his approaches, and there found himself engaged hand to hand with the obscene, and that to his horror he found that it had involved his own mother.

Here, the erotic flow between mother and the son came to a primal, violent crisis point, foreshadowed by his early childhood encounter with the neighbor girls in Selma. "When the mother comes in this situation," the poet recalled years later, "she is both your mother and the archetypal woman, embodiment both of radiant beauty and seductive openness. With each night's dream and each day's writing, she became more and more primal, until at the last she turned into pure animal, a cat":

She made in her throat a kind of animal mewling, a sound of primordial imprecation, at once slavish and imperious, as of some magnificent and intelligent beast persuading its master to comply to its needs. The broad mouth opens . . . She stops her mewling a moment to lick her lips, and a muffled purring trembles around her throat. The breasts stir, a ripple of impatience flitting across them, shaking them in the charged and hushed air.

Finally,

He takes her in his hands and strangles her, tears the beautiful maternal body limb from kicking limb, rips out the belly, tramples the obscene womb that gave him life. He kicks, claws, hacks, slashes. Member by member he tears her apart and reduces her down to nothing. He blots her out of his existence. And utterly exhausted he falls into slumber, he sleeps the long sleep of unbroken peace. He sleeps the immemorial sleep of a man who has thrown off his devil.

But rather then throwing off his "devil," he had simply awakened her, and through the next months Antoninus was obsessed with the complexities of this recognition, and his embracing of the psychological approach. Morning after morning he would wake to record the night's dreams in great detail, then attempt analysis focusing primarily on the Oedipus theme, which preoccupied him.

Following White's advice, Antoninus was now reading Jung closely, though not without a certain trepidation.

I went into the library and signed out Jung's *Psychology and Alchemy*. Heretofore I have never read through one of Jung's works. I dabble in *Two Essays*, but I have always relied upon his disciples, because I cannot abide the way he toys with the problem of religion, and the almost compulsive way that he expatiates himself upon that subject, whereas his disciples do not see it so necessary to treat of it, simply laying out their material as they see it. But I can no longer postpone the master himself. Back in my cell I worked until late.

He reread Sophocles *Oedipus* carefully, as well as a number of related works like Eric Wellisch's *Isaac and Oedipus* and Gustav Swab's *Gods and Heroes*. "It was sexual impetuosity," he meditated, "that led to Oedipus' birth, just as sexual impetuosity led my mother to marry my father, a divorced man, though she was a Catholic and she knew it was wrong. I am illegitimate in the sense that my parents' marriage was invalid." Further, he was finding "astonishing parallels in both the myth and my life between the castration complex and the foot."

Castration, as well as masturbation, came to hold his attention especially. In these voluminous unpublished writings the axe seems to embody the castration motif, as he recalls, "In CPS in 1944 we brushed off an old lumber train road bed to make a road for trucks, and I misused my axe in trimming a pole, cutting a deep gash in the index finger of my left hand, the scar of which I still have." In these pages he remembers taking a broken axe on a camping trip with Edwa. Further, he examines the body of his work to ferret out such references, and discovers that the first such image appeared as early as the 1935 "Fisheaters," and that even the Peter Martyr poem came from an account he had read of martyrdom by "billhook," or axe.

As for masturbation, a perpetual problem now magnified by his plunge into the unconscious, he wrote on August 31,

When I was in my teens and deep in the masturbation vice a sensational murder occurred near our district in which an unbalanced young man finding his interest in a young woman unreciprocated murdered her and her suitor. My father took me to one side and began talking in a general way about this man's insanity. He gave me to understand that his insanity had sprung from the fact that he had "played with himself," developed a vice in childhood that demented him as a man. He added that boys who did such things ought to have their hands tied behind their backs at night.

And, he argued, his task was to somehow "universalize" his situation: "There are thousands of clinical studies but little literature and little spirituality. I have to show the universality of the castration complex. Man is castrated, cut off, truncated. That is the meaning of the Fall. I have to relate my castration to the castration of the race, when the penis-envy of Eve emboldened her to castrate God in the garden of Eden by stealing His fruit. My castration complex is historical and metaphysical. All men live in me, are emasculate in me." And it was through masturbation, "reverting to the underlying psychology of childhood," that he could "more nearly approximate the unresolved incest desire latent yet in the unconscious . . . .Masturbation was not simply a rut, a deed of pure carnality, but rather a tragic gesture, a heartbreak, a lost attempt to commune with the mother."

"Bit by bit," he wrote in late September, "the darkness is driven back." By Christmas he had completed the *Oedipus* trilogy, Ernest Jones's *Hamlet and Oedipus*, F. R. Leavis's study of D. H. Lawrence, and Erich Neumann's *The Origins and History of Consciousness*, which "has given me the key by which to correlate all the findings of the summer." As he wrote Victor White in January,

Things have happened so fast on the interior level that I am still in that state of transcendent awe when one looks about with new eyes, and wonders how he could have been so blind for so long. Since my last letter to you I read Neumann's *The Origins and History of Consciousness*, which gave me the perspective to make the large-scale correlations and threw me definitely out of the camp of the Freudians, where I had tended to stay for reductive purposes.

He recounts a dream he had at Waldport in the summer of 1943 involving "a most marvellous maternal voice" which told him that "the chaos of the world was fate . . . . This dream I now see provided the Reconciling Symbol that coincided with the passage through the patriarchal struggle. As a CO I had taken my stand against my father's values, and made my quits."

But the matriarchal deliverance which should have proceeded it had never been achieved, due to certain defects in my home life, and clear up through the post-war conversion, the entry into the Order, until at last, this past summer, the whole thing boiled over, and I was delivered the Reconciling Symbol, this time the Host and Paten, the true Mandala.

And yet, as he continued to White, the recurrence of the castration motif in his dreams, and his obsession with masturbation, demonstrated that the matriarchal conflict had not yet been worked through. But Neumann opened the door:

Here, by relating the masculine-phallic element under the unconscious and hence under the maternal I was led to seek the cause of the castration complex under its true location, and learned that despite my emergence of the summer I had out of fear re-repressed the maternal element. . . . So that on Epiphany, of all wonderful days, through some other studies I had been making on the fall of satan as the beginning of evil, I was led to see that the satanic and the maternal are closely intermixed due to their adhesion to the material unconscious side, and by an act of discrimination the unconscious must clarify between them, distinguish between maternal-unconsciousness fear and straight diabolical fear, and out of this emerged the Blessed Mother, who through her maternity gave us life, but through her virginity seals us off from the devouring womb of our fear, and furthermore is placed by God as victor over the devil, so that in her all our unconscious fears may be dispelled.

vvv

In the spring of 1956, before Fr. White left for London, Antoninus had given him a copy of the "Prodigious Thrust" manuscript to read. He had started the project in 1952, pretty much finished it by 1954, then had made various revisions while at Kentfield. The book is a 500-page "autobiography," though it is written far more on the order of Augustine's *Confessions* or Pascal's *Pensées*, that is more of a meditation on various aspects of Church doctrine, than like Thomas Merton's popular *The Seven Storey Mountain*, which had appeared in 1948. The manuscript was

divided into five parts: a brief preface, three long prose meditations, the poem-sequence "The Falling of the Grain," and a prose
epilogue. It began as a collection of poems, as Antoninus remarked
in the preface, "supported by an autobiographical context," but as
the narrative took over "the poems survived only as a kind of
archipelago awash in an ocean of prose." Given the history of the
manuscript, perhaps the most remarkable aspect of the piece to a
contemporary reader is the rather thoroughly nonsensational tone
and subject matter. Aside from the second part, "From the Depths
of a Void," which among other things presents the poet's conversion experience, generally the focus is on topics ranging from printing, monasticism, and marriage to Catholic views of the
Incarnation, contraception, homosexuality, and the Eden myth.
As with Augustine, the texture of the prose throughout gives a
sense of a soul caught in some heightened battle between the spirit
and the flesh, but compared to any page of the "breakthrough"
document, there is little if any overtly profane material here.

Which makes it all the more curious that from the start
Antoninus had worried about the reaction of a friend who figures
in the narrative. Fr. White saw the book as a classic conversion
account, and enthusiastically urged publication. With the priest's
encouragement, Antoninus submitted it to the censors:

They read it, but they thought it was too strong. Victor White himself
did not, and his authority was so great that, just a behind-the-scenes talking about it, they were kind of loath to make a decision. Anyway, they
decided that my friend's attempt to separate herself from the book was
not very realistic since she was going to be the one that would have to
bear any of the repercussions that the book would have on the public.

So, nervously, Antoninus gave her the manuscript, and, two days
later, she returned it, refusing publication permission of those passages in which she appeared.

During this time, a salesman for the Catholic publisher Sheed
and Ward was passing through San Francisco, and got word of the

manuscript from the owner of a Catholic arts shop. Suddenly, Antoninus received a letter from Frank Sheed himself, asking to read the narrative for possible publication. Hoping his friend would eventually relent, the poet sent the autobiography off to New York, and waited.

Meanwhile, having gone through his almost manic psychic breakthrough, the monk was in a state of high inflation, and some confusion. He was not at all sure that he should remain in the Order—White himself felt that Antoninus most probably should leave, that the stress was too great—yet he could not bring himself to make the break. Antoninus continued to insist even more strongly on the re-establishment of the rigors of traditional monastic life—strict discipline, strict diet, and so forth—and, as at Kentfield, had little patience with what he thought to be his fellow religious's attempts to liberalize the monastic lifestyle. As Fr. Antoninus Wall recalled,

he was such an extreme—the hyper-disciplined, hyper-ascetical, which made no gentle allowance for the affective to enter into his life. Then suddenly the affective would assert itself. It was always an either/or situation. His ascetic dimension, especially in the early years, was a drag. You couldn't do some innocent thing without him moaning and reminding you that you were corrupt. When Fr. Fulton was Provincial, and he was as innocent as they come, he took the novices up into the Sierras for a picnic. We stopped at a little hamburger place and Antoninus spent his time letting us know that we were all tainted by our presence there. He seemed to have a vision of the monastery as a citadel into which you'd withdraw from the corruption outside. He was very much like the reformed alcoholic who can't move gracefully in the outside world because of his previous experience; it's all or nothing. For him this was a very honest dynamic, but often it was a pain to everybody else.

Though in fact, according to Finnbar Hayes, the life continued to be quite rigorously structured, and it seemed as if the poet enjoyed the drama he generated by his embracing of the ascetic as much as anything else.

For instance, we'd rise at 6 a.m. Every morning there would be two masses before breakfast, the first a silent mass, the second sung. All through the year we would put on our black hoods and black cloaks for the purpose of receiving communion. At St. Albert's the floor tiles are black and white, in a chess board pattern. Before receiving communion, we would recite the Confetior in Latin, and to do that we would stretch out full length on the floor. It was a gesture called the *venia*, meaning pardon or forgiveness. When one arrived at a community function late, the same gesture was used. One knelt down with the tip of the scapula in one's hand, then sprawled out and layed there until the superior gave a signal. Now Antoninus did this more dramatically than most. When he'd come in and crash down, whatever his transgressions were, it was nothing to be taken lightly. It added color to an otherwise sometimes boring life.

First there was the film incident at Kentfield. Now, suddenly, one day in October Antoninus happened into the priests' recreation room to find a television, and he exploded. "That television set formed a catalyst for the whole movement; it was just a symbol. I was clinging to the old monastic norms and every invasion of the world into the monastery was cutting it down, watering it down; the world was triumphing. We were jealous of our ancient monastic heritage. The television had entered every other house in the province but that one." He angrily packed his clothes, manuscripts, and a number of books and stormed out of the monastery for the LaPlacas, where he stayed for a little over two weeks.

While there, he got in touch with Fr. Duggan, who besides his Maurin House duties was in charge of a parish in Decoto, a Mexican barrio outside Hayward. He offered to let Antoninus live in a small room there, and Fr. Thomas, who after White's departure had become his spiritual advisor, and Finnbar Hayes picked him up from the LaPlacas and drove him to Decoto. According to Hayes, "He had with him a large sack of grain, maybe wheat, and he planned to live on this. Gruel and grain. There were sins to be atoned for. Television was to him the vehicle of sin entering the monastery."

The first night there, Antoninus woke from a nightmare, apparently caused by the hostility of some young Chicanos who resented his presence there, and, certain he had made the wrong decision, immediately made his way back to St. Albert's and asked to return. Fr. Thomas was adamant—it was too soon, he needed more time to think—and Antoninus obeyed. The next night passed without incident, and the following morning he took an eight-mile walk through the fields and orchards, feeling a sense of elation and making plans to find an "even more remote penetration into the wilderness." But when he returned, as he wrote the LaPlacas on November 10, he found a note from Fr. Thomas saying that he was waiting in the chapel.

I went over to the church, and we came back together, and brewed a cup of coffee, sitting there on the floor of that vacant little shack. He seemed agitated and nervous. He said that after I left him at St. Albert's the day before . . . he had given himself over to prayer, and that over the course of the day and night he came to believe with increasing conviction that I belonged back in the monastery. At an administration meeting that morning he had broached the matter of my return, and found it welcomed. I asked him directly what he advised for the immediate prospect. "I think," he said slowly and seriously, "that you should come back with me now. There is nothing to be gained by waiting."

We loaded all those books and manuscripts into his car and came on home. It was sundown, and the traffic was terrific. Friday night, three weeks to the day, three weeks to the hour, since I had left. I was neither high nor low at this turn of events, being possessed rather of an attitude of resignation, of inevitability. I did not feel crushed and defeated like the return to St. Albert's from Kentfield. This was no retreat. We reached the monastery with the community just going to supper, and got all my stuff into my cell unobserved. Then I put on my habit and went down to the second table, and made the *venia* as I entered the refectory. The brothers came up and kissed my hands. Later I learned that the day after I left both masses were offered for me, and an announcement made to the community to that effect.

The next morning, a special delivery letter arrived from Frank Sheed, asking Antoninus to fly to New York at his expense to discuss the publication of "Prodigious Thrust." Antoninus, of course, saw this as a dramatic indication of the hand of God. As he concluded to the LaPlacas, "If this letter had come one day earlier is it not obvious that in all probability I would never have returned to the Dominican Order?" Fr. Thomas's attitude was a little more mundane. "Every once in awhile a Dominican needs a vacation, and this was typical—it took three weeks and cost us a hundred and fifty dollars." In any case, the television remained in the recreation room, and Antoninus was back, seemingly for good.

▼▼▼

During the last week of November, Antoninus flew to New York to discuss his autobiography. This was the first time he had ever been on an airplane, and the night before he left he drew up a will, leaving his literary papers and manuscripts to UCLA (under the custody of Lawrence Clark Powell), the publication rights to "Prodigious Thrust" to Frank Sheed, the royalties from the book and any other literary work split evenly between a friend and the Province of the Holy Names, his printing equipment and other properties to the Province; further, he named Naomi Burton, who was handling "Prodigious Thrust" negotiations, his literary agent. His meeting with Frank Sheed went very well, as he noted in his journal:

For me it was a magical meeting. Here I was in the heart of the great city, at the request of a real publisher, discussing my book and things intellectual with one of the leading Catholics of the day. Frank Sheed was the only layman ever to be accorded an honorary degree in theology in Rome. . . . He was radically different than I expected. I looked forward to a tall, tweedy, pipesmoking man, but he was nothing like that. He was rosy and almost jolly, free and open in his responses. We had only to exchange a few words and we took to each other. I had come expecting to work over the Ms. but he had no such intention. He wanted to take it to England and go over it with Fr. White, to make a version of it which would be acceptable.

Sheed's attitude was that the book would not only be an important Catholic document, but a best-seller as well. And Antoninus
signed a contract, then headed back to Oakland, ecstatic.

Just before leaving for New York, Antoninus had written his
friend a long letter, explaining the purpose of his trip, pointing out
that he had been very clear with Sheed about the permissions
problem. He had hoped for the best, but on his return he found
a note from her refusing permission for publishing anything relating to her, and threatening legal action if he did. Antoninus,
stunned, passed this word on to Sheed, who still proposed to go
ahead with attempting to edit a version of the narrative that would
be acceptable. But Antoninus held out little hope. Sheed took the
manuscript to England, and eventually produced a much-
abbreviated version, which he passed on to Victor White. White
was not at all pleased, and strongly suggested to Antoninus in a letter that the whole matter be dropped. Antoninus agreed, pointing
out that as White had confirmed his "fears, I can see no reason for
carrying on the subterfuge." Antoninus was particularly grateful
that White offered to handle the matter himself while Sheed was
in England—"It is a godsend to me that you are there, a country-
man of his, to put the issue so directly."

Sheed, however, was not yet ready to give the project up, and
on White's advice simply restored many of the cuts. But when in
August of 1957 Antoninus finally received the edited version of
the manuscript, he was incensed. As he wrote the publisher,

For all my advance assurances, when the thing was actually before my
eyes I became so disgusted, furious and depressed, that I could do nothing for a couple days. . . . My spontaneous reaction to the edited version
you returned to me demonstrates that it is impossible for me to sanction
a version sufficiently drastically cut (apparently) to meet the approval of
both my friend and the diocesan censors. I have written my life as I lived
it. I have written it from an authentically Catholic point of view. I am
not a political man. If my life in its integrity is unpublishable, then I will
keep silent. It is bad enough to have to expose oneself to the world
(though one does that for the sake of the apostolic end) but if the terms

by which he can relate to the world are denied him, so that others cut out for him the mask he is obliged to wear, it is better he keep still.

Later in the year, both Sheed and Naomi Burton made further overtures in an attempt to rescue the project, but to no avail. Antoninus reconciled himself to the fact that his longest and most personal prose work would remain unpublished.

The
Rose of
Solitude

According to the poet Philip Whalen,

The term "beat" actually denotes people who were around Times Square in 1947. When we had the first big poetry reading in San Francisco in 1955, I had never heard of the Beat Generation. Some journalist or other somehow got hold of the term from an ancient copy of the *New York Times Book Review* and hung it on what some people called the San Francisco Renaissance. Now the San Francisco Renaissance was not the right word either as that belonged to the people who were earlier, and they resented our identification with it. People like Jack Spicer, Robert Duncan, and Brother Antoninus rather resented us carpetbaggers being called San Francisco poets. After all, we were all from out of town—I was from Oregon, Ginsberg and Kerouac were from New York, give or take a few states, Burroughs from St. Louis, and so on. Gary Snyder was actually the only native San Franciscan of our group, but even he very early on was removed to Seattle. Here we were all being tagged San Francisco or beat poets in 1955, which made no sense, and a lot of people resented it, but it did bring new attention to the scene.

Preoccupied first with his breakthrough then with the difficulties and excitement surrounding the "Prodigious Thrust," Antoninus kept pace with all the literary activity across the Bay only vaguely. As he wrote a friend in early 1962, "Although as a poet I am identified with the San Francisco Renaissance, actually I am not a group poet. . . . My archetype has been the solitary visionary who isolates himself in nature and views the concerns of man from afar . . . . I am not a man of literary movements, and owe almost nothing to them. I do not despise them, but simply say that my gestation does not proceed by that kind of literary stimulus. I identify with the Beat Generation because of its mystical concerns, its emphasis on the oral as opposed to the academic tradition. But typical Beat poetry leaves me cold. I remain the solitary poet-utterer that I began."

But certainly the interest in the autobiography turned him from introspection to a renewed interest in his public life as a writer. And, as Robert Duncan sensed, he was a natural for the burgeoning scene. In the late fall, just before he left for New York, Antoninus was contacted by Duncan, who asked him to give a joint reading with Madeline Gleason at a hall in San Francisco for the Poetry Center. Although he had not given a public reading of his work since entering the Order, Antoninus, anxious to assert himself as one of the region's legitimate figures, agreed, after getting the blessing of Fr. Thomas. In the confusion of his preparations for his trip, however, he mistook the date, and when the night came for the reading he failed to show, to Duncan's consternation. A second appearance for the two poets was scheduled for the following week, however, this time on the San Francisco State College campus, and Antoninus gave his first public reading as a Dominican, presenting a number of poems he had written since the Catholic Worker experience to a packed house.

Two weeks later, Leonard Wolf invited him to read at St. Mary's College in Moraga. He had not yet developed his well-known charismatic reading style, but already the experience was beginning to have an effect on him. As Antoninus noted in his journal,

I was on the stand almost two hours, and ended in a great ovation, a real triumph. In other words I was exalted. It was an experience of great frustration, great realization, after my months of frustration and oppression here under the indifferent super-ego. Moreover it confirmed my impression after the San Francisco State reading that this was my vocation in the Church. People will not read my poems, but when I read to them I can spellbind. Everything engages, all my faculties converge here, and I become for this brief time transcendently myself . . . The ideational heart of the poem burns with an inexplicable revelation. It is this realization of my poems as vehicles for establishing contact between God and other souls that gives me the understanding of their prophetic character, and led me back to writing again.

The readings soon pulled him into the welter of San Francisco literary life. He was present at Kenneth Rexroth's apartment for an evening of poetry readings—along with Michael McClure, Philip Lamantia, and others—on February 3, staged for the benefit of *Life* magazine photographers, which in September ran an article on the "Howl" obscenity trial. And in the fall of 1957, when the second issue of *Evergreen Review* was coedited by Rexroth and devoted to the San Francisco Renaissance, Antoninus's poetry stood alongside work by Duncan, Lamantia, and others, and Ginsberg's "Howl." In his essay on these writers which served as a preface, Rexroth wrote of Antoninus that he is "probably the most profoundly moving and durable of the poets of the San Francisco Renaissance . . . .His work has a gnarled, even tortured honesty, a rugged unliterary diction, a relentless probing and searching, which are not just engaging, but almost overwhelming. . . . Anything less like the verse of the fashionable quarterlies would be hard to imagine."

   In his afterword to his long erotic poem *River-Root*, which was not published until 1976, Everson explains that the work was actually undertaken just a few weeks after the *Evergreen Review* appeared. It served as a breakthrough for him, a return to verse after his two years of monastic silence. As he notes in the afterward (written, interestingly, in the third person), the poem is a direct "reaction to the *Evergreen Review* appearance of only a few weeks earlier. The 'holy is the phallos' assertion is too suggestive an echo of Allen Ginsberg's 'Howl' to doubt of it. . . . And indeed the poet-monk seems consciously to be trying to redeem the libidinous Beat energies from the insane horror of Ginsberg's poem—to canonize them." Where "Howl" is a litany, *River-Root* is narrative; where "Howl" focuses on the city, *River-Root*'s setting is rural; where "Howl" ranges through American history and politics with Jewish mystic/socialist sympathies, *River-Root* is ahistorical, nontopical, and of course Catholic; finally, while both the "coda" to "Howl" and *River-Root* celebrate the body, Ginsberg's poem is homoerotic, while Antoninus's is frankly, almost to the point of cliché, heterosexual. It is this last point which is of particular interest. Subtitled "A Syzygy," the poem is overtly Jungian. Here, following his encounters with White, his extensive reading in analytical psychology, and his breakthrough, Antoninus attempts a synthesis of his Catholicism with his early concerns for the natural environment and the well of primal sexuality.

Originally, an early draft of the poem concluded with a "triumph for the maternal images of the sea," Antoninus wrote in his 1957 notebook, on All Saints' Day. Now, employing Jung's sense of the conjunction of the masculine and the feminine, he made his synthesis a movement toward psychic harmony.

I got deeply involved in it and wrote far into the night, and today all the freetime went into it too. Whereas in the first drafts I had established the maternal frame, here, in bringing the maleness to bear in the images of animal copulation, I finally brought the scene down to intercourse between man and woman. By late afternoon I had exhausted my energy

(I got little sleep last night, dominated by the creative energy of the poem) and could look back. As I conceive it, the poem will be divided into two main sections, the earth-images background of the first section (the river) and the archetypal sexual act of the second. This, I see now, is what I was trying to do—establish a basic or archetypal version of the sex act. But actually I was trying to achieve a reconciliation point between my conscious and unconscious selves in terms of the sex act as symbol. This, it seems to me, has been what all my sex-poems have been. They are all attempts to establish the act in its archetypal character, but the task keeps needing to be done over because the components in my psyche have not achieved resolution. The poem "Orion" was the first. Part IX "The flesh waits on" from *A Privacy of Speech* was the next. Prologue to *The Blowing of the Seed* was the next after that. Then no more again until *Prodigious Thrust*. Now this river poem, which is the most ambitious so far.

And thus for Antoninus the poem, as Albert Gelpi has observed, "opened the way back to poetry—and to the world."

vvv

In early 1959, Steve Eisner, a student at the University of Detroit, invited Antoninus for a reading. This occasioned the poet's first performance outside of California. As he remembered,

It was a stunning week. I made the AP wire service on the strength of the reading and my interviews. They regarded it as sensational—a Dominican monk part of the Beat Generation, which was getting bad press at that time. As far as the Beat Generation goes, it was a creation of *Time* magazine and *Life*. The second Eisenhower administration was becoming so bland that the press was looking for something. They gave it negative publicity, though, and "beatnik" became a household word, like "hippie" in the sixties. I was proud to be identified with them, however. I knew it was a revolt needed in American letters.

Eisner had gotten in touch with Paul Carroll, editor of *Big Table*, who made arrangements for radio interviews and an appearance on "Kup's Show," an early television talk show.

A few months earlier, Robert Frost had given a reading in Detroit, drawing over three hundred people. Eisner was determined that Antoninus would do even better. To publicize the event he took a photograph of motorcycles, then superimposed an image of a monk standing in front of them. He posted these all over the city—in coffee houses, bookstores, "everywhere anybody might be beat, post-beat, hippie, whatever. Where the motorcycles hung out. I practically made him the father confessor of Allen Ginsberg and Jack Kerouac," Eisner remembers. He picked the poet up in a borrowed Cadillac from the airport and as it was late, they immediately went to dinner at a friend's posh restaurant. "We started with turtle soup, and soon as he saw it he fell to his knees saying, 'Sweet Jesus!' And between every bite he'd beat his breast because he felt so guilty eating this kind of thing while the other brothers were back in the monastery working. 'O Lord, forgive me!' Then he'd take another mouthful. He could drink like a fish, so we had wine, scotch, after-dinner drinks, everything. But in between every drink, he'd beat his breast again. Everyone in the restaurant was stopped short."

Because of Eisner's efforts, the reading drew well over five hundred and was a triumph. After an introduction, Antoninus stood up and, in an attempt to make a psychological bridge with the audience, he just stared out at them. According to Eisner, who was just off-stage, "He kept staring and staring, walking back and forth, saying nothing. Everybody started shifting in their chairs, and I was ready to cut my throat. I thought I'd turned a maniac loose. But then he broke into 'Canticle to the Waterbirds'— looking right at the women lined up in the front row, he started, 'Clack your beaks!' They almost passed out; they thought he was saying this to them and didn't know at first it was a poem. After about thirty minutes of reading, he suddenly looked out and said, 'I've come two thousand miles, and I've got nothing to say to you.' The place broke up, and he got a ten or fifteen minute standing ovation. They just wouldn't let him off the stage." The next evening he gave a reading at the University of Chicago, to a packed house and another standing ovation.

When Antoninus returned to Oakland the following day he was exhausted. "I'd wrapped the monastery around me for years, and this first going out into the world was a terrific strain. I had to come home and just lock myself in to recover. I just couldn't capitalize on it. It was like after I got my Guggenheim when *The Residual Years* came out. If I could have gone east and met people, I'd have sold out the edition. But that just isn't the way my life goes." In fact, he had drawn enough attention through his Detroit and Chicago appearances that on May 25, *Time* did a feature on him as the "Beat Friar," but even had he been psychologically able to capitalize on the moment, events back in the Bay Area would have made this impossible.

Although the Dominicans are a democratic Order, before the election of Fr. Fulton to the Provincial's office, a rather severe priest named Fr. Benedict Blank had held the office for twenty years, through a special arrangement with both the Dominican headquarters in Rome and Archbishop John Mitty of San Francisco, his close friend. When Fulton finally succeeded him, Blank was furious, as the priest had not been one of his close associates, and he soon attempted to continue running the Province through the Archbishop's chancery office. As Antoninus started drawing attention, Blank began protesting to Archbishop Mitty about the situation. The *Time* article was the last straw. The Archbishop insisted to Fulton that Antoninus no longer be allowed to read in the diocese, nor anywhere in his habit (which, as a donatus, he had no right to wear in public anyway). Also, Fulton suggested that the poet remove the acronym O.P. (Order of Preachers) following his name whenever it appeared in print, and he insisted that he turn down a chance at popular national recognition, an invitation to be a guest on the Jack Parr television show.

Actually, the magazine piece was simply another event in a series of difficulties which had disturbed the house. Almost two years earlier, as Antoninus wrote Victor White, there had been

a stir here now over the defection of some of the more adventurous young philosophers to Alan Watts. They went to S.F. to see him, became enamored, and kicked up trouble when forbidden to attend his current series of lectures on Zen in Berkeley. Fr. Parmisano went to hear him once to make an appraisal, tangled with Watts in the discussion period, and turned thumbs down on the whole show. He and the Provincial are worried about this trend to what looks like straight pantheism.

Just a few years before, Watts had left the Anglican ministry to pursue studies in Buddhism and had become one of the west coast's most charismatic popularizers of Zen. When the *Time* article appeared linking Antoninus and the Beat Generation (with whom Watts was often identified), traces of the animosities and suspicions generated by this incident still lingered. Perhaps because of this, in an attempt to discourage the "free-lance character" of his activity, further pressure included the withholding of permission to make a commercial recording of his poems with Lawrence Ferlinghetti, as well as the cancellation of an interview with a reporter from the *Wall Street Journal* on Bay Area poets. As Antoninus noted in his journal, March 5, 1959, "I went to San Francisco and talked to the Provincial about my 'silencing.' It developed that the Archbishop had called him in and rebuked him in a most insulting way. One of the things he protested was my lecturing. He said people might think I am a cleric and that I speak for the Church. He objected to the fact that I had been a pacifist. He objected to the article I had submitted called 'Dionysus and the Beat Generation.' The attack obviously was stimulated by Fr. Blank, our past Provincial. I have not been sufficiently in the limelight to draw the Archbishop's attention. Fr. Blank's last source of power is his friendship with Archbishop Mitty. He is using this to attack Fr. Fulton in every way."

Further, Fulton had shown an interest in the Order moving more fully into the world of the arts, and to that end had helped establish Blackfriars in San Francisco, a Dominican arts center. Antoninus had been asked to contribute a group of poems to become the center's first publication, and Warren Hinckle, who would later edit *Ramparts,* gathered the manuscript, typed it over a weekend, and had *An Age Insurgent* printed by a job printer. Fulton insisted that this book be withdrawn also, arguing that if the Archbishop had placed strictures on Antoninus's public performances, this injunction should reasonably include printed work as well. Antoninus was obviously caught up as a pawn in a classic clerical struggle for power. As he remembers, "This was devastating to me, but I swallowed my pride and did not protest. In the long run it paid off. When Mitty died, and yet another new Provincial came in in 1960, Fr. Joseph Agius, he took me from my chores and the press, said I'd earned my spurs, and gave me permission to return to the platform in my habit. He gave me full time to write."

By the time of Mitty's restrictions, Antoninus had assembled his Catholic poems into a volume called *The Crooked Lines of God.* He had sent the manuscript to Naomi Burton, who had no luck in placing it. For a time, the poet held out hope that it would be picked up by New Directions, but *The Residual Years* had sold relatively few copies, and the firm had no interest in cutting into the sales of its best-selling Catholic author, Thomas Merton.

At this point, Steve Eisner suggested that he would publish the book under the auspices of the University of Detroit Press, and he and a Jesuit priest, Fr. Charles McGlynn, set out to raise money for publication through subscriptions. Antoninus had the type set by Monotype in San Francisco, then printed a thousand copies himself on a job press during the summer. Eisner made sure that the book was ready for Christmas sales, and it sold out its complete edition of a thousand copies in just thirty-one days. Because the book was not published in Archbishop Mitty's territory, it carried both the Dominican and Jesuit imprimaturs, and it was widely reviewed, with mixed reactions. In *The Nation* Kenneth Rexroth argued that "the ultimate, agonized sincerity that makes for a great truly personal style" was at the book's core, while in *The Sewanee Review* James Dickey quipped that the collection contained "enough solemn, dead metaphors to fill the stuffed owl's mouth for generations to come." Reviewing the book for *Poetry*, John Engels complained of the seemingly prosaic lines, that one couldn't tell "where to breathe"; to this criticism, Antoninus responded in a letter to the editor that it was "really very simple. It is accomplished in the following way: You read like hell till you run out of air. Then you do it." In any case the volume proved very popular. In January of 1960, Antoninus printed a second run, which again sold out quickly; this was followed by three more offset printings before the year was out, and it was nominated for the Pulitzer Prize.

vvv

By 1960, Edwa seemed like part of another life long forgotten, and it was at this juncture that another woman, Rose Moreno Tannlund, entered the poet's life. She had been born in Austin, Texas, had married young, soon had two daughters and a son, and had eventually gotten divorced. As Antoninus told David Meltzer in 1969, "Rose brought a new dimension into my life, a new version of woman. Beautiful and ardent and adamant, she took over . . . and for five years my life was hers . . . Rose is a Mexican and a mystic—an altogether primitive sensibility, capable of fanatical Mexican asceticism, spikes in the flesh, that sort of thing. Yet with an overlay of sophistication that was nothing like I had ever experienced. She never missed daily Mass, but her perfume was My Sin!" She introduced the monk, as he remembers, to the "world of cafe society. She was preparing me for the cocktail rounds every poet has to survive as a literary lion on the lecture circuit. She taught me the art of holding a contemplative life in the midst of

the social whirl, the mystic encounter with people in a highly tran-
sitory social milieu, how to go the limit until you collapse, then
bounce back." And in short order, the poet found himself once
again in love.

Antoninus met Rose because of her relationship with Finnbar
Hayes, who since the spring of 1959 had been stationed at St.
Dominics in San Francisco, where he worked for the Provincial as
his secretary. One day Rose showed up at the parish asking for
advice on a problem relating to her children. According to Hayes,

> She was unlike anybody I'd ever met. The thing that was extraordinary
> about her was the dramatic quality to her life. She was a classic Latin
> beauty, with long black hair and an immediate physical quality about
> her. One of those women who will come up and kiss you as a greeting.
> She also had this intense Latin piety, an enormous devotion to Jesus and
> his Blessed Mother, while always driving a convertible. I was 27 years
> old, and soon Rose had more than a passing interest.

Hayes, however, while obviously attracted to her, remained rather
aloof and diffident as a matter of self-protection. After a few
months, Rose got frustrated: "'How am I going to understand
you?' she asked. I said that if she wanted to understand me she
should go talk to Brother Antoninus. She wrote down his name,
walked out the door, got into her convertible with her hair flying
out the back, drove across the Bay to St. Albert's, and pounded
on the door asking to see Antoninus. Well, he came down and
there she was. The rest is history."

But in terms of Antoninus's relationship to women, it is a rather
complicated history, as when Rose entered his life two other
women were already vying for his attention. By the fall of 1960
the monk had been freed of all household duties, though he continued counseling. As he continued his studies in analytical psychology, he made forays into autohypnosis, attempting to use it as
a mystical technique. About the time he met Rose, a woman was
seeing him once a week for spiritual advice. It soon became apparent, according to the poet, that she had fallen in love with him.

My interest in self-analysis and autohypnosis left me incredibly exposed. I was trying to overcome all the forces of resistance. In *The Hazards of Holiness* I went step by step through my encounters with the shadow. Part of my assault on the psyche was an attempt to depotentiate the shadow, get it in the open where I could cope with it. This worked, but at the same time made me very vulnerable to the anima, when she came directly in the form of a woman.

Suddenly, in early February of 1960, the whole situation got out of hand. As the poet remembers, "I was already falling in love with Rose, but I didn't know it. This other woman was all dolled up and on the make. She didn't make the move, though, I did. I took her in my arms and began to kiss her. She was incredulous, but became very passionate. I told her of my love for her and called her my bride. But I was really falling in love with Rose." As he recorded in his journal, "The effect upon me was profound, from an unconscious point of view. There had been no erotic reaction, yet the physical contact did something. I noticed washing the pots and pans later that my voice was deep and baritone, masculine, as when my voice changed before."

As if this triangle were not complicated enough, a third woman, Yvonne Winslow, had entered the picture. Though a non-Catholic, she too had come to Antoninus for counseling. She was two years older than the monk, born in fact in the same year as his sister, but in very poor health. She was quite wealthy, and soon took to inviting him to her house where she had a fine library he enjoyed browsing through. Like the other woman, Yvonne found herself in love with the poet, though in this case he did nothing to reciprocate. She was deeply attached to Jungian thought and had undergone serious analysis for years, and the two of them spent many afternoons discussing analytical psychology. Though her feelings for him were apparent, the monk continued to see her frequently throughout his whole relationship with Rose, and for a long time the two women knew nothing of each other.

It was Rose, however, "the Mexican cross" as he called her in

his powerful love-poem sequence *The Rose of Solitude*, to whom
Antoninus was drawn with an intensity he hadn't felt for many
years. Growing up in Texas, the daughter of an Hispanic business-
man, she had married a German when she was very young, and
moved with him to San Francisco where her three children were
born. Eventually, she divorced, and took a job at the Arthur
Murray Dance Studio as a dance instructor to support herself and
the children. To make of her a Scarlett O'Hara might be an exag-
geration, but certainly she was a contradiction. Working at Arthur
Murray's and a great beauty, she was constantly surrounded by
suitors. According to the poet, she seemed to enjoy playing these
men off each other. Yet like McCool at Maurin House, she was
very simple in her Catholicism, almost superstitious, and very
devout. Occasionally for penance she'd tape the sharp pieces of
aluminum used to hold altar candles to her palms to produce stig-
mata. Other times, she'd enter into prolonged fasts.

Yet twenty-five years later, Fr. Hayes still doesn't know exactly
what to make of her house. She had invited him often to her home
and he had always refused. Finally, on New Year's Eve in 1960,
both he and Antoninus went together for dinner. "She had this
kind of subdued lighting," he remembers, "with bar, lots of col-
ored glass, and a great view of the city in the distance. She showed
us the bedroom, which was elegant. There was a very large bed
with a bookcase behind it. On top of the bookcase there were portrait photographs of at least six and maybe eight or ten priests that
she knew. Later that evening, when she had left the room, I said
to Antoninus—and by this time it was obvious that they too had
an intense relationship going on—'I don't want to become another
moosehead on that mantelpiece.' He laughed and laughed." Still,
Hayes insists, part of Rose's extraordinary quality was that she was
"erotic and attractive, but *not* a seductress. She was not destructive
at all, but rather a real 'earth-mother' type."

Like Yvonne, Rose began to see Antoninus for counsel; one of
the monk's long journal entries dated October 6, 1959, mentions
simply, "In the afternoon Finnbar's friend and charge, Rose, came

to visit me. I talked with her a couple hours. I was highly keyed psychically from the morning's thought and engaged very intensely." Soon Rose began going regularly to Antoninus to get advice:

I was able to talk to Brother about my feelings of guilt over my separation from my husband. Although I was outgoing, I was rather naive when I was married—I didn't believe that your husband could cheat on you. So when it happened, I was in shock. For about four years before I met Brother, I felt somehow responsible for this; I just wasn't able to let it out. Why didn't I take my husband back so that my children would have two parents? Was I being too stubborn? Maybe because he had been through a similar thing with his first wife, we were somehow kindred souls, and this enabled me to talk about it. In time, talking to him I found myself able to release my sense of guilt.

And quickly, Antoninus found himself obsessed, almost dangerously, with the first woman in years to utterly capture both his erotic and spiritual imaginations. By December, the two were seeing each other very often, and speaking on the telephone almost every day. Whenever they had a chance, they would drive somewhere scenic, like Vista Point at the Golden Gate Bridge. As the poet remembered, "It had something to do with the spiritual core of our relationship, which was not sexual. We seemed to intuitively understand that it would have to happen to get things on a certain plane. In a sense, it relieved the relationship of squalor. What was going on in the spiritual dimension was that Rose was leading me, teaching me how to sustain myself on platform. On those poetry circuits you drink like a fish, there are groupies, and when I first started going out I'd often have to put my appearances a week apart just to recover my balance. Rose got me through that."

In fact, in both their conversation and letters Antoninus repeatedly stressed the spiritual aspect of their relationship, though certainly a measure of this might be sourced in guilt over a physical relationship with a woman. But as he wrote her in January,

I have discovered that I need a Queen to serve, to keep my energies and spirit in focus, not dissipated into fragmented reaction, as St. John of the Cross needed St. Theresa to serve and Blessed Raymond needed Catherine of Siena . . . It is apparent that we are not perfect, and God wants us to be perfect, and has brought us together so that we may find perfection through each other. I know that in the history of the saints there has been no relation like ours. The erotic phase is the phase that is difficult precisely because it seems to fly in the face of history, and the witness of all the saints before us. Given their testament, either our erotic relationship is the work of the devil, or we stand on the verge of a new era of man's relationship to himself . . . When our two erotic natures come together a holocaust occurs which every time threatens to overcome us with its tremendous passion.

Rose herself made a conscious effort not to let the relationship deteriorate, to the extent that whenever they went out together she'd introduce the poet as Brother Antoninus, never allowing him to hide the fact that he was a monk. She led him into her world of San Francisco nightlife, and they often might be found at Club 365, a popular cabaret. For his part, Antoninus introduced her to various literary friends and acquaintances. One afternoon following a writing workshop, Don Carpenter and Philip Whalen gave the poet a ride to her house, and the four of them spent a pleasant afternoon talking over drinks to Rose's mother, who was visiting from Austin. On another occasion, Antoninus took her to a birthday party at Kenneth Rexroth's. He was a little nervous about the meeting, but as it turned out, "She was sensational. It wasn't as if she was center stage. She was in deep conversation with several people, including Philip Lamantia and the woman he was with. But she made a hell of an impact. Rexroth was amazed, and a little taken aback. He thought I'd given up women. And here was the beautiful Rose on my shoulder." The main landing of Rexroth's apartment was up a flight of stairs, and he'd have to go down to unlock the door and let his guests in. When he first opened the door and saw Rose, "his eyes got bigger and bigger. He followed her up the stairs, staring, then when he got to the top and took her coat, he looked at her breasts in a tight dress. I thought he was going to faint on the spot!"

That Antoninus experienced love again is not so curious. Of all of Jung's concepts, it is the idea of the anima/animus which has taken a central place in the poet's program; that each man carries "a spontaneous product of the unconscious" which is the feminine within him, while "each woman's unconscious has, so to speak, a masculine imprint." These contra-sexual aspects, Jung argues, must be recognized and reconciled within each individual and finally, by extension, within the collective to form an androgynous whole if psychic stability is to be realized. In the poet's preface to *The Rose of Solitude*, his finest achievement as Antoninus and written as the relationship with Rose progressed, he recognizes this theme: "The spiritual life is both speculative and practical, but a painful tension obtains between the world of the ideal and the world of immediate experience." *Rose* appeared finally in 1967 (though as early as 1964 the poet was reading long passages during his performances, at Rose's insistence) as his third and final full-length Catholic collection, and its subject is a monk's interior struggle with sexuality in his relationship with a divorced Mexican dancer. "Every time something particular happened in our lives," Rose recalls, "there would be a poem coming out of it. He'd always give me the first copy in a letter." Yet even deeper, the sequence of poems shows a path to *gnosis* by tracing the transformation of a sexual struggle through a Jungian mergence of the masculine and feminine aspects of the self.

This process is traced rather dramatically in the monk's journal from this period, as his obsession with masturbation intensified. Following his confrontation with the mother during the 1956 breakthrough, the next few years record any number of free-floating heterosexual masturbatory fantasies. By early 1959, however, without any particular explanation, these give way to graphic homoerotic imaginings, sometimes relating to specific figures in the poet's life, sometimes not. Interestingly, about the time he begins counseling a friend, these fantasies take yet another turn of the androgynous wheel, as the monk moves from a preoccupation with male anal intercourse to imagining himself a woman. As he records on the Feast of St. Jerome,

I was a woman awaiting the approach of my lover, who was my divine son. I had conceived him of God when I was pubescent and now he is grown and coming to possess me. . . . I am a woman of early thirties [Rose, whom he had first met a month before, was thirty], he a man of twenty in perfect physique. I have the proportions of a Hindu goddess, small ankles, large calves and hips, narrow waist, deep navel, perfect fruit-like breasts, round full shoulders and arms. I have never known man and am a virgin, and my divine son ventures to possess me.

In possessing me he knows no laws. If he puts his phallus in my anus it is not because it is obscene but because there is a connaturality between phallus as penetrator and anal cavity as receiver that is true and exists in potentiality and this potentiality has to be activated in order that reality be complete. He possesses me every possible way. Sometimes his phallus is sound and penetrates the womb of my ear, fertilizes my brain. Sometimes his phallus is sight, penetrating my eyes and impregnating my mind.

It is at this point in early February, when he embraces his friend and his voice becomes "deep and baritone, masculine" again, that these entries, and presumably the fantasies, come to an end.

Certainly, from a literary standpoint, *Rose* is anticipated in the poet's earlier work, especially *River-Root*. Further, Antoninus's concern with "the woman within" appears as early as the pre-Catholic, pre-Jungian *In the Fictive Wish*, though it becomes progressively more important through the Catholic poetry. As Albert Gelpi points out in his afterword to the poet's collected Catholic work, *The Veritable Years*, "in 'The Encounter' and several other remarkable poems towards the end of *Crooked Lines* Antoninus becomes the woman before God, his/her whole being called into activity by His totally mastering love." Additionally, in "Annul in Me My Manhood" the poet reverses Lady Macbeth's apostrophe "unsex me here," asking that God might make him "woman-sexed and weak, / If by that total transformation / I might know Thee more," while the later "God Germed in Raw Granite" asks "is this she? Woman within!/ . . . when we / Well-wedded merge, by Him / Twained into one and solved there." But it is not until *Rose* (his encounters first with his friend and Yvonne Winslow setting the stage for his full-blown affair) that Antoninus moves beyond a sense of the recognition of the anima as a facet of his quest to a realization that in fact the woman is its object.

The "Prologue" to *Rose* announces the book's theme:

> The dark roots of the rose cry in my heart.
> They pierce through rock-ribs of my stony flesh,
> Invest the element, the loam of life.
> They twist and mesh . . .
> The Sign of God evoked from the splendid flesh
> Of the Rose revealed.

The opening lines of the poem present a traditional symbol, though the situation is ambiguous: we have a rose (and we think here of Dante or, perhaps because the "roots" are "dark," of Theodore Roethke), yet at the same instant the rose seems to be a thing both external to the poet (i.e., a woman) and part of him as well. The question becomes one of direction—is the rose something that has invaded him (his infatuation with an Other) or is it something already resident in the poet, buried deeply in his soul, crying to emerge? The sequence *is* autobiographical; Antoninus does have a relationship that causes him both great joy and great anguish. He is after all a religious under vows. And yet the first line is telling: the rose is crying *in* his heart; that is, we do not necessarily have a movement outward to the "loam of life" which is psychic wholeness. In this sense, the rose becomes symbolic of the poet's feminine aspect, and the movement of the poem, the unfolding "petal by crimson petal, leaf by leaf" of the rose, becomes as much a figurative enactment of the poet's emerging recognition of his own androgynous nature as a specifically sexual circumstance. On the one hand, the monk finds in the body of his woman "The Sign of God"; on the other, it is the "splendid flesh of the Rose" of his anima which reveals to him the core of his religion and affords regeneration.

Throughout the sequence's five sections, then, the poet is transformed into the crucified Christ, having nailed himself to "the Mexican cross, / The flint knife of her beauty." Of course such symbolism is perhaps rather unextraordinary given both the poet's situation—a monk whose vow of celibacy is undergoing a rigorous test—and his interest in martyrdom, yet it works on a level deeper than the immediate. According to Jung's studies, the cross (which is the primary symbol in *Rose*, after the rose itself) "is a many-faceted symbol, and its chief meaning is that of the 'tree of life' and the 'mother,'" certainly an instrument of pain, but one leading to regeneration. Further, Christ's crucifixion, which the poet here re-creates in the passion of his own life, is often identified with a passing into androgyny. As Finnbar Hayes, who at this time was his closest male friend, seemed to realize, "Rose served as the catalyst for thoughts and feelings which were in him already."

Fr. William Ruddy, a poet himself who had known Antoninus since 1961, recalled,

In the monastery he was always harping on the notion that the soul is feminine to God, and people in the house were always wondering why he pushed it. But living in the monastery is an unnatural life; you castrate yourself when you live as a religious. You can't use psychological techniques to establish your validity as a religious. We are supposed to be preaching a beautiful embracing kind of Christian love, yet the most embracing kind of human love is found between man and woman in the sexual act itself. So we have to, as Thomas Merton said, care and not care at all. That's where the tension of religious life comes from, and if you don't see it you are going to live blandly, pat babies on the head and think you are living a fulfilling life when deep down you know better. This was what Antoninus was agonizing out.

And it is as the Christ figure in *Rose* that Antoninus finds regeneration not finally in the moritification and denial of "A Frost Lay White on California" and his midnight battles with demons, but rather in his submission to the erotic passion of the Rose—the woman within.

As Rose remembers, "Our relationship was close to touching the deepest part of oneself, the very depth of the soul."

I really grew through my relationship with him. No one ever touched me the way he did. Around him I could suddenly express myself, say what I needed to say. For my part, I allowed him to come out of his cocoon. In the monastery you have to be sure that you are always in check; he always used to say to me that he felt like he was pulling a nail out of a wall. With me he too began to be able to truly express himself.

vvv

As difficult as his personal life was at this point, however, the poet's public life following the lifting of the Archbishop's ban on his readings was beginning to flourish. He wrote Steve Eisner in 1961, "The new Provincial wants me to set up with an agency and make a tour, get East, get going. I am resisting somewhat, afraid to make the change over from the passive, let-them-come-to-me attitude of the past, to the aggressive go-out-and-get-em attitude of this new superior. I guess I will start designing a poster and a circular. I am in a difficult in-between stage. The contemplative withdrawal is solving certain interior problems, but it does not make for decisive crystallization." Antoninus put together an extended press release under the name Virginia Spanner, and by the end of the year he had participated in a writers' conference at the University of Washington, and given readings at universities in Minneapolis, Madison, Chicago, South Bend, Detroit, and Cleveland, as well as Los Angeles. By mid-March he had gone on a second tour, reading at Boston College, Boston University, Brandeis, Providence College, and Harvard. October and early November took him through the southwest, with readings at the

University of Oklahoma, St. Michael's College, the University of New Mexico, and New Mexico State University at Las Cruces. Usually the performances were sponsored by campus Newman Clubs.

None of these performances was ever quite the same, though all followed a similar pattern. Antoninus titled his reading/talk "Poetry and the Life of the Spirit" because, as he wrote one program director in 1961, "although I do read poems the discourse between the poems is usually not about poetry but about the general problems of the spiritual and moral life as all men confront it, related to as wide an audience level as I can make it to avoid literary aestheticism on the one hand or religious sectarianism on the other." He would begin with "A Canticle to the Waterbirds," then "start the free-associations, delving down into the roots of the mind for spontaneous correlations, groping out into unexplored areas, trying to find the creative areas within *myself*, probe the unknown, find new leaders and terminals, cross-references, intuitions, smokey conjectures, etc. To *risk*. To suffer exposure, find the cross, the moment of agonized realization. And in the end, to *be*." And it was primarily for this reason, that these performances were as much intense excursions into the dark well of his psyche, that the poet was forced to allow at least a few days, if not a full week, between each event.

Almost always, these readings, or really public meditations, were a great success. As Thomas McDonnell reported on the Harvard reading for *Commonweal*, "It was clear that something quite different was taking place, that this was not just another poet at the lectern: poem, polite applause, repeat as scheduled, thank you, good night. . . . Antoninus had subsumed the method of Bertholt Brecht's 'epic' theater to the ritual of the poetry reading. . . . It is nothing less than a breakthrough from the poem as a platform recitation piece to the poem as the meaningful charismatic gesture in art that it was always meant to be." The reporter for the *Washington Daily News* saw him as "God's own showman . . . a man possessed. His face and eyes and hands were never still"; the

Columbia University *Owl* recalled that "he read his poems with a strong vibrant voice which did not declare them but sang them with enormous feeling . . . .It was between the poems, in his spontaneous remarks, in which the power of his personality transformed an over-heated, crowded lecture hall into a place of genuine human encounter"; according to The Dominican College *Meadowlark*, "The first word echoed from every corner of the room—a word no one remembered because of the emotion and love from which it sprung. It was a cry in the wilderness . . . a communion with the people sitting before him."

As charismatic encounters, the events were far more draining for the poet than traditional readings. As he noted in his journal, "these public appearances put a demand upon the psyche which it has to face in no other way. There is a tremendous calling forth of psychic energy in the act of engagement. As you face a group of people and seek out to engage their souls." On occasion he would read as few as four or five poems, though the event might go on as long as two hours. And Antoninus would, if things went well, emerge from each of these sessions with a deepened perception. "Less and less I offer ideas," he continued,

I call them "encounters" because they are like an encounter in the woods between a man and a strange animal. The acuteness, alertness, intense interest in one another is there, but no operating at the level of ideas. I introduce ideas only to establish the relation. The audience is the animal, latent, potential, alerted but not in act. I am the man, analysing, projecting, seeking discovery and meaning. My own trajectory is the sequence of these encounters, each contributing something to me, each changing me, so that I approach each encounter a different being from the last.

Because Antoninus would rely on a very tenuous balance between himself and his audience, however, on occasion things did not go well. As he notes in his journal, at one point he was asked to speak on "Art and Christianity" as a preface to a showing of experimental films by Bay Area film makers: "It was shambles. I started out, but never did get related. I could have, in time, but time ran out. I began with the imagination and aesthetic intuition. I got over to mystical intuition. Then I began to establish the nature of the abyss that separates man from God. But as I was establishing the unknowableness of God preparatory to leading God into life by virtue of the Incarnation—as I said 'God Himself, as He is, cannot be known. . . . If you can know anything it cannot be God.' . . . At this point an artist in the front row convulsed in revulsion, and I was finished. I couldn't pick it up again, and quit."

Other times, the very size of the audience might cause problems. In early December of 1962, for example, the poet performed at the University of California at Berkeley. He was scheduled to read in a lecture hall with good acoustics. That evening, however, fifteen minutes before the reading was scheduled to begin, over two hundred people crowded outside the door of the room, unable to find seats. Everyone moved into a much larger room, but there was no sound equipment, so Antoninus was forced to read without a mike; for a week following, the student newspaper *The Daily Californian* ran numerous letters by irate audience members who couldn't hear. The poet Czeslaw Milosz, who had translated a few of Antoninus's poems for a Polish newspaper, had been one of those who couldn't hear, and had complained to the poet in a personal letter. "In defense of my style," Antoninus replied in a letter to Milosz on December 12, "I maintain that there are some truths that cannot be uttered at the top of your voice. When I said that it didn't make any difference whether I was heard or not I didn't mean my ideas were irrelevant, but that the *event* was larger than the concepts, and in terms of *event* everyone there could participate in it. And did so, whether they liked it or not. My appearances are not lectures, but encounters, and as encounters do not depend upon my concepts, though my concepts are important. The intensity of the voice, the tenseness of the audience, the vision of the poet, the psychological dynamism of the engagement—all were there."

In addition to his own psychological and sexual problems, the poet suffered an additional shock during this period, the death of his "spiritual father" Robinson Jeffers. Antoninus had never met Jeffers, nor had even made the attempt to meet him, though he had sent him a copy of *Crooked Lines*, inscribed to "the greatest living poet." When Jeffers died, suddenly, on January 20 of 1962, the monk wrote his friend Lawrence Clark Powell, who had written the first full-length study of Jeffers's work, reminding him that his was a shared enthusiasm for the elder poet's work which had brought the two of them into contact. At Jeffers's death, Powell remained one of the few critics to continue to show any interest in his work, and certainly Antoninus was his only poetic disciple. "I have spent the day thinking about him," Antoninus wrote Powell,

taking out his books, touching them, looking at his picture . . . .The news articles speak only of his vast reputation and prestige—no hint of the snarling refusal of the literary critics to give him his honor. . . . He was my spiritual father. It was he who broke my own father's agnosticism, and proved to me there is a God. It was he who taught me how to worship. It was he who woke up my soul, related me to the whole of things. It was he who made me a religious man, gave me the dignity of faith in life and in God. Without him I would probably never have found my voice as a poet. He taught me to write. I mourn the passing of my father. For me it is the end of an epoch, an era of my life and experience. I wish to God I had met him, touched his hands.

A month earlier, the poet James Schevill had asked Antoninus and other poets to write work to be performed at a poetry festival to be held at the San Francisco Museum of Art in June. At first the monk declined, explaining that he had never done an occasional poem and that he didn't think he could. Schevill suggested that he write something on Jeffers, but as Antoninus related in a letter to John Ciardi, poetry editor of the *Saturday Review*, this seemed improbable. "But when I took up my pen this thing came boiling out. I was in it for days, completely submerged, hardly coming up for air. Some real archetype in me was touched. I know what it was too: the Father. The great old man. God it was terrific the way it came out." Antoninus completed "The Poet Is Dead" by late spring, and read it for the first time at Schevill's festival, performing alongside M. L. Rosenthal and Thomas Parkinson. Audience response was overwhelming, though the reviewer for the *San Francisco Chronicle* complained that he had hoped to attend a celebration not a wake. In any case, as Antoninus concluded to Ciardi, "What astonishes me is that there is not a Christian concept in the poem, as if I had been groping back to something way before my conversion that had to be taken up and laid to rest."

Brother Antoninus
setting type in St.
Albert's basement,
1954

Brother Antoninus reading at Blackfriars opening in San Francisco

Brother Antoninus
and Rose Tannlund,
1964

*(Courtesy of the Bancroft
Library, University of
California, Berkeley)*

Profession at Kentfield, with Father Antoninus Wall presiding, Gary
Snyder standing in the middle, far right　*(Courtesy of the Bancroft Library,
University of California, Berkeley)*

With Lawrence
Powell at Wesleyan,
1968

*(Courtesy of the Bancroft
Library, University of
California, Berkeley)*

Sharing the podium with Mayor Joseph Alioto, reading "This City Does
Not Die," April 18, 1969

Brother Antoninus reading at Grace Cathedral in San Francisco in
support of People's Park, 1969 *(Courtesy of the Bancroft Library,
University of California, Berkeley)*

William Everson and Susanna at Kingfisher Flat *(Courtesy of Leigh Wiener)*

NINE

The
Spirit
and the
Flesh

In the early 1960's, following the liberalization of Vatican II, the western Dominican province decided to upgrade the vocation of lay brothers and offer in the formative years a specialized training. To this end, the novice clerics were sent to a house in Thousand Oaks in southern California, while their former novitiate, the English Tudor priory at Kentfield, was given over to the brothers. Fr. Antoninus Wall was made the prior, Fr. Louis Robinson the novice master, and Fr. Hayes remained in residence. Eventually they were joined by eight brothers from St. Albert's, including Antoninus. Antoninus had never quite given up his dream of a closer, more permanent connection to the Order—he was still at this point a donatus—and while he saw no more hope of entering the priesthood, he seriously considered taking the vows of a First Order brother, which would make him permanently a member of the Dominicans, as well as enable him to legitimately wear his habit in public. Rose did everything she could to encourage this, though for many months the monk resisted. To take such a vow, a brother (whether or not he had been in the Order for a day or a decade) was required to spend a year in relative seclusion and prayer, unless a dispensation was granted. In March of 1963, Antoninus wrote to Fr. Basil Lamb, now master of the lay brothers at St. Albert's, requesting the novitiate period be waived. "I have served twelve years in the Order under obedience and have amply fulfilled all the purposes the novitiate period is meant to provide," he argued. Further, "the restriction of my activities to those permissible under novitiate conditions will seriously jeopardize my apostolate (if I may presume to so designate it) at the present time."

He was particularly concerned that he not repeat the loss of momentum in his writing and reading career that had occurred first when he entered the Order in 1951, and again when he had fallen under the Archbishop's ban in 1959. "I need now the ability to respond wherever and whenever the call comes," he continued to Lamb. "I believe the Church does not mean for us to be slaves to mere formulas, not even meaningful formulas." For better or worse, however, the request was denied, and if he hoped to become a First Order Dominican, Antoninus was forced to once again reconcile himself to withdrawing from the public eye.

As the dispensation for the marriage to Edwa had never been granted, he had to reapply to Rome for that before he could legitimately enter the novitiate. On September 18 he finally received his dispensation, and on the following day canceled upcoming readings at the San Francisco Public Library, the University of Dayton, Iowa State University, Texas Western College, and Siena College in New York with the excuse that "by the Grace of God I have learned that my dispensation has been granted in Rome and I am leaving immediately for the novitiate in Kentfield, California. I will be sealed up this coming year."

In fact, Antoninus was not cloistered absolutely—he spent a few afternoons in his robes on the priory's tennis court playing tennis with Rose, chasing down balls—but the following year was spent in relative seclusion. The monk's room had a bed, closet, and wash basin, with a window looking out onto the oak and madrone trees. His routine was similar to that at St. Albert's: up at 6 a.m. to chant the office, Mass, then breakfast. As the idea was to make the brothers more than simply menials, several would then attend class or head to nearby Catholic schools to teach. Because he was tied to the house, Antoninus couldn't do this, and thus had his mornings free for writing and prayer. Following lunch, after a recreation period where he took walks or read, he would return to his writing. At 5 p.m. the community would gather again for vespers, followed by a rosary, then supper. He'd spend the rest of the evening reading, until Compline at nine.

Throughout the year, the poet's only specific chore was, once again, washing dishes twice a day. "Actually, the Provincial had intended," he recalled,

the same exemption from chore-work to apply in the novitiate, but he had neglected to inform the Kentfield superiors, and I took up my task. Once on a visit the Provincial saw me in the scullery and exclaimed, "Brother Antoninus is sprouting wings!" but I only grinned in acknowledgement and never pressed. Truthfully, I expected to be returning to St. Albert's the following year, preferring the house of Studies for its intellectual atmosphere, but later I learned I wasn't welcome there. Fr. William Lewis, a venerable parochial Dominican appointed Prior there to serve as benign father figure, had been unhappy with my exemption, on one occasion going so far as to refuse allowing another lay brother to drive me to a performance. "Let Brother Antoninus provide his own transportation," he said. "He doesn't contribute to this house." Thus I found myself permanently assigned to Kentfield.

Along with work by White and Vann, he continued to read everything of Jung's that he could get his hands on, and studied especially *Symbols of Transformation*, along with Erich Neumann's *The Origins and History of Consciousness*. As an outgrowth of this study he also began to develop an intense interest in astrology. A friend named Terry Nichols, who had been a student at Harvard, came to San Francisco to meet Gavin Arthur, the most well-known astrologer in the city at the time. One afternoon, Nichols visited Antoninus, bringing with him the poet's chart, which he had prepared.

There I saw the disposition of my psyche with remarkable objectivity. What amazed me most were the House positions in the career and creative areas. Saturn in the 9th House, the religious, was the perfect embodiment of a formal conservative religion, and explained to me how I could accept Catholicism. In the Tenth House, career, I had Pluto, which I had in common with both Richard Nixon and Ronald Reagan— the great shift in career is explained there, a terrific oscillation. In the Fifth House I had Uranus; this is the house of love affairs, platform appearances, charismatic intensity. There was the moon in the 12th, the classic position of the monk, with Venus and Mars conjoined in the First House, a sexual orientation with the power to overcome the moon in the 12th. And so on.

He was so startled at what he perceived to be the accuracy of Nichols's chart, that he immediately began serious study and within a short time had assembled a substantial library of astrological materials. Soon he was proselytizing astrology to his Jungian friends as he "came to see the archetypes objectified in the horoscope. Jung dismissed astrology in favor of alchemy, which to me was a fatal mistake. The alchemy work does apply to the assimilation of the psyche in the transformation process, yet it isn't a valid parable of the process of psychological integration. It can't begin to compare with the social dynamic of astrology in terms of understanding the disposition of one's archetypal situation, the temperament and personality."

Antoninus did not find reconciling astrology to Catholicism difficult, as the Dominicans themselves had introduced it to the Church in the thirteenth century. "Saint Albert the Great," he reasoned,

was an early scientist. The first monasteries were in the deserts, and with the fall of Rome Saint Benedict took those principles into the city. In the time of Augustine astrology was equated with paganism, but with the Dominican revival of the Aristotelian in the thirteenth century, astrology made a comeback. Soon even the Popes had their personal astrologers as an official office. Astrology disappeared again with the shift into Newtonian physics, but then returned with Einstein and the relativist universe which could accommodate it. I soon found myself drawn especially to the work of Dane Rudhyar because he had a Jungian orientation. I attempted to calculate charts, but I was never really successful at it as they are too mathematical. I was adept at interpreting them, however.

Aside from his reading and prayer, the monk's primary preoccupation during this period was his writing, and two projects consumed him, concluding his *Rose of Solitude* poem-sequence and his second major extended prose work, a Jungian meditation on the death of John F. Kennedy. Like everyone else, the poet was stricken by the assassination of the President on November 22, 1963, and like everyone—from political commentators to conspiracy fanatics—he tried in his own way to make some sense of the national tragedy, for many months losing himself in an archetypal consideration of the event. "When a nation falsifies the vision of its creative destiny with a specious logic," he conjectured, "and in so doing rationalizes the corruptness that no logic can justify, God himself assumes the initiative, and visits upon it the most paralyzing rebukes producible from the forces latent in the historic situation." Sometimes, he continued, such rebukes might be natural disasters, sometimes wars. At other points in history, however, there "comes the hour of great moral or spiritual crisis, and something keener, something more acute, more precisely specified to the deceptive complaisance fattening in the entrails of the people is mysteriously prepared and held in readiness, until the finger of God moves ever so slightly, and there occurs an act destined to take its place forever in its heart and in its soul." Such was the death of John F. Kennedy. Interestingly, he argued that because Lee Harvey Oswald was close to the President's age, and thus a brother rather than a father figure, "the event fell more compre-

hensively within the American ethos than the other might have,"
an acting out of the Cain and Abel myth. He went on to point out
that while he himself could never have been Kennedy, "I can only
tremble before the tissue-paper division of fate that kept me from
being Lee Harvey Oswald . . . proud, sensitive, morose, 'disaffil-
iated,' he had the Kerouac cut, but lacked that redemptive
Kerouac buoyancy and elan." And Oswald himself was of necessity sacrificed in this archetypal drama, shot in front of television
cameras by the "ubiquitous Master of Strippers and buddy of the
police," Jack Ruby.

By April of 1964, the manuscript was finished, and a selection
appeared in the spring issue of *Ramparts*. He sent the complete
manuscript to Doubleday, which had published *The Hazards of
Holiness* with moderate commercial success in 1962, the book
going through three printings. Within six weeks, however, *Tongs
of Jeopardy* was rejected, perhaps because it was too eccentric, perhaps, as Antoninus wrote a friend, because it was too soon for serious analysis, that such a study would be "resisted in the hallowed
atmosphere that has prevailed." Naomi Burton, the agent who
had worked with him on the autobiography and had seen *Hazards*
through Doubleday, where she was now employed as a full-time
editor, attempted to interest other publishers in the manuscript,
but to no avail. Like "Prodigious Thrust," this second major prose
effort would remain unpublished.

When his novitiate year was up, Antoninus took his first three-
year vow, which made him a member of the First Order. As
Antoninus wrote Naomi Burton,

My vows-taking was terrific. As too many people were coming for the
chapel we held it out in our redwood grove. A beautiful morning. The
sun coming through the great trunks in shafts. The birds coming right
down in great moments of silence. All the people hushed. Friends from
my old college days back in '35 showed up. Certainly the peak of my
days in the religious life. My psyche is still out there, stunned, looking
up, overwhelmed.

Other guests included the poet Gary Snyder, who had been brought by Andrew Hoyem, and Rose.

He had seen Rose occasionally during the year, though with no regularity. Working at the dance studio she had met a tall, good-looking man named Amir, and unbeknownst to the monk, during his seclusion had been involved in a fairly serious affair with him. As Antoninus remembered, "When I took vows in the fall, she didn't want to come. She arrived late and was very solemn." The poet had expected to pick up their relationship where it had left off, and after the ceremony drove with a mutual friend to Rose's house. That evening Rose acted diffident. Within a few days, she broke down and told him about Amir, which first astounded Antoninus, then outraged him. Antoninus Wall happened to cross his path one evening not long after the vow-taking ceremony. "I made a big mistake," he remembers. "I realized what he was depressed about and told him that the whole thing wasn't really all that important. That really put him in a low mood. His response was simply, 'I hope you never find out what *you* really think about *your* mother.'"

He had planned a reading trip while in seclusion, one which would take him through Iowa, Missouri, Kentucky (where he met with Thomas Merton), Maryland, Washington, D.C., and Pennsylvania, and he hoped that the trip would take his mind off his disappointment. In fact, however, it only worked to intensify it. Just before he left, Rose telephoned him and insisted that he read only the poems from the *Rose* sequence. "I thought I couldn't do that," he recalled, "but she said I must. I'd been hiding them all the time because of their erotic content. She told me that if I didn't she'd marry Amir. That's the way she'd play one off against the other. She asked me if she'd ever miscalculated. Tell them the work is from your heart and it must be spoken. After some time, she convinced me and I gave her my word. My God, sometimes it would be pure torture to read the work, but the audiences reacted terrifically." And in fact according to the student newspaper at the University of St. Louis, following the reading of the

sequence a crowd of a thousand gave the poet an extended standing ovation. "We left the auditorium," a student commented,
"walking on air."

By the time he returned to San Francisco, Rose's affair with
Amir had progressed, and she had become his fiancée. The poet
was devastated. "I had hoped to write long before this," he wrote
Albert Gelpi on January 22 of 1965, "but I have been going
through my most prolonged bout with heartache in twenty years,
coming back from my trip to find my relationship with Rose
marred by an intruder, and all the storms of anxiety and depression that brings in the train. My room is a shambles, nothing filed
away, my correspondence neglected, all heaps and stacks of papers
and books." And in the midst of this shambles Antoninus wrote
the final agonized section of his long love poem:

> Wherever I go
> The burn of that beauty
> Brands me, bludgeons me.
> I am thrown.
> I slew sideways.
> Grinning I go down.
> Getting up I mouth
> Blasphemes of incomprehension
> The stutter of gall.
>
> A forked, naked man?
>
> One spasm of pain in the world's womb.
> One wince in the dark.

As the monk wrote in a final letter to Rose, "This is to say goodbye. The pruning shears are tearing me to pieces. I can't stand it
any longer. I can't go on. I have to cut back and get my feet under
me again. I have to save myself." Ironically, within a few weeks,
Rose broke off her engagement to Amir, whom, perhaps, she had

become involved with simply to bring her relationship to Antoninus to some kind of resolution.

Although he thought there might be problems with the censors over *Rose*, all along Antoninus was writing the poem for publication, not as a private diary. Before sending the finished manuscript to Naomi Burton, he submitted it to the Provincial, who passed it on to Frs. Meagher and Fearon, the Province censors. As Antoninus remembered, "the book fell between two monolithic forces, the ancient tradition and the awesome revolt following Vatican II. I was surprised when they passed it, though I suppose after Vatican II there was no longer any unanimity of prejudice." The Provincial himself was greatly displeased with the book and went through it very carefully. "He didn't want to cause a furor because so many were leaving the Order as it was, and by that time I was the best-known Dominican in the country. Also, to block the thing he would have had to publicly defy his own censors. He would have vetoed it if he could have gotten away with it, but he would have had a hell of a time arguing with Fr. Meagher, who was the ranking Dominican intellectual in the west."

Antoninus had sent Naomi Burton a few early passages from the manuscript, and she was a bit scandalized, writing him a letter of mild rebuke over the sexual explicitness of the poems. Once she got the whole book, though, she became quite enthusiastic, and convinced Doubleday to risk publication. The collection proved the most widely reviewed and successful of all his books, and won the Commonwealth Silver Medal for 1968.

But with the publication of *Rose*, Antoninus's relationship to many of his fellow Dominicans became more problematic. As Fr. William Ruddy recalled,

The feeling in the monastery was mixed. Some people thought he was using the monastery as a persona, a sounding board for his own creative expression, in such a way that he really couldn't get involved in the life of the community itself. Others would say that it was just our not being able to understand his attitudes toward the contemplative life, his going through the violation to achieve the resolution of problems—it just wasn't in the mainstream of traditional religious life. And his work could be shocking. Still, for all the years I knew him, as far as I could see, he participated in the daily religious exercises in a very humble and genuine fashion. And in *Rose* his level was not a level of confessional exposure of sin. It was a directive approach toward the whole problem of original sin, the whole problem of God's absolution and forgiveness. When he says in Rose that he is "murdering Christ"—there just aren't many other religious poems that can come to that.

▼▼▼

In the late fifties while still in St. Albert's, Antoninus had regularly counseled a woman named Cris Markee, a student of Thomas Parkinson's at Berkeley. Eventually, she came to him less often, but by the fall of 1965 they were still in touch occasionally, and one afternoon she telephoned Antoninus asking him to speak with her stepdaughter. Because of his experience with Rose, Antoninus had decided to give up counseling women, but Cris pleaded with him and he consented. The following week, Susanna Rickson, who had just turned eighteen, showed up at Kentfield for an hour's session.

Her background was both sad and fascinating. As a girl she grew up on a ranch in Almaden with her mother and grandparents, having never met her father, who lived in Chicago. When her grandfather died, the family left the ranch, and moved to San Jose. Leaving both her friends and her familiar rural environment so soon following the death of her grandfather, the only father figure she had known, was traumatic. Not long after this, she was involved in her first physical love affair with a boy. Her mother died, leaving her entirely in the care of her grandmother, and very soon she fell, as the Victorians would say, into bad company. Her grandmother felt that she had lost all control over her, and day by day the situation grew worse. Finally, late one Saturday night, she was arrested, drunk and disheveled. She was only fourteen years old, and the court determined that she be taken away from her grandmother and given over to the care of a near relative, Edie Fitzpatrick Hampton, Cris Markee's mother, who lived in Oakland.

In turn, Cris and her husband Chuck took Susanna into their home in Walnut Creek. Cris was a convert and with her husband not only had a number of her own children but adopted others as well. Sue blended into the family and started high school, seemingly happily, and for a time did well. The Markees, however, who worked with the Physics Department at the University of California, started a related business which forced them to spend much time away from home. As they got busier, more and more responsibility for household chores fell to Sue, who began to feel constrained and put upon. By this time she had graduated from high school, had her own car, and was preparing for her first semester at San Francisco State. One evening, feeling especially depressed, she picked up a man on impulse and they decided to head for Las Vegas. Once there, she left him, and started for Chicago to find the father she had never seen. Thinking she had been kidnapped, the Markees alerted the police, but within a few days, broke and exhausted she returned home on her own, not having made it farther than the middle of a Utah plain. Cris, furious, wanted to take her to a psychiatrist immediately, but Sue pleaded that she speak instead with the famous Brother Antoninus Cris had talked about so often.

For a time, she made her way out to Kentfield each week to speak with the monk, who was still reeling from his separation from Rose. Because of this, and her age, Antoninus took great care to keep an emotional distance from her. Still, obviously in the best of circumstances the counseling situation produces a certain intimacy which can be dangerous, and both Antoninus and Sue were very vulnerable. Before his second reading trip in the fall of 1965, he was already beginning to feel attracted to her. When he left on his trip, Sue broke down in the parlor, certain she would never see him again. He reassured her that he would return within a few weeks and they'd pick up the sessions where they left off, and she agreed to bide her time by continuing school while living back with the Markees.

In January of 1966, Richard Moore contacted Antoninus about participating in a series of films on contemporary American poets called "Poetry U.S.A.," which he was producing for National Educational Television. Antoninus agreed to do the film, and the film crew, feeling that Kentfield didn't look "monastic" enough, descended on St. Albert's. By this time Antoninus hadn't been connected with the house of studies for several years, and he felt it somewhat presumptuous to approach the fathers to request the cooperation of the community in the filming. Looking now at the film it is obvious that the poet was uncomfortable, out of phase with the community. The fathers were in fact in favor of the project, though in the film the poet doesn't join in the chanting, but rather sits sullenly off to the side saying his rosary. Most members of St. Albert's community showed up for the filming, along with a few invited lay guests.

Taking the stage he began with difficulty, rebuking the audience like an angry John the Baptist, talking haltingly about his own pain. "He said to the audience," recalled Fr. William Ruddy, "'You're not with me, you're not with me.' Our silent response was, 'How can we be? You have people here we don't know, and here are these bright lights for filming, and we don't know the people who are doing the filming. You are looking into the lights, not into us.' There was the feeling among many at that point that he was just using the monastery for his own ends." But eventually he got his stride and began reading his poems. Cris Markee and Susanna had been invited and had come in late, and when the poet read "Annul in Me My Manhood,"

> Make me then
> Girl-hearted, virgin-souled, woman-docile, maiden-meek;
> Cancel in me the rude compulsive tide

That like an angry river surges through,
Flouts off Thy soft lip-touches, froth-blinds
The soul-gaze from its very delight,
Outbrawls the rare celestial melody.
Restless I churn. The use of sex is union . . .

Susanna, mortified, slipped out of the hall, without Antoninus noticing. At the conclusion of the reading, as Fr. Ruddy remembered, "a woman became hysterical, screaming out from the back that she'd just come from a hospital where a black woman with a baby had been denied admission. 'How can you stand there reading poetry with things like this going on in the world? Why does God allow this?' What would happen to Robert Frost in such a situation? Well, Antoninus held the woman until she stopped crying." Unbeknownst to Fr. Ruddy, the woman was Cris.

As Antoninus calmed her, the brothers looked on, appalled by the whole scene. "For some reason," the poet remembers, "this filled me with despair. I felt things were closing in on me. The woman problem was just too much to handle. The next time Sue came to visit, I was in her arms."

Susanna didn't tell anyone of this, and began to visit Antoninus even more frequently, picking him up in her automobile. The poet had fallen in love with her—it was at this moment that he started writing his long love poem "Tendril in the Mesh," a hymn to Susanna as celebratory of woman as was his poem "Blowing of the Seed" twenty years earlier. Though Antoninus didn't contemplate leaving the Order, the pair took little care to hide their relationship from strangers. "We especially delighted astonishing people in parking lots in the city," the poet recalled. "And we'd go to places like Point Reyes and Tamalpias, all along the coast." Interestingly, Antoninus felt no guilt about this new relationship. As he wrote Susanna in April from Providence College, where he was giving a reading, "I understand and acknowledge the mystery of the physical intensity of our love. I accept this as a great mystery and a great good. I do not, strangely enough, suffer from guilts in this regard. It is as if the mystery of your physical belief in me, and mine in yours, were a sign of great spiritual truth. I know that God brought us together for our mutual understanding, and happiness, and good." Further, while their physical intimacy had been frequent and intense, they had stopped short of sexual intercourse. "I long," the poet concludes, "to consummate that love totally, in total possession of, and fulfillment in you."

While he continued his duties at the house and gave frequent readings, during this period the monk was obsessed with his new relationship with Susanna, "the perfect one, who is my discovery, whom I have named and seen, who comes to me in sleep, and blesses me with her presence—Persephone, the goddess of rebirth and all beginnings." However, besides the obvious problems of the difference in age and Antoninus's position in the Order, there suddenly appeared another stumbling block to consummation— the recurrence of impotence. "Then too," he wrote Susanna from his April northeast reading tour, "the humiliation of my impotence. I become exasperated with these liberated moderns who speak so assuredly of sex who know nothing of its mightiness, nothing of its awesome, smashing, obliterating power. You had experienced its whole destructive power and come through it unscathed. That fascinated me . . . . But I have come, in these two weeks away from you, to realize that my impotence is no transient thing. That it is here to stay, at least as long as I accept monastic life. It is the brand of my spiritual condition." And two days later, "In me my impotence subsists like a block. There is a story of St. Thomas Aquinas who cinctured his loins with a cord so that he might be chaste. Have I not done so much? What an irony of God."

Unlike Rose or Edwa, Susanna had little interest in the monk's career as a poet, or even his work, perhaps feeling that it took him away from her. Soon after their affair began, Antoninus had given her a number of his books; her only response came in a letter while he was reading in Michigan—the poetry was "belabored." Such a judgment, he wrote back, "punctured my vanity and I felt so foolish for having pressed my books on you. I just didn't want anything like that to stand between us—like my being a poet and a well-known speaker, etc. If I could just be as anonymous as anybody else and simply love you as you are and I am, that would be enough for me. When I am back with you and in your arms all those things become nothing. I promise I will never impose my world-self (poet, speaker, big deal, etc.) on you again, and I really do most sincerely and profoundly ask your forgiveness for having tried to impress you with that. It was a typical masculine foible, but I should have learned better by this time."

During the summer of 1966, Susanna, who was then attending San Francisco State College, decided to go with a Catholic-sponsored group of young people into rural areas of Mexico. Antoninus was of course depressed by her going, and to make matters worse within a few weeks she wrote him that she had become involved with a young Mexican. In late July he wrote her that "Rose I worshipped as a phenomenon of Nature and of God. But Sue I *experienced* as the archetype of my instinctual self." Now, "I am going to try to fall out of love with you this coming month . . . to dispell the physical attraction, your spell over me." When she returned in September, however, her affair was over, and Susanna and Antoninus were back in each other's arms.

Returning to school, she took a room above a coffee house in the Haight Ashbury district, and for a time she and the poet were again constant companions. By June, Susanna wanted more stability in the relationship and one afternoon suddenly asked Antoninus to marry her. He wrote her just a few weeks later, after she had left on a second summer trip, this time a San Francisco State College tour of Europe.

I was so taken by surprise. From the beginning any passing suggestion or inference from me that marriage might be desirable, had been resisted by you. Finally you told me not to speak of or suggest any such thing, so for the last year at least I was careful not to get near the subject . . . . You asked me for a ring to show your state of commitment. At first I went along with it until I actually began to look them over preparatory to purchasing, and I realized that I could not.

It was two weeks ago in the little alcove by the sea, between Muir Beach and Stinson, that I told you I could not. That I could not give you a ring unless it was "for real." It was then that you embraced my knees and tried to tell me—and I was dense and did not understand. And never understood until up the road, in your car, that you had to overcome my stupidity and spell it out. You hated to say it, for it is the man's place to ask the girl, but I am stupid. You were at last forced to confess to me that you wanted to get married.

Then here on the hill above the Priory, where we climbed in the sunset, the last of the light, and it came up between us, and finally I told you that if it's my destiny to do so, then truly I will marry you. That I will let no abstraction stand between us if it is our destiny. That I will leave the Order and even the Church to marry you. Not really leave the Church in my heart. Never that. But I would step aside her proscription to marry you.

I *want* to marry you. I know we could live a beautiful life. Never have I known such compatibility of spirit. I know beyond a shadow of a doubt that our life could be a most beautiful life—a most beautiful love. So I await the working-out of God, beautiful Susanna, placing it in His hands, and in His Providence, ready to follow as He decrees.

By Susanna's return, however, the monk had decided that such a drastic move as leaving the Order was impossible, that he would like to keep up their relationship but there could be no marriage. Rebuffed, Susanna soon took up with a man nearer her own age, who had moved into her apartment building. One afternoon Antoninus took her to one of their favorite restaurants in San Francisco, the Tadish Grill, where she told him of this new relationship. As he recounted in the interview with David Meltzer, "She was so radiant and daughterly that I could only rejoice in her. Although I was in mufti at the time, it so happened that I was recognized by an entering family of Catholics—no one I knew, but the fact of recognition was evident. Normally, I would have conducted myself prudently, but in view of what Sue had just told me,

and since it was apparent that this occasion was to be one of fare-
well, I would not think of being anything less than true to the state
of poignancy and relinquishment we were experiencing. So I took
her hand and gazed, with all the meaning I could muster, into her
eyes as we shared that meal."

By the summer of 1968, Susanna was pregnant. The young man
soon left her, but she was ecstatic. Years before a physician had
told her that she would never be able to have children, which
haunted her. Now, suddenly, she was expecting a baby the following March. She withdrew from San Francisco State and moved to
Hayward, enrolling in the state college there. Over the next
months she continued to see Antoninus fairly often, and the following spring her son Jude was born.

vvv

While Antoninus hadn't been doing much writing during these
years, his reputation was again on the rise as he traveled back and
forth across the country doing readings, which continued to be
very popular. His old friend Lawrence Clark Powell, who was
spending a year as Resident Fellow at the Center for Advanced
Studies at Wesleyan University in Connecticut, for example,
recalled Antoninus's performance there in the spring of 1968 in
his autobiography *Life Goes On*:

Antoninus was our house guest. I assured him that the vestiges of
Edmund Wilson, that austere critic who had occupied our house when
he was a Fellow, had vanished. The first night I was awakened by the
anguished sound of the poet's praying. The next morning we walked in
the nearby Indian Hill cemetery while he gathered his forces for the reading. We paused to decipher inscriptions dating to the 18th century. It
was a bitterly cold day. Antoninus was obviously still moved by inner
torment which had led him to his nocturnal prayers.

We must have made a sight walking across campus to the Honors
College, he in a white robe and black surplice, a head taller than I am,
so long legged that I had to trot to keep up with him. . . . Then at four
o'clock came the reading to an overflow crowd of students sitting, stand-

ing, and lying on the floor around the edges of the room. After my introduction he read for an hour and twenty minutes his *Rose of Solitude*. It
was a spellbinding performance punctuated by long pauses while he
strode the platform, and the only sounds were of trucks grinding up the
Hartford road. . . . It left him drained and the audience enraptured and
bemused.

Following the release of the NET film, his early poems were collected into *Single Source*, with an introduction by Robert Duncan.
A few months later, an expanded edition of *The Residual Years*
appeared to generally favorable reviews, his short writings on
Robinson Jeffers were gathered into *Fragments of an Older Fury*,
and "A Savagery of Love" was released on Caedmon Records. In
the spring of 1969 Joseph Alioto, the mayor of San Francisco,
approached Antoninus to perform, and on April 18th the poet
read "The City Does Not Die" to a vast crowd that had gathered
at daybreak to commemorate the San Francisco earthquake.

Antoninus's poetry was known in Europe, and for years he had
been hoping to make a trip there to give readings. In 1967, his
friend Fr. Antoninus Wall had left Kentfield for the Graduate
Theological Union in Berkeley to do advanced work in theology.
In August of 1969, on the Feast of St. Dominic, various
Dominican groups met at St. Albert's for a mass and cocktails. Fr.
Wall was there, and he told Antoninus of his plans to leave for
Rome in just two weeks to write his thesis. Spontaneously, he
asked the poet to go along, and before the evening was over,
Antoninus agreed. The next day Wall took the brother to apply
for a passport, and he wrote the State Department to inquire about
the possibility of government-sponsored readings abroad at
American cultural centers. Mayor Alioto provided a letter with
the seal of San Francisco, indicating that Brother Antoninus was
the unofficial poet-laureate of San Francisco. According to Wall,
"part of my thinking behind the invitation was that I knew
Antoninus was coming up for solemn vows in about three months,
and as he was a convert who'd never seen the Church or the Order

in Europe, I thought this would be very helpful. Antoninus, dressed in black, white shirt and black tie, had grey hair down to his shoulders, though no beard yet. He looked like a proper ecclesiastical poet. I was hoping there'd be no hitch with the plane because I felt he might turn off at any moment. Europe was a big apple to bite. He had a great desire to go, but strong misgivings about how well he'd be received." Further, Antoninus looked at this as an opportunity to distance himself for a period from Susanna, with the hope that she and her baby's father might reconcile.

The pair arrived in Dublin in late August, where they were to stay at the Dominican house for a week. "Soon as we got settled, we went out," Wall remembers. "I noticed that he was a little sensitive to the way people looked at him, with his long hair. In 1969 in Europe this was still a bit of a novelty. But he seemed to get friendly responses and this exhilarated him." The two spent their first evening in a pub, where as the night wore on they struck up conversation with a couple of people who insisted they go immediately to the Merriman Festival. There, they insisted, Antoninus would be allowed to read his poetry. So early the next morning, hungover, they took a train to Ennis.

The Merriman Festival at Ennis was a yearly event meant to serve as a counter to the annual Yeats Festival in Sligo, which had a reputation for being academic and dull. When the two arrived, however, they were disappointed. As Fr. Wall remembers,

We went with the impression that it would be a guitar-strumming poets event, and Antoninus would be a hit. We got to the hotel and there was a group of tweedy-looking middle-aged people there. It looked like a convention of librarians. They were sitting there with Irish coffee in their hands, the most staid, stiff, formal, lifeless scene possible. Antoninus has a great streak of paranoia in those situations, where immediately he'd expect the worse—like a great joke had been played on the Yanks, that we had been set up and the people at the bar were laughing their heads off. We decided to spend the night, and when we got to our room Antoninus collapsed on the bed moaning and groaning. He was really down. Later that evening we went down to dinner, Antoninus really dragging. We walked into a large group of people, all talking and drinking, and suddenly Antoninus yelled out "Jack!" and rushed excitedly across the room.

It turned out to be Jack Sullivan, the curator of the Harvard Library's Woodbury Poetry Room, who had been responsible for setting up readings at Harvard for the poet years before. He was now retired and living in Ireland. "Immediately Jack started introducing Antoninus around as one of the premier poets of the United States. The people running the festival invited us to sit at the head dinner table, and Antoninus underwent a radical transformation in his mood. From that point on we were treated like special guests. The next night he shared the stage with the Irish poet John Montague, and was a great success."

On their return to Dublin, Antoninus gave a reading at Sennet's pub, one of the city's most famous gathering places for poets and writers. The reading had been publicized with an article and photograph in *The Irish Times*, and it was so crowded that for the first time in its history Sennet's had to turn away over half the people who showed up. The young American poet James Tate happened to be there, as did Thomas Kinsella. A young female poet preceded Antoninus, then the monk finished the evening with a number of both secular and religious poems, including "The Springing of the Blade" and "The Encounter," work that, Fr. Wall recalls, "made a tremendous impact, left everyone in ecstasy. There was a kind of excitement and adulation that he didn't get again through the rest of the trip. Christianity and creativity came together that night." Further, as Antoninus wrote Susanna on August 27, "we found ourselves visiting all the ancient and massive ruins of that country—bronze age dolmans, cairns, Christian monasteries and beautiful round towers, high crosses of incredible austerity and beauty. It was so profound and unspeakably moving for me to see these things at last. I thought of you among them, just as I do standing among the immense columnar redwoods on the Coast."

Thus ended their week in Ireland, as Antoninus and Wall

headed to London. "We got into London Friday night, crossing the Irish sea by boat and angling across England by train—just to establish some transitional space between it and Ireland," the poet wrote Susanna on August 31 from St. Dominic's Priory in London. "It is well that we did. Ireland was innocent. London is lecherous. Everywhere the senses are assailed and the advertisements more pornographic than the States, the miniskirts just cutting the cheek of the hip. I am invaded by the impact of it all, and my last night in your arms burns my mind blue."

Antoninus was scheduled to read at the Institute of Contemporary Arts, not far from Buckingham Palace, within two days of his arrival, and an extended article on the event along with a photograph appeared in *The Times*. As with the Sennet's reading, there was again a full house, and Antoninus read for well over an hour. Unlike the Irish, though, the audience was at first reserved, and the poet was a bit uncomfortable. But a heckler soon broke the ice. Taking offense at Antoninus's Catholic poems and the fact of his habit (which he wore through all the European readings), early into the performance he shouted out, "Christianity makes my penis shrink!" Undaunted, the monk didn't miss a beat. He paused for just a moment, then shot back, "I wish it did the same for me!" And from that point on, the audience, which included such luminaries as A. Alvarez and Stuart Montgomery, publisher of Fulcrum Press, was his.

Over the next few days Antoninus and Fr. Wall took in the sights, then boarded the ferry to France, ending up in the Dominican house in Paris. Antoninus spent his birthday in bed with "the continental curse—the trots," though the following day he was well enough to visit the Louvre. He had hoped to give a reading in Paris, but nothing could be arranged until a reading at the American Embassy two weeks later. Before leaving England Antoninus had gone to Stonehenge and Salisbury Cathedral, and now Fr. Wall rented a Fiat and the two drove to Chartres, then headed down the coast to Spain for a few days prior to readings in Hamburg, Berlin, and Munich. Following the German appear-

ances, which were sponsored by the State Department, the two
men drove to Zurich, stopping briefly at the Jung Institute. Venice
followed, then Florence, then finally, in mid-October, Rome,
where Antoninus read at the U.S. Information Service Library.
There they visited the Vatican, but were unsuccessful in getting an
audience with the Pope. On October 19, Antoninus left Fr. Wall
in Rome, flying first to Paris, where he gave his final European
reading, then back to San Francisco.

In leaving for Europe, one of Antoninus's hopes was that by
putting space between himself and Susanna, she might reconcile
with the father of her son, and he might mute his obsession with
her. Neither proved the case, however. Soon after his departure,
Susanna and Jude moved alone to a small house near the ocean at
Stinson Beach, where she set out to wait for his return. On his
part, separation only intensified his feelings. As he wrote Susanna
from Lake Lucerne, "I love you beautiful girl and lovely presence
of woman in my life! I hold you! I am yours!"

Within just a few days of his return to San Francisco, during
which time he saw Susanna for only a few hours, the poet was off
again on another reading tour, this time to New York,
Massachusetts, and Rhode Island. "I think of you constantly," he
wrote Susanna from Boston College on November 21. "I have the
feeling of shaping consequence, of something important about to
happen, or being decided. I do not know what will emerge, what
the future course will be, but I do have this profound sense of
approaching decision." And the following day, "I just want to say
now I love you despite my confusion, that I long for you, long to
hold you, to feel your glorious body in my arms, your beautiful
mouth on my mouth. You seem to me so unpossessable, so
remotely close to me, so bafflingly simple and complex. I ache for
you and ever will, beautiful Susanna."

For Thanksgiving Antoninus made his way to Spring Lake,
Michigan, where his friend Steve Eisner and his wife were living.
According to Eisner, "When we started talking about it, he
seemed to be looking for someone to tell him whether or not he

should leave the Order. For some years I had felt he should detach himself from the Dominicans given his way of life. It was just fatal for him to come into contact with people while he was in the Order. So I told him that he would leave the Order, not that he necessarily should, but that he would. Everything in his attitude seemed to suggest it. When he left to return home, he told me that whatever he decided to do, he'd do it with peace, dignity, quiet, and decorum."

Immediately upon his return, the monk went to his confessor, hoping to get some kind of clarification. "'Don't give up your vocation for an episode, Antoninus,' he told me," the poet remembers. "'You are in the male menopause. The girl is thirty-five years younger than you.' I understood what he was saying, but I was still wildly in love. Now, with the birth of Jude, it seemed as if there was another structure just waiting for me." That night, over eighteen years after entering the Dominican Order, he went to Susanna and asked her to marry him.

At first the pair planned to slip away and marry quietly, and Antoninus returned to St. Albert's to make preparations. Speaking with a few friends whom he felt he owed warning of what he was about to do, however, the monk became convinced that to simply disappear would be a betrayal of the many people who had supported him throughout his years in the Order. The final reading of the group of post-European performances was scheduled at the University of California at Davis, December 7, and he decided that there he would announce his forthcoming marriage, making his last appearance as Brother Antoninus. Before leaving St. Albert's for Davis, the poet prepared a news release and left it with his Oyez publisher Robert Hawley, to be sent to the media after the reading. Though he could bring himself to tell no one at St. Albert's of his plan, he did meet with Fr. Paul Scanlon, who had been his brother-master at Kentfield and was now Provincial, and in a tearful scene explained what he was about to do.

The Sunday afternoon reading had been very well publicized and was packed, though no one there had any notion of what was to happen. Antoninus took the stage wearing his robes, and as usual there was an exaggerated period of silence as the poet alternately paced and stopped short, staring out at the audience. He began haltingly, explaining the myth of Pluto and Persephone, then read the prologue to "Tendril in the Mesh," his love poem to Susanna, which he had finished some months before but had never read publicly:

> Persephone smiles,
> The pomegranate seed in her pouch, her jewel of rape, and the stain
> Of his lust on her lip. She measures his term. Cringing,
> He sleeps on unappeased, in the hush of the solemnly slain . . .
> Oh my God the terrible torch of her power!

"Thus far," he continued, "I've been talking about Pluto and Persephone, but I can no longer do that. I was writing about myself, and when this reading is over I am going to remove my habit and leave the Dominican order to marry."

The audience was of course stunned. "Right away I waded into the opening strophes of the poem proper," the poet recalls,

> In the glimmer of night a wedge of fern configures her croft.
> Maidenhair snuggles the cleft. Its shadow conceals and defines.
> When I dip my lips to drink of that spring I throat the torrent of life . . .
> I have fastened my heart on the stitch of your voice.

Between the sections of the poem he meditated on his life as a Dominican and the forces that were taking him out of the Order, concluding with the poem's rhymed epilogue,

> Call to me Christ, sound in my twittering blood,
> Nor suffer me to scamp what I should know
> Of the being's unsubduable will to grow.
> Do thou invest the passion in the flood
> And keep inviolate what thou created good!

He paused for a moment, then slowly drew his robes over his head, dropped them to the floor, and walked out of the hall.

EPILOGUE

The
Integral
Years

The next morning, Frs. Hayes and Leo Thomas were summoned to the Provincial's office to hold "a conference as to how we would respond to the media. We decided that as far as attitude was concerned we would respond by saying simply, 'The Western Dominicans have been greatly enriched and blessed by his presence and are grateful for it.' We took a positive approach, and," according to Hayes, "I don't think the reporter was too thrilled by that." Actually, a number of Antoninus's brethren were stunned. As Fr. Schauer remembered, "I was in Frankfurt when I got the news. I was shocked, walking around for days in a daze. It was not totally unthinkable, but it shocked me. He had such a profound understanding of the value of the contemplative life. I was upset and disappointed."

To many, though, it seemed not to be the monk's leaving the Order that upset them (he had not, after all, taken final vows) but rather the manner of his leaving. "People would quickly forget the fact of his leaving," Antoninus Wall surmised, "but to go on stage and remove his habit . . . I think many people felt used. In fact, I would say this was a universal feeling among the Dominicans. It was just so unnecessary. For eighteen years he was involved in the community and had a lot of friendships, and generally the community was very supportive. Had he left quietly, there would have been support, but suddenly, because of the way he left, when he needed support most of all it wasn't there."

Still, an early effort was made to convince the poet to return to the monastery. When Rose read the morning paper, she was aghast and went immediately to the Provincial's office to see if the news was true. Fr. Scanlon, she recalled,

told me that it was. He told me that I was the only one who could go talk to him—that none of the priests or brothers could do it. He asked me to tell him that if he would return, no one would say anything. So, very frightened, that night I made my way up to Stinson Beach. I'd never been there before, but somehow found their cottage, and I pounded on the door. The three of them were there—Brother, Susanna, and her baby—and I talked to him for at least two or three hours. He told me that he felt he had an obligation to help, and I replied that was fine but he was doing it at the expense of his vocation and the Order. That he would lose everything he had built. It was obvious Susanna was not happy hearing what I was saying, but I kept it up because I kept remembering Fr. Scanlon's words.

And obviously she felt hurt and betrayed. The meeting grew progressively heated.

I said some pretty serious things to her. "How dare you? Don't you realize that I could have had him at any time? But he belongs to God! You are responsible for this man's future!" I said painful things, but I was trying desperately to make him see what he was doing. He was listening to me, but he was just so caught up in the drama of the moment.

Rose also felt a certain amount of guilt. "I felt that I may have let Brother down. If in fact leading him out into the world of the readings, the social world, I was really leading him eventually out of the Order, maybe it was a mistake." Everson had told Eisner that he would make his exit from the Order quietly, and yet just a few weeks later the Davis performance was on the front page of the newspaper. Eventually, Rose would come to sense that the reason for this was to prove to Susanna that she herself was part of his past. And to an extent, this was probably true. "It's not as if Susanna said that he had to make a big show of it so that she could take her rightful place, to prove to the world that she is the one. But, and I don't think I'm being egotistical, Brother felt that he had to prove to her that I was out of his life. So I said goodbye."

The two had planned to marry the following Saturday in Mendocino, a lovely, small northern California town. A Church marriage was of course out of the question, and as Susanna had no religious affiliation, they decided to get married by a justice of the peace. Susanna was particularly attracted to the location because a large nineteenth-century statue of Father Time and the Maiden rested on the courthouse steps. The ceremony was quiet, with only Robert and Dorothy Hawley and the photographer Allen Say attending. Over the next months, the couple settled into Susanna's small wood-frame house just up from the beach, occasionally troubled by hate mail from strangers accusing Everson of having betrayed the Church and his vows. For a time money was not a problem, as Everson had a few thousand dollars in his traveling account. "One of the reasons I had been dissatisfied with the Order," the poet remembered, "was Vatican II's emphasis on Orders shifting over from the contemplative to social action. This meant that the monasteries were being penetrated with a different spirit. It even struck the cloistered monasteries, like the Trappists. By the end, my readings were drawing enormous fees, which went to the Dominicans. But they set me up with a special bank account to facilitate my travel expenses, and when I left there was money there." Further, Susanna had a trust fund generated from the sale of the Almaden farm years before, so that for the near future at least neither contemplated getting a job.

Everson hoped to retire from public life for awhile, and during the next year he and Susanna lived in relative seclusion. He began work on the poems that would be published along with "Tendril in the Mesh" as *Man-Fate: The Swan Song of Brother Antoninus*. "I was very confused," he remembers, "and I wrote those poems to clarify my confusion":

> Susanna: girl and bride,
> You sleep in the adjoining room,
> And I sense the sea, at solstice,
> Tide-turn, pivot and close in.
>
> This turning of my life,
> Swings back and resurges.
>
> The fate of man
> Turns on the body of woman.
> She takes the long advance
> And the long recession.
> By what she is
> She defines them . . .

"The poems expressed an urgency I was feeling, an attempt to come up with something integrative, somewhere to stand in terms of my shattered sense of identity," Everson wrote James Laughlin, in August. "Life is very good. The new marriage is tranquil and lovely, and my experience with the boy is new and vital and long overdue in my life." However, apparently the energy he put into this attempt at integration did at times cause marital strain. As Susanna wrote to friends a few years later remembering this period, "Instead of working at marriage, Bill become obsessed with his loss of vocation and his need to reestablish himself, as you can read at the beginning of *Man-Fate*. He couldn't see the scars on me and my need to be reestablished. But then I couldn't see through the scar tissue on my soul either."

In fact, in terms of his faith, Everson's first prolonged reaction to leaving the Order "was hunger; being out of the sacraments was like famine." He complained of this to Steve Eisner, who in turn told Fr. McGlynn in Detroit of the problem. In the priest's diocese there was an understanding that "people who had good faith" but were not allowed to participate in the sacraments because of legalistic problems with Rome might be allowed back into them without comment. Through Eisner, Fr. McGlynn offered to remarry Susanna and Everson in a Catholic ceremony in Detroit.

This second wedding was as circumspect as the first, with Eisner and his wife acting as witnesses, and that day, for the first time since leaving the Order six months before, Everson received communion. His leaving the Order had not been occasioned, after all, by a crisis in faith, but rather by his inability to continue living a celibate life. In fact, in a real sense, his faith now was stronger than ever, and for many months after the marriage the poet attended Mass each Sunday quietly and by himself, and continued to take communion. Fr. McGlynn had told Everson that if any problem arose over this matter with Church authorities he should be contacted, but he was suddenly killed in a car accident. About the same time the Vatican insisted that American priests conform their practice to Church doctrine. At this point, demoralized by his friend's death and Rome's explicitness on the matter of remarriage, Everson sadly decided he would once again have to remove himself from the sacraments, and thus again stopped attending Mass, this time for good.

The new collection, first composed of "Tendril in the Mesh" and a number of earlier uncollected poems, was entitled *Inceptions*. Everson sent the manuscript to Doubleday, which summarily rejected it. Next the poet sent the gathering to James Laughlin, but while New Directions was considering it, he had second thoughts and decided to withdraw it. Originally, he told the publisher,

I had planned to publish the book under my religious name, depending upon my status and the authority of the Order to carry its extreme sensuality. But now in a period of transition I do not have these supports, and I fear that such a book, coming at this time, will compromise the

whole force of my witness as an exponent of erotic mysticism, a witness
that I painfully developed over much suspicion and many sneers,
throughout the whole course of my life in the monastery. So that now,
if the public took this work as merely a raunchy offering by a defrocked
monk, all would be lost.

Instead, now he opted to publish much of this material first in limited editions, such as *Tendril in the Mesh* and *Who Is She That
Looketh Forth as the Morning*. By May of 1973, however, he had
completed his cycle of love poems to Susanna, and resubmitted the
manuscript under the title *Tide-Turn: A Cycle of Renewal*, changed
finally to *Man-Fate* by the book's publication in 1974.

A few of Everson's lay brother friends brought his library to him
from St. Albert's, and he managed to use a small lean-to near the
house for his studio. Besides the poetry, which occupied much of
his time, he also worked on another prose project, *Archetype West*.
In February of 1970, John G. Burke, associate editor of *American
Libraries*, had approached the poet about contributing to a volume
of five essays, each exploring "the literary heritage of a given geo-
graphical region of the United States, and to come to some conclusion about the qualities which defined the region as a region in
literature." Everson accepted, then realized that while he was
fairly fluent in his knowledge of west coast poetry, he had read
almost no west coast fiction. Thus, while writing, he "read ener-
getically to make up for the lack of a lifetime" work by Harte,
Twain, London, Norris, and Steinbeck, as well as contemporaries
like Ken Kesey and Charles Bukowski. He had a year to do the
piece, and at its conclusion it ran to over three times the
10,000-word limit, metamorphosing into a book, which was published in 1976 as *Archetype West: The Pacific Coast as a Literary
Region*. His approach, like that of *Tongs of Jeopardy*, was Jungian:

Of course, regionalism has had a bad press since the advent of the
Modernist movement early in this century. That movement was international in its outlook and regarded the regional accent as provincial and
myopic, emphasizing content at the expense of quality, and hence con-

stituting a threat to both culture and art. Over against this perspective I believe that the impress of place on man's artifacts is something not only authentic but absolutely ineradicable, and in affirming it I have sought to isolate the energy shaping the specific Western experience. We have to make bare the basic power below the mere decorative details usually attributed to regionalism considered as an influence in art. In reaching for this source of power I have had recourse to the uses of depth psychology as it applies to collective factors, and have employed its techniques to grasp the root forces with which we are dealing; chief among these is the concept of the archetype.

Like similar studies by D. H. Lawrence and William Carlos Williams, the book is as quirky as it is perceptive, as Everson ranges from work by Joaquin Miller to poetry by Gary Snyder, Philip Whalen, and Lew Welch in his attempt to argue that "the Western writer stands as term of the American impulse, and that as term he constitutes its mainstream rather than a merely peripheral and incidental relevance."

▼▼▼

In mid-1971, Robert Hawley got word that a Washington hand-press had been donated to the library at the University of California at Santa Cruz, with the proviso that the university set up a working press for both teaching and publication, and he began trying to arrange for Everson to take over as master printer there. Earlier, in 1968, Esalen Institute in Big Sur had asked Everson to attend one of their encounter groups to analyze it from a theological point of view. There he had met Michael Kahn, one of Esalen's counselors, and the two had become friends. Now Kahn was teaching at Kresge College at the University, and he worked with Hawley to convince the administration to hire Everson as both a lecturer and master-printer of what became the Lime Kiln Press.

Kresge itself was a radical university experiment, attempting to teach values in an encounter group environment as much as a regular core curriculum. The grading was simply pass/fail, and a number of innovative thinkers and scholars were hired to teach there, including Norman O. Brown and Page Smith, offering such programs as The History of Consciousness. Everson had no real interest in teaching per se: "I had a lot of hesitation making the move," he remembers. "I'd been an anti-academic poet all my life, and I saw no real reason to move to Santa Cruz. By now I was reading again off and on, and making pretty good money at it; I was worried that teaching would inhibit that. Also, I just felt that I'd be more consistent philosophically if I made my living from the platform and royalties, like Robert Bly does. But the lure of the handpress was strong, and the pressure of Bob Hawley finally convinced me. The thing fell into my lap."

Santa Cruz is a small coastal city, and with the coming of the university housing problems arose. Everson and Susanna spent much of the spring of 1971 taking trips down from Stinson Beach looking for a place to live, but to no avail. The poet was particularly attracted to Swanton, just north of the city, which because it is an agricultural area was not developed. By chance one afternoon in the early summer he drove along the main Swanton Road and ended up at the office of Big Creek Lumber. He introduced himself as a writer and new university faculty member to the woman in the office, Marsha McDougal, who it turned out had known Everson's CPS friend Hackett. She put in a good word with the McCrary brothers, owners of much of the Swanton forest property, and by mid-September Everson, Susanna, and Jude moved from Stinson Beach into an old forest-service house owned by the McCrarys, nestled among massive redwoods.

Within a few weeks Everson began teaching. In designing his course, he had decided to focus on the problem of vocation, not in the sense of learning a trade but rather the notion of a calling. Perhaps as a combination of his own lack of formal university training and the years in the Order, he sought to redefine the traditional lecture in terms of that with which he was most familiar—the poetry reading. Rather than a course in the writing of poetry or critical analysis, Everson hoped to develop a series of meditations around the theme of vocation. It would be "an approach to ascesis as applying to the vocation of poet," he wrote in an early course outline:

While not itself a rite of passage, the course of study will point to that crisis of consciousness in which vocation is revealed. The key activity will naturally be verse-writing, but the emphasis will not be on how to write a poem but on what a poet is . . . . The acquisition of technique will be pursued, certainly, for vocation is only confirmed in competence. Nevertheless, technical mastery will go forward strictly in the context of a deeper dimension—surrender to a call. Not that such a call can be elicited through a course—any course. Rather, for one who seeks to be a poet, study and practice will attempt to clarify that he is in fact seeking.

Such themes as The Archetype of the Poet, Call and Surrender, The Charismatic and the Institutional, Extasis and Entasis, Rhythm Versus Pattern, Subject Versus Method, Beauty—Increment of Form, Rhetoric—Increment of Purpose, Aesthetic Faith as the Constituent of Transcendent Form, and many others will be explored. Encounter group atmospherics will doubtless prevail, but what is sought is not togetherness, however excoriating. Traditionally, withdrawal, silence, and solitude have been catalysts of vocation. Toward these the work will be directed.

Everson eventually fine-tuned the year-long course, so that in the fall he focused on the vocational archetype itself, with special attention given to the nature of myth and dream in terms of the poet's call; the winter quarter stressed the national consciousness, what it means to be a poet in America; finally, the spring quarter emphasized the regional element, what it means to be a poet living on the Pacific coast. Each meditation took on a particular aspect of the broader topic, eventually moving into the heart of the interior castle of the poet's vocation.

The course reading list reflected the reading Everson had discovered through his friendship with Victor White: Joseph Campbell's *The Hero with a Thousand Faces*, Mircea Eliade's *Rites and Symbols of Initiation*, Heinrich Zimmer's *The King and the Corpse*, F. C.

Happold's *Mysticism*, and of course Jung's *Four Archetypes*, as well as Emerson's *Essays* and Everson's own *Residual Years*. The poet enjoyed his course, but continued to be discouraged by academic life. "The Santa Cruz effort to break up the vast impersonal American campus by reinstating the Oxford-type college system," he wrote Laughlin, "has merely resulted in the old, inbred monastic enclaves, with their petty rivalries, which the vast impersonal American campus was designed to circumvent. Round and round the little ball goes." According to the students' quarterly course evaluations, a few each term found Everson's meditations too diffuse to hold their interest, or had hoped for a more traditional writing workshop. Generally, however, the reports were glowing: "Bill asks us to explore our unconscious, to see life in an archetypal, symbolic way"; "although I get angry with my classmates who 'guruize' the poet, the class is like a magnificent song." Later, a student would recall, "I had taken Everson's class during my first year of college. In the intervening years, I have come to know him as being a forceful reader of his own poems, in contrast with his milder lecturing style. In class he always spoke spontaneously, allowing time for the absorption of thought, musing as he stroked the long grey beard, contemplating his next idea. On the platform at a poetry reading, he unleased an unexpected torrent of energy, enunciating each syllable with an attack. In class we felt his words as if they were touch itself." The course, listed as "Birth of a Poet," proved to be one of the most popular on campus, drawing at times as many as two hundred students a session.

Once he began teaching, Everson again began to put a lot of energy into readings. He felt that his writing career as Brother Antoninus had blossomed primarily because of his public performances, and now, as he wrote Galen Williams, Director of Poets & Writers, "my principal reason for going on the circuit is to reestablish my image as William Everson rather than Brother Antoninus." Between 1972 and 1975, for example, he once again became a regular campus visitor, giving readings at Fordham, Queens College, Central Connecticut State, the University of

Kansas, St. Cloud State College, Cabrillo College, Fresno State, San Francisco State, and numerous other schools. Further, he participated as a featured guest at such events as Stanford's "Myth, Symbol, and Culture Conference," an Ezra Pound Conference in San Francisco, and the Robinson Jeffers Memorial Festival in Carmel. On January 19, 1974, he read at the University of California at Berkeley to celebrate the Bancroft Library's purchase of his archive to a large audience which included Robert Duncan, Allen Campo, and Steve Eisner; the following November he gave a joint reading at the de Young Museum in Golden Gate Park with Duncan and Diane DiPrima as part of a major showing of "San Francisco Poets of the Beat Generation: The Prints of Peter LeBlanc," again to a sellout crowd, as slowly he worked to reacquaint audiences with the poet who had entered the Dominicans twenty years before.

By this time Everson had become obsessed with natural world again, as if to compensate for the separation enforced by religious life. The later poems of *Man-Fate*, which attempt "to work out the implications of his break," as he relates in the preface, offer the controlling image of the sea, its ebb and flow reflective of the ex-monk's own uncertain psyche. At one moment he celebrates his new life with Susanna, his "girl bride"; at another, he broods on the implications of yet another major shift in his life. The long poem "A Time to Mourn" is an extended meditation on this problem of separation and renewal, as the poet contemplates his sundering from the Order which has rendered him "nondescript, / Rootless and unbelonging, a fugitive identity: / Monk without a monastery, / A friar without vows." He cannot, he considers, expect either his religious or secular friends to understand his break, but even those creatures closest to God, the birds, seem to chide him. Yet, while man has free will, it "Is subsumed in the inscrutable, / The savagely oblique will of God," and thus there is hope for his soul even in the traditional Catholic schema. But at the close of the poem, as if to return to the pantheism of his youth in the Central Valley a half century before, the former monk turns to the "Old sea, old mother, / Grant me surcease! / Lave my wounds / And lift me home!"

Two of the last poems in the volume, "The Scout" and "The Black Hills" are of particular interest as they describe the poet's transformation into the identity of his old age. First the poet-farmer, then the conscientious objector, and finally the monk. Now, as he writes in "The Scout," "back in the monastery, / My black and white habit is worn by another. / . . . I assume the regalia of the Old West: / Beads, buckskin and bearclaws." As William Ruddy, visiting Everson while he was at work on this poem, recalled, "He had a badger skin that he himself had tanned. At one point he put it on his head and talked about the assimilation of animal spirits that the American Indian had achieved." Everson's vivid dream in "The Black Hills" of coming upon the remnants of Sioux ambushed and massacred by the United States cavalry, and his later vision of chiefs confirmed for him the direction of his last phase—to attempt to recapture in both his life and his verse "The fabulous, unspeakable vision, / Primitive and elegant, / The unquenchable glory of primal man." As he wrote a Native American friend,

When we talked I said the animal was a kind of prism through which we beheld God . . . . But such talk is on the mental level and is no longer satisfactory to me. I believe that when it happens it really happens as a kind of gut experience. I know that when I encounter an animal or especially a bird my heart stops. Something in me turns over. All such concepts as the animal as a God-person or such vanish. I get excited, my breath slows then quickens.

Yet this new emphasis meant not the abandoning of his Catholicism, but rather an attempt at integration. Reading Pierre Teilhard de Chardin, he wrote Allen Campo, gave him a "way to work toward a synthesis in a more cosmic sense, drawing back to the primordial sources in my preoccupation with Indian attitudes, but also, through De Chardin, employing the cosmic evolutionary sense to tie in the prevalent Eastern mysticism which seems so important right now while retaining my Catholicism."

One of the innovations at Santa Cruz was the notion that creativity should be given as much support as scholarship, and to that end the university stressed the importance of small groups and independent study. It was on this basis that Everson was able to establish his handpress workshop, the Lime Kiln Press, a course he taught each semester without pay. The Press's first project was a series of broadsides by local poets called *West to the Water*, produced in a year by Everson and five apprentices. *Tragedy Has Obligations*, a Robinson Jeffers poem with an afterword by Everson, followed as the Press's first book. *Granite & Cypress*, a collection of Jeffers's poems, was finished in 1975; *Blame It On the Jet Stream*, Everson's commencement poem, in 1979; *American Bard* (a verse rendering of Walt Whitman's Preface to the *Leaves of Grass*) in 1982. Everson chose each project himself, though because the items were produced by a group he never thought as highly of them as the books he himself did earlier. "The only reason that the colophons didn't give the students credit," he reasoned,

was the fact that I was concerned that the books be successful. In America the arts are a matter of personality. Things move here in terms of personality, so that is what I stressed. As far as I know I was the first to institute the signing of books by the printer. The Grabhorns didn't do it. Even John Henry Nash didn't sign his books in the colophon. The reason I introduced it was that because by the time I began work at the Lime Kiln the rare book market had turned my signature into gold. In fact, it was almost as if a book didn't have my signature it wasn't of the canon, at least from the point of view of the sellers. So in order to ensure the success of the Lime Kiln books I signed them.

By far the most intricate of these projects was *Granite & Cypress*, a group of Jeffers poems Everson conceived of (according to the book's subtitle) as "rubbings from the rock poems gathered from his stone-mason years when submission to the spirit of granite in the building of house and tower and wall focused his imagination and gave massive romance to his verse." In an attempt for the first time to give full range to Jeffers's long lines, the pages of the book were very wide. According to Everson's prospectus, "it became apparent that to present each poem at its best only the recto, the righthand page, must be used. However, a uniformly blank page on the left, the verso, becomes tedious, then disturbing. It is like an unsounded note in music: the ear craves correspondence, and flinches when it is not there. So with the eye and an open book: confronted with endless blanks on the left, the recto sinks like lead."

To solve this problem "each sheet was skip fed. The first pull was made on the naked tympan, then the damped sheet of hand-made paper, placed over it, was run through the press. The second pull, the true one, thus received a reverse imprint of itself, offset from the backup, so that in the finished book when the reader turns the page the shadow of the previous poem in effect provides its own image to enliven the verso." Obviously, such a project of 33 leaves in a hundred copies was exceedingly difficult. Further, there was the problem of the book's presentation. Everson envisioned some kind of slipcase, but he was at a loss as to how such a thing might be effected. A neighbor, Don Longavan, who worked as a woodcraftsman, one day suggested to the poet that each copy of the book have its own slipcase fashioned out of Monterey cypress, with a small window of granite from Jeffers's own stoneyard. "The whole idea was his," Everson remembers. "I didn't think anything so elaborate was possible. On the face of it I would have said it was an Herculean task, but somehow he brought it off." "Readers will find here, then, four unprecedented features," concluded the prospectus:

In the book itself they will read together for the first time the nuclear body of poems which Jeffers wrote under the impact of stone, the transforming symbol of his creative emergence. They will see the long Jeffers line extended to its natural outreach, like the pulse and withdrawal of the tides to which he attributed his prosody. They will find a typography in which the implication of stone is carried to the ultimate, registering the wave-worn permanence of his mood and themes. And in the incomparable case which enshrines the whole they will possess the architectonic resolution of all these elements, memorializing the achievement of a spirit intense but serene, and the passionate instinct, immoderate and fierce, by which he will always live.

The entire edition sold out long in advance of publication, and two years later Joseph Blumenthal's exhibition "The Printed Book in America" chose *Granite & Cypress*, Everson's crowning homage to the master of his youth, as one of the seventy best-printed books in American history.

The fact that Everson was able to see this project through to completion so quickly was fortunate, in light of an impending change in his health. For all his psychological traumas and except for the problem with his knee caused by his high school football injury, throughout his life Everson had had very few physical ailments; even colds were quite rare. Suddenly, in the spring of 1977, however, he came down with a severe viral infection, which caused a high fever and kept him away from his university duties for a month. His physician couldn't locate the cause of the disorder exactly, though after a few weeks the poet began to feel a bit stronger. "I had a reading coming up," he recalls,

but I still hadn't returned to teaching and my course was going to hell. I was shaking a bit, but I attributed that to the virus. My reactions were often uncontrollable. I happened to talk to the poet Morton Marcus one afternoon and he told me of an acupuncturist in Watsonville who was a specialist in this kind of thing and urged me to get in touch with him. When I did, he suggested that first I should talk to a neurologist in Santa Cruz.

The following day Everson went to a neurologist's office for an examination. After watching the poet walk and perform a few manual tasks, the physician gave him the bad news—he was not suffering the aftereffects of a virus, but rather the onset of

Parkinson's Disease, a progressively debilitating nervous disorder.

vvv

In 1978, Everson collected the body of his Dominican verse into *The Veritable Years*, which won both that year's Shelley Memorial Award as well as the Book of the Year Award by the Modern Language Association's Conference on Christianity. Two years later, his most recent full-length volume of poetry, *The Masks of Drought*, appeared, and poets as diverse as Karl Shapiro and Diane Wakoski greeted it with high praise. Unlike most of the earlier books, *The Masks of Drought* carried no preface by the poet and was not divided into sections. Rather, it simply contained nineteen narrative poems inspired by the California drought of 1976–77, arranged not in order of composition but, according to a note, in "the line of the seasons." The setting of all the poems save one ("Moongate" recounts a visit to his brother in Baja California) is northern California, usually the wooded area surrounding his home, which he came to call "Kingfisher Flat." The poems describe various events of the drought year—the poet's cutting of a firebreak, his labrador being bitten by a rattlesnake, the hunting of a buck, and the experience of spotfires throughout the dry summer. Yet most of these simple events are dramatically transformed into the Lawrencian symbolic. In "Cutting the Firebreak," for example, the "mad scythe"

> Hisses in the vetch, a snake denied, moans in the yarrow.
> Whumph! Whumph! Oh, the grunt of lovers biting each other
> Stroke on stroke coupling through hell. It makes the sex
> Growl in my groin to call them down, wild iris, lily,
> The moan and the shudder. All the women in my life
> Sprawled in the weeds—drunk in death.

Further, with the drought as either stated or implied background throughout, most of these poems grapple once again with the problem of the poet's impotence. In "Kingfisher Flat," the most focused statement of this theme, the poet likens himself to the Fisher King, "his domain parched in a sterile fixation of purpose," as his young "woman and earth lie sunk in sleep, unsatisfied. / Each holds that bruise to her heart like a stone / And aches for rain."

By the time Everson had left the Order, both Lee Watkins and Victor White were dead. Soon he lost touch with most of his Catholic friends, including Finnbar Hayes, Blaise Schauer, and Antoninus Wall. In the spring of 1982, Kenneth Rexroth died, and soon after Robert Duncan fell gravely ill. Everson had not spoken to Edwa or Rose for years. And finally, after endless treatment and medication, the Parkinson's Disease had begun to take its toll. He was often in great discomfort and had to resign his teaching duties and close up the Lime Kiln Press with the publication of *American Bard*. Although he continued to do readings, he could no longer perform at great length or without a podium. Each day the physical act of writing became more difficult.

Yet he continued to work every day, finishing his long-planned book-length study of Robinson Jeffers as a religious figure, publishing the first canto of a long autobiographical poem in progress, writing numerous essays and prefaces. Even though the simple act of gathering firewood had become a chore in his weakened condition, he had lost none of his belief in the value of poetry as a transformative principle. Forty-five years before, as a young man living in the San Joaquin Valley he had written C. F. MacIntyre, "Where the romanticists deserve the black eye is in their assumption that by talking passionately enough about the infinite they achieve it, but I don't think criticism of their means invalidates their ends. I'm a romanticist because I believe life hasn't any meaning when the infinite is ignored. Whatever I think of human potentiality, I feel that a man is given an occasional Revelation, and I think of a poem as a means to that end: the poems as a wire, the Ultimate the vitality that charges it."

And now, at the close of *The Masks of Drought*, Everson once again offered as the regenerative force, the vital wire, the conjunction of the male and the female. In "Stone Face Falls," Susanna stands naked in a pool under a waterfall, holding out her arms to him. He drops his clothes and like the New Adam approaches her,

> It is the longest walk—
> Out of the glacial
> Past, through the pulsing present,
> Into the clenched
> Future—man to woman
> Through time-dark waters.

APPENDIXES

APPENDIX A: "The Sign," by William Herber (1940)

Under the docks the dark water slurs, swashes,
The men look down to it, their thin lips straighten:
At the given word they move pier-ward, close-packed,
Their eyes hard with meaning.

The men on the narrow street
Gather together: few words spoken:
Twos and threes out of the gutter-dusk:
The groups form. One man moving among them
Talks quickly, the quick short gestures:
The groups thicken.

And the wind: slow on the Rockies
The wind prickles the eyes of the last hunter, the last fur-taker:
He sees the far plane high on the peak of the Great Divide
Burn west and vanish.

In box-car corners, roaring through Kansas, roaring through Utah,
Two men talking, three men speaking,
One man dreaming alone in the loud darkness,
Not hearing the wheels, not seeing the stark poles
Flick on the moon as miles break under.

And one man in the thundering dark
Guiding the tractor hour by hour,
The thin light piercing
The great blades ripping the loam,
Hour by hour, the one man, dreaming his one dream through the blind
                                                                    hours,
Guiding and dreaming.

You see them heel-squatting night after night,
Round all the hidden fires of America.

When the freight pulled past he lay in the weeds,
His heart pounding: he heard the long whistle far down the tracks:
The speed gathering: and seeing the bull turn finally back,
Broke for it, plunging out through the first dusk,
And sprang, and catching flung back on the car, and held,
And pulled panting into the suck and safety of the inside cleats.

You see them night after night:
They meet on the corners,
They say few words, quietly, and part quietly,
They go on their way dreaming the one dream,
In a whore's bed, or a ship's berth, or a bum's blanket,
Sad and persistent, running through the lonely rivers of their minds.
The one dream: like a bond: the one future.

And he in the field, hoeing,
Heard the near train,
And watching the cars saw who huddled in the cold light,
And their hands lifted, a sign,
A symbol between them,
The one sign caught between earth and sky,
Like the meeting touch of their palms.

APPENDIX B: From "The Bancroft Notebooks"

1956

I grew up totally dependent upon my father. To him I owed my existence, and furthermore my continuing existence. He had gotten me out
of my mother, and though she formed the immediate context of my life,
for my father spent most of his time earning our living away from home,
nevertheless it was only to him that we owed our daily existence.

Yet such was my nature, and so intimate was my contact and association with my mother during these years, that I developed an attachment
for her that maintained its predominately physical character instead of
broadening out into the normal sublimations. Perhaps the fact that my
mother was some fifteen years younger than my father inclined her to
unconsciously seek in her son something of the youth of the bridegroom
she missed in the father.

Yet though she unconsciously stimulated this physicality in me, at the
same time its too exuberant manifestation must have disturbed her, so
that she reproved me sharply when my efforts sought to invade areas
which she associated only with the part of the husband. But this reproof,
incomprehensible to me, aggrieved me, and caused me to set up an
ambivalence to her, and filled me with resentment towards my father,
whom she permitted to enjoy the same sentiments which she both stimulated and reproved in me.

But in my immaturity I was absolutely impotent to effect in any real
way my powerful repressed carnal passion for her, so that when I at last
met a girl who related to her physically, though not spiritually, I seduced
her. In committing this sin by projecting my mother on this girl, I committed actually five sins: I usurped the authority of my father; preempted
his paternal potency, not an adult I had no patrimony to support; cuck-
olded his wife, under the form of my mother; violated my mother, by
projecting her on this girl; and deflowered my sister, who, because she
related to my mother, became by association my daughter.

My father could not be blind, of course, to my oppressively sexual
attachment to my mother and my consequent hostility to him. He
rejected me, and withdrew from me the welcome of the home.

And since my guilt was undeniable, and since my support was derived only from my father, his punishment of me was, in effect, castration. With no means of my own I simply couldn't prosper.

And though my mother by instinct and nature tried to help me despite my father's rejection, for she saw me begin to split up and go to pieces under his hostility. But even though in her sympathy for me she began to unconsciously project those very signs of attachment which as a child I craved (embraces, kisses, etc.), now, in my own separation, they could only oppress and disquiet me, so that I found on both levels, both that of my father and my mother, existence there was simply not possible for me any longer. But since I had no place to go I could only wither, killed by his rejection and her attachment.

This reversal of position between that of my childhood and my manhood in regard to my mother, caused me to vaguely repress the memory of my early carnal desires for her, so that even when I did sufficiently transfer these to the girl I had seduced, I could not achieve the detachment of real patrimony and parenthood. My symbolic castration was consummated by vasectomy, and I projected so intensely this oppressive sexuality upon my wife, that lacking the fruition of children, our marriage had to break up. I was, to the last, cut off from the sources of potency in myself. My life as a husband and father, a potent man, was doomed.

vvv

1957

If in childhood the Oedipus Complex was never resolved, if the gravitation toward the father that should have occurred in pre-puberty was thwarted by the hostility of the father, and at the crisis of puberty the crossover from mother to father never occurred, then the identification with the mother remains fixated through the growth of true sexuality in adolescence, and the castration complex which gains its full sexual dimension at this time can be seen as an unconscious resistance to the very biological classification in which he finds himself.

The castration complex is an attempt to eradicate his masculinity, to cancel out the very life-process that is inexorably thrusting him onward to the status of a man, a status he has rejected. For in rejecting the father he is retaining the status of maternal adhesion. And when this cannot be accomplished, his incest-motivation toward the mother is to be seen not as the incipient masculine need to dominate and impregnate the female, the only female he knows, the mother, but as a means of union at the pre-sexual level, an extension of the pre-sexual attitude into full sexual status. He uses his ineradicable masculine sexuality as a means of maintaining his unrelinquished pre-sexual adhesion, burying his genitals in the mother, the phallos becoming a kind of umbilical cord, the root of sensation that joins him to her. But since this is morally and psychologically unfaceable, he takes a maternal wife and uses his phallos as an umbilical cord to retain his sensational contact with this surrogate mother, his wife. Here the super-ego does not revolt against what in actuality would be intolerable.

But still the buried guilt of what the unconscious is doing effects him, and this ambivalence in regard to his actual status—biologically a male, but unconsciously fixated to the mother and resisting the masculine status of the father—tortures him. So that in his phantasies he finds himself mutilating himself, or being mutilated. Thus by mutilation several things are accomplished. He makes himself non-masculine and hence pro-maternal. He eradicates the offending member that leads him to the unconscious incestuous act. He eradicates the offending member that leads him into the substitute act, masturbation. He "prunes his vine," fulfills the archetype of rebirth, transformation into a more preferred state of being. In short, he liberates himself from his sin. "If your hand or eye offend you, cast it out . . ."

It seems likely that I have at last come to the heart of both my castration complex and the specific nature of my maternal sexuality. I see now why I was not homosexual. For the homosexual enacts the role of woman; he disposes himself and opens himself, woman-like, to receive the masculine act. He identifies with the mother to the point of imitating her. Rather than being physically attracted to the other man's masculinity he is actually attracted to the role of the woman. In his act he is not looking at the other man, he is looking at himself, his own role as woman. The other man serves only to make that role actual, concrete, bring the illusion as close as possible to reality. In the embrace of the other he achieves almost the actuality of a woman.

This was not my problem, not my level of infantile fixation, although if fate had thrown me as a youth into the hands of a mature pederast I might have crystalized into one. Rather I remained at an infantile fixation to the mother as protector, nourisher. I did not seek to imitate her; I only wanted to remain conjoined to her, sustained by her. At the level of conscious imitation I imitated my father; the super-ego formation was strong enough to insist on a conscious masculine persona. But on the unconscious level I remained adhered to my mother, caught by the archetype of the maternal. . . .

It is necessary not to oversimplify. By temperament, as poet and artist, I was drawn to the feminine, maternal side because that is where the unconscious power lies. And I still am. It is the anima that gives me power and life. If I do not recognize and stimulate the anima I dry up. If there is no feminine presence in my life I have no interior activation. Thus it has been the association with the LaPlacas, where the feminine anima presence is active but protected and sealed off from danger by the presence of the animus, the husband, that I have turned these last months for my inspiration. That I need the feminine presence, the anima, is undeniable. Nor is this an impurity: I am chaste. Look at the fructifying presence of women in the life of St. Dominic. Look at the creative relationship between Blessed Jordan and Diana. Certainly I would have preferred to retain the relationship with——. She was the true muse, and it was she who evoked *Prodigious Thrust*. But she would not tolerate the role. Her Electra complex would not permit it. Her superego was always in a state of alarm. When I showed her the Tamalpias poem in 1953 she was upset; she refused the role of muse by rejecting it. When I showed her *Prodigious Thrust* wherein she *is* the muse she broke off entirely. What can I do if the muse revolts? Without a muse I am helpless. I have no direction.

▼▼▼

1958
One astonishing thing occurred which I must set down here. Sometime, I think around the first of December, Brother Damien—no, this was during my last sickness, after my entry of November 13—yes, actually the night of November 15, Feast of St. Albert the Great. I met Brother Damien in the hall and he acted strange, stopped me, and told me that I "understood," and etc. I could see he was going through some kind of psychic illumination, but thought nothing more of it. He was never one of my close friends among the students, there was something disconcert-

ingly naive about him that made me kind of keep clear of him, so that morning I put the matter out of my mind. That night at 10:00 I was in my room propped up in bed from the last of my cold, my capuce up and reading a book, when someone knocked and it was Damien. He flung himself into my arms and began a fast speech that was difficult for me to follow. He had a newspaper in which he purported to see the meaning of his life, symbolically. As he went on I began to get the sickening feeling that he was disoriented, out of his head. He acted so strange.

After he went I went immediately to Fr. Thomas and told him the boy was disoriented. He went to Fr. Parmisano, the student master. In the morning they took him off to Livermore hospital where the doctor pronounced him a very bad case indeed.

Still, he recovered fast. Early in December he was back. I heard occasional comments on him. I knew that his father and brother had both committed suicide, and it seemed to me a case in which the images had been jolted. I took some pride in disassociating myself from him. I was grateful that if anyone was going to crack up it was not one of those with whom I was working. I took some pride in being the one who had detected the extreme nature of the case and reported him. It seemed to put me in better with the patriarchy, the authorities, justify me, somehow, make me seem safer.

Once he asked me what the symbol meant of being in the Virgin's womb. I told him I would tell Fr. Thomas, who was also his own advisor. I told Fr. that in this case it was best to give a mystical interpretation—like the devotion of hiding in the wounds of Christ. I did not think it safe to give him a more concrete sexual interpretation.

Just before Christmas he asked if he could see me. I told him yes, but meant to tell Fr. Thomas I did not think it wise. I certainly did not wish to see him. His case seemed dangerous to me, and I did not wish to jeopardize my position by advising him. But I forgot to warn either Fr. Thomas or Fr. Parmisano.

Saturday he came and told me he had permission. I was dumbfounded and apprehensive, but decided it was the will of God, and I saw him at 2:00 here in my cell.

I began very patiently with him. I went into laborious detail with the fundamentals, through which he listened patiently and with interest. But as he talked more and more I began to see that this man understood the mystic life. And as I began to question him I realized that I had done him a great injustice. He had come through a stage where his psychic intuition was so high that he was seeing symbols everywhere, so much so that I and everyone else thought that he was "gone." His state was actually deeply mystical—his intuitions highly psychic and mystical. I saw that he had been undergoing a most profound mystical experience. When I saw this I flung myself at his feet on the floor of my cell and wept, and begged his forgiveness. It was a great teaching to me that I should be the one to send a mystic to the sanitarium. The irony was crushing.

Yesterday Damien got permission to come again. This time I most carefully went over many details of the psychic life with him. I am convinced that everything he experienced was authentic. Even his most extravagant symbolisms were actually coherent when reduced to the principles of the psychic life. He has suffered greatly and nobly. He had come through hell, and triumphed.

vvvvvvvvvvvvvvvvvvvvvvvvvvvvvvv
ACKNOWLEDGEMENTS
vvvvvvvvvvvvvvvvvvvvvvvvvvvvvvv

Without William Everson's patience in allowing me to interview him at length over a period of many months much of this narrative would have been far more speculative. Further, he generously gave me full access to his own archive, as well as the enormous Everson/Antoninus archives at the Bancroft and William Andrews Clark Memorial libraries, and *carte blanche* permission to quote from his letters, notebooks, manuscripts, and published writings. He did not suggest tampering with the writing or conclusions of this study, however, and obviously all errors and misreadings are my own.

From the outset, Everson's family, friends, and associates agreed to interviews, answered questions through the mail, and lent me relevant letters and documents. Susanna Everson was especially kind in this regard, not only responding honestly to numerous rather personal questions, but allowing me to examine her substantial correspondence with the poet, housed in the Bancroft Library collection; throughout the writing of this book she endured my disruptive sorties to her Davenport home with great cheer. Other informants who allowed extended taped interviews include Allan Campo, Christopher Eskelli, Fr. Finnbar Hayes,

O.P., Fr. Blaise Schauer, O.P., and Adrian and Joyce Wilson. Further, Allen Campo lent me tapes of important discussions with Steve Eisner, Fr. William Ruddy, O.P., and Fr. Antoninus Wall, O.P., while A. V. Krebs sent me a taped autobiographical reminiscence which Antoninus recorded for him in the late sixties.

Everson's siblings, Vera and Lloyd, shared early memories of their brother and their parents. Others I must thank include Fr. Joseph M. Agius, O.P., Claire Braz-Valentine, Robert Duncan, Micaela Martinez Du Casse, William Eshelman, Albert Gelpi, Robert Hawley, Fr. Kiernan Healy, O.P., John Knight, Larry and Deena Laufenberg, Bob Liebman, John Martin, Fr. John Hilary Martin, O.P., Carroll McCool, Fr. William Monihan, S.J., Thomas Parkinson, Karl Shapiro, Dan Stolpe, Janelle Viglini, Diane Wakoski, Philip Whalen, James and Roberta Woodress, and Fr. Paul A. Zammit, O.P. I am especially grateful to Mary Tyler for providing me with both an extended handwritten memoir of her acquaintance with Everson and two photographs included here, as well as Rose Tannlund for allowing me to examine a manuscript and letters in her possession, and allowing an interview.

No mention of the poet's second wife, poet and artist Mary Fabilli, was made in deference to her wish for privacy. The couple was married on June 12, 1948, separated on June 30, 1949, and divorced on May 13, 1963.

Both James and Ann Laughlin showed great interest in this project from the start, and wisely insisted the book be held to a reasonable length; further, James Laughlin shared memories of Everson and Kenneth Rexroth with me. My colleagues Hamlin Hill, Patrick Gallacher, Barry Gaines, Sam Girgus, David McPherson, Robert Fleming, Louis Owens, and Peter White were very supportive during the writing of this book, and offered intelligent suggestions along the way. Passages from this material appeared in greatly different form in both *Sagetrieb* and *The Centennial Review*, and I thank editors Burton Hatlen and Linda Wagner-Martin for their interest. Over the past two years Nathaniel Tarn has become a close friend and offered much encouragement even at a time when his own life was difficult at best.

I am grateful to the Directors and staffs of both the Bancroft and William Andrews Clark Memorial Libraries for their constant and kind cooperation, and for their permission to allow me to quote from materials in their possession. I am also grateful to the Research Allocation Committee at the University of New Mexico for providing a series of small grants which allowed me to travel to these collections and conduct various interviews. Permission to quote from Everson's work was graciously granted by James Laughlin of New Directions Publishing Corporation, as well as John Martin of Black Sparrow Press. Peter Glassgold at New Directions has been an astute and patient editor. Elizabeth Abbot offered numerous good suggestions while typing the final manuscript.

Next to William Everson himself, I am most grateful to my family for enduring a project which because of countless disruptions must have seemed endless. I'd like to thank especially Al and Jean Bartlett, Clancy and Charlotte Imislund, Gar Clarke, and my daughters Jennifer, Katy, Emma, and Marisa. Finally, without the constant encouragement (and occasional firm hand) of my wife Mary this book would never have been completed.

vvvvvvvvv
NOTES
vvvvvvvvv

Manuscripts, notebooks, and letters from the pre-Catholic period are housed at the William Andrews Clark Library, University of California, Los Angeles (Clark). Materials from the conversion period through the present, The Bancroft Library, University of California, Berkeley (Bancroft). All unattributed quotations are drawn from interviews conducted by the author with William Everson, 1983–86. Full citations of his published works are given in the Bibliography.

CHAPTER ONE: The Valley

P.4 "Dad spoke without a trace . . ." In 1980, J. Randall McFarland published his *Centennial Selma*, a 300-page history of the city, in conjunction with *The Selma Enterprise*. A few months later, Lloyd Everson responded to McFarland's project with a 56-page letter with additional information, including discussion of his family. The quotations from Lloyd Everson in this chapter are drawn from that letter.

P.4 "He was self taught . . ." A. V. Krebs interview with Antoninus (1968); unpublished.

P.6 "He became fascinated . . ." Vera L. Shorey letter to the author, Jan. 21, 1987.

P.9 "Dad was quite handsome . . ." *Ibid.*

P.12 "his poem 'Gypsy Dance,' " *The Caravan* (Fresno State College), V, 1 (Dec. 1931), 40.

P.13 "I propose . . ." See John A. Salmond, *The Civilian Conservation Corps, 1933–1942* (Durham, NC: Duke University Press, 1967) and Kenneth Holland and Frank Ernest Hill, *Youth in the CCC* (Washington, DC: American Council on Education, 1942).

P.15 "Our mother was born . . ." Vera Shorey letter.

P.16 "I took it home . . ." Unpublished lecture (Nov. 1975), University of California, Santa Cruz; Bancroft.

P.16 "October Tragedy," *The Caravan* (Fresno State College), VIII, 2 (April 1935), 6.

P.18 "Do Not Brood for Long," *Westward*, IV, 8 (Aug. 1935), 13; "Winter Plowing," *Westward*, IV, 10 (Oct. 1935), 25.

P.19 "The Watchers," *Poetry*, L, 3 (June 1937), 130–32.

P.19 "Sleep," *Saturday Review of Literature*, XVI, 16 (Aug. 14, 1937), 5.

P.21 "which mentioned the book . . ." See Jean Prussing, "Four Poets," *Poetry*, LVI, 4 (July 1940), 220–22.

P.21 "Your 'POEM' in Phoenix . . ." Clark; the full text of Duncan's letters appears in "Where As Giant Kings We Gatherd," *Sagetrieb* (Fall 1985), 137–74.

P.22 "I am glad to see . . ." Ekbert Faas, *Young Robert Duncan: Portrait of the Poet as a Homosexual in Society* (Santa Barbara: Black Sparrow Press, 1983), 70.

P.25 "The Sign," *Poetry*, LV, 5 (Feb. 1949), 243–45; the letter to Dillon appeared in *Poetry*, LVI, 2 (May 1940), 108–9.

P.27 "It is unthinkable . . ." Everson letter to James Decker, Sept. 18, 1942.

P.27 "to all the magazines . . ." Everson letter to Decker, Sept. 28, 1942.

P.30 "Her funeral was Masonic Rite . . ." See Everson's narrative poem *In Medias Res.*

P.31 "When a man . . ." Everson to Louis Everson, Dec. 22, 1942.

CHAPTER TWO: Waldport

P.34 "It is true . . ." Clark.

P.38 "As the bus rounded . . ." Everson letter to Edwa, Feb. 12, 1943.

P.39 "I must have stood about there . . ." Everson letter to Edwa, Jan. 21, 1943.

P.41 "a bearded Poe . . ." Everson letter to Edwa, Jan. 26, 1943.

P.41 "The camp itself . . ." See Jacqueline A. Taylor's unpublished thesis, "Civilian Public Service in Waldport, Oregon, 1941–1945," Department of History, University of Oregon, 1966. Everson included a sketch of the camp grounds in his Feb. 3, 1943 letter to Edwa.

P.42 "In devising the general . . ." See *The Conscientious Objector* pamphlet published by the National Service Board for Religious Objectors, Washington, DC, 1941.

P.42 "Everson would rise . . ." Everson letter to Edwa, Jan. 21, 1943.

P.42 "At the first Everson attended . . ." *Ibid.*

P.44 "Camp Waldport had an official . . ." See the extended "Waldport: An Interview with William Everson" with Guido Palandri, *Imprint: Oregon* (University of Oregon Library), 5, 1–2 (Fall/Spring 1978–79), 1–30; see also William Eshelman's "Bibliography of the Untide Press," same issue (pp. 30–39).

P.45 "Helped get the *Untide* . . ." Everson letter to Edwa, March 7, 1943.

P.45 "kind of a game . . ." *Imprint: Oregon*, 15–16.

P.46 "Here, where great tensions . . ." Everson letter to Edwa, Feb. 28, 1943.

P.46 "When Everson sauntered . . ." Everson letter to Edwa, March 12, 1943.

P.47 "is certainly a superb . . ." Everson letter to Edwa, March 17, 1943.

P.47 "the one that scored . . ." *Imprint: Oregon*, 16.

P.48 "It was a discussion group . . ." Everson letter to Edwa, March 21, 1943.

P.49 "Hackett and three others . . ." Everson letter to Edwa, April 13, 1943.

P.51 "that the fellows are . . ." Everson letter to Edwa, April 21, 1943.

P.51 "My biggest objection . . ." Everson letter to Edwa, May 18, 1943.

P.53 "If at Christmas . . ." Edwa letter to Harold Hackett, Sept. 4, 1943.

P.53 "Harmon and I got leave . . ." David Meltzer, ed., *The San Francisco Poets* (New York: Ballantine Books, 1971), 77–79.

P.55 "While the red . . ." Everson letter to Edwa, Oct. 17, 1943.

P.56 "Came home early . . ." Edwa letter to Everson, Feb. 13, 1943.

P.58 "His main occupation . . ." Letter from Mary Tyler to the author, Sept. 25, 1986.

CHAPTER THREE: The Fine Arts Project

P.59 "Early in 1944 . . ." Much of this chapter is drawn from Adrian Wilson's interview with the author (May 9, 1984).

P.61 "Thus, Mills was fairly isolated . . ." *Imprint: Oregon*, 22.

P.63 "At present Harold Row . . ." Everson letter to Edwa, July 31, 1943.

P.64 "As far as the camp . . ." Ruth Teiser's unpublished interview with Everson (as Antoninus), Dec. 13, 1965; Bancroft.

P.65 "James and I were down there . . ." *Imprint: Oregon*, 27.

P.66 "there were a bunch of snobs . . ." *Ibid.*, 21.

P.72 "Judges in Portland . . ." Teiser interview.

P.73 "The Tylers were . . ." Letter from Mary Tyler to the author, Sept. 25, 1986.

P.74 "hatred toward him . . ." Edwa letter to Everson, Aug. 13, 1943.

P.74 "It seems impossible . . ." Everson letter to Edwa, Nov. 17, 1944.

P.75 "Finally, earlier Robert Duncan . . ." Meltzer, 96.

CHAPTER FOUR: Berkeley

P.81 "While in San Francisco . . ." Teiser interview.

P.82 "In July of 1945 . . ." Ham and Mary Tyler, "In the Beginning, or Recatching the Years as Catches," in *Robert Duncan: Scales of the Marvellous*, ed. Robert J. Bertholf and Ian W. Reid (New York: New Directions, 1979), 1–13.

P.82 "Many unknown visitors . . ." *Ibid.*, 10.

P.83 "By this time, Duncan . . ." Letter from Mary Tyler to the author, Sept. 25, 1986.

P.84 "Everson was . . ." Thomas Parkinson, "William Everson," *American Poetry* 4, 2 (1987), 69–74

P.84 "We were particularly fond . . ." *Ibid.*

P.88 "Carefully fitted, its parts . . ." " Latter-Day Handpress," *Earth Poetry*, 122–23.

P.89 "For one thing . . ." *Ibid.*, 126.

P.90 "To this also . . ." *Ibid.*

P.91 "Cyril Connolly was in town . . ." Connolly briefly recalls his visit to the West Coast (with no reference to Rexroth) in "American Injection," *Ideas and Places* (London: Weidenfeld and Nicolson, 1953), 179: "San Francisco and its surroundings . . . probably represent the most attractive all-the-year-round alternative to Europe which the world can provide."

P.93 "Pity this girl . . ." "The Stranger," *poems: mcmxlii.*

P.95 "a weekly seminar . . ." See Rexroth, "A Selected Bibliography of Poetics/Modern [1947]," *American Poetry*, 1, 2:65.

P.95 "quarrels with his friends . . ." Everson, "Rexroth: Shaker and Maker," *For Rexroth: The Ark 14*, edited by Geoffrey Gardner (New York: The Ark, 1980), 25–26.

P.96 "the long honorable . . ." Bartlett, *The Beats: Essays in Criticism* (Jefferson, North Carolina: McFarland, 1981), 1.

P.96 "Any bright young man . . ." D. H. Lawrence, *Selected Poems*, edited by Kenneth Rexroth (New York: New Directions, 1948), 18–19.

P.96 "During the war . . ." Everson, "Four Letters on the Archetype," collected in *The Beats*, 186–94.

P.99 "From the start . . ." See Faas, *Robert Duncan*, 274–80.

P.101 "Everson thinks Rexroth's memory . . ." Further confirmation comes from Everson's presentation copy of *San Joaquin* to Rexroth. Inscribed by Everson, November 26, 1945, it was sent following Everson's return to Waldport after his first meeting with Rexroth.

P.101 "Cry *peace.* . . ." "On the Anniversary of the Versailles Peace, 1936," *San Joaquin.*

P.101 "Like so many . . ." Rexroth, "San Francisco Letter," *Evergreen Review*, 2 (1957), 9.

P.102 "The honor is all mine . . ." Rexroth letter to Everson, undated (dated "1946" in pencil in Everson's hand).

P.103 "What makes this more . . ." Everson letter to the author, May 4, 1985.

P.104 "full of the hatred . . ." James Dickey, *Babel to Byzantium* (New York: Grosset & Dunlap, 1968), 124–26.

P.105 "The jacket blurb . . ." Leslie Fiedler, "Some Uses and Failures of Feeling," *Partisan Review*, 15, 8 (August 1948), 924–31.

P.106 "raging literary civil war . . ." This feud between Rexroth and Fiedler for capo de capo was not imagined, and it was long standing. In a 1968 review, "Leslie Fiedler: Custer's Last Stand," Rexroth would write, "Leslie Fielder is possessed by a number of obsessions which destroy his convincingness, except amongst people who don't know better. First, as is well known, is his favorite term of abuse, 'WASP.' He uses it the way Stalinists used to write 'Trotskyite,' for the most incongruous assortment of writers and tendencies. Since he sees White Anglo-Saxon Protestants under every bed and in every woodpile, it is easy for him to so identify the main line of American culture with their works and to prove that this culture has been continuously challenged and is now collapsing from within. Ultimately this is an incurable distortion of vision due to membership in a small circle of extremely ethnocentric people—the self-styled New York Establishment, triangulated by the *Partisan Review*, *The New York Review of Books*, and *Commentary* . . . . The United States is a big country, and this tiny set is not even an epi-center, but a small disturbance of an epicycle." ("Ids and Animuses," *New York Times Book Review*, March 17, 1968, 4).

P.106 "When James Laughlin . . ." Laughlin in conversation with the author, Sept. 21, 1983.

P.107 "Despite of which . . ." Dudley Fitts, "Subjective Weighing and Writhing," *Saturday Review of Literature*, 31:47 (Nov. 20, 1948), 32.

CHAPTER FIVE: Conversion and The Catholic Worker

P.111 "My pantheism had suffered . . ." Teiser interview.

P.112 "broke both my Jeffersian . . ." *Ibid.*

P.112 "The candor is wholly winning . . ." Everson letter to the author, May 30, 1984.

P.112 "the nuns had prepared . . ." "Prodigious Thrust"; Bancroft.

P.114 "Triptych for the Living," *The Crooked Lines of God.*

P.114 "he wrote 28 poems . . ." 1948 notebook; Bancroft.

P.115 "It is inexcusable . . ." Dorothy Day letter to Everson, Nov. 16, 1948.

P.116 "to realize in the individual . . ." See *By Little and by Little: The Selected Writings of Dorothy Day*, ed. by Robert Ellsberg (New York: Alfred A. Knopf, 1983).

P.116 "those who think there . . ." *Ibid*, pp. 51–52.

P.120 "I was seized . . ." 1950 notebook; Bancroft.

P.120 "I realized . . ." *Ibid.*

P.121 "My second conference . . ." *Ibid.*

P.122 "disgust with . . ." Everson letter to Fr. Osborn, undated [1950]; Bancroft.

P.122 "Yesterday God made . . ." 1950 notebook; Bancroft.

P.123 "In the long summer . . ." Preface to *A Canticle to the Waterbirds.*

P.123 "Hospice of the Word," *The Crooked Lines of God.*

P.124 "The Seraphim is one . . ." Teiser interview.

P.125 "He will not let me . . ." Everson letter to Fr. Osborn, undated [1951].

P.126 "Now I will say . . ." *Ibid.*

CHAPTER SIX: Brother Antoninus

P.130 "deliberate on the improvement . . ." *The Catholic Encyclopedia* (New York: Encyclopedia Press, 1913), XIII, 354–70.

P.131 "a context intense . . ." "Prodigious Thrust" manuscript.

P.132 "So much then . . ." *Ibid.*

P.133 "It was a mistake . . ." Teiser interview.

P.133 "The rumble of the thing . . ." Fr. Finnbar Hayes, O.P., interview with the author, May 12, 1984.

P.134 "I can see . . ." Teiser interview.

P.134 "I had never worked . . ." *Ibid.*

P.135 "It is this that determined . . ." See preface to *Novum Psalterium Pii XII* in *On Writing the Waterbirds and Other Presentations*, 126.

P.135 "Such was the manner . . ." *Ibid.*, 132.

P.136 "gravely disappointed with his results . . ." On his obsession with typographical perfection, Antoninus would note in his 1957 notebook (Bancroft) that C. G. Jung's *Psychology and Alchemy* "in which he demonstrated that the alchemists were actually projecting their unconscious upon their material manipulations impressed me and convinced me because I was enabled thus to see that this is precisely what I was doing with my printing. The lack of resolution in my own soul, was projected upon the typographical problem, and my tremendous effort to bring every level of the work into harmony and resolution corresponded with my effort to make the material and the psychological perfectly poised."

"In printing there are two phases, design and execution. In design the supreme attempt, as I have seen it, has been one of orchestration. I began with relatively simple designs, but as time goes on I am more and more challenged by the problem of intricate typographical harmonization. Production printing is torture to me, I see now, because it does not permit time nor permission to achieve the resolution. But yet that is always my attempt. Here the mandala as a typographical center might be studied. I think of my Aquinas Institute poster, with its graded elements of caps and lowercase in Centaur, with only the small cross in the center in color. This cross is certainly a mandala; rather the whole poster is a mandala, a square sheet with a red cross in the center of complex typographical elements. Perhaps I will make a collection of title pages or display pages I have done, from the point of view of the mandala resolution of psychic difficulty."

P.137 "Antoninus was at that time . . ." Hayes interview.

P.137 "The whole thing blew sky high . . ." Teiser interview.

P.138 "The material I have . . ." Antoninus letter to Muir Dawson, undated [1954].

P.139 "I certainly did not know . . ." Teiser interview.

P.140 "There were very strict . . ." Hayes interview.

P.140 "There was a little pamphlet . . ." *Ibid.*

P.141 "Thomas especially . . ." *Ibid.*

P.141 "They were a different breed . . ." *Ibid.*

P.142 "A Frost Lay White on California," *The Hazards of Holiness.*

P.142 "That was part . . ." Hayes interview.

P.143 "Antoninus always had . . ." Fr. Blaise Schauer, O.P., interview with the author, May 20, 1984.

P.144 "A Jubilee for St. Peter Martyr," *The Crooked Lines of God.*

P.145 "Ever since I entered the Faith . . ." Everson letter to Fr. Meagher, undated [1952].

P.146 "The Thomistic view . . ." Lewis Hill acted as a coordinator between the Quakers and the government in the administration of the CO camps. In 1949, along with William Trieste and Richard Moore, he founded the first listener-sponsored radio station, KPFA, in the Bay Area. Everson letter, undated [April, 1954].

CHAPTER SEVEN: Kentfield, Breakthrough, and "Prodigious Thrust"

P.148 "I thought I would . . ." Teiser interview.

P.149 "It was a typical . . ." Hayes interview.

P.151 "Now, as time goes on . . ." Antoninus letter to Fr. Fulton, Oct. 16, 1954.

P.152 "the relationship between . . ." Antoninus letter to Fr. Duffner, Jan. 9, 1955.

P.153 "suspicious of depth . . ." Preface, *God and the Unconscious* by Victor White.

P.154 "those who live by the sword . . ." Antoninus letter to Charles H. Carver, July 24, 1956. In this early poem, he continued, "what I did intuitively grasp then was the relationship between love and violence. I have never flown, but remember reading of the island warfare in the Pacific, bombing raids, etc., with photographs of aerial views, vast expanses of water, with little focal points where the islands cropped up. In the prevalent tactical discussion I picked up the fact that the Japanese flyers at Pearl Harbor probably never reached their carriers, the carriers abandoned them to escape. Out of these elements the poem was built."

"The island, then, tropical and verdant, seen from the air, rounded, appealing, feminine, erotic, is definitely maternal. The raid is a rape, an act of violence, and the raid is punished, for in the end the flyers, who attacked the island, are themselves betrayed. The brute power principle, here the aggressor nation, which uses its destructive violence against the maternal, passive principle, orders its sons, the flyers, to attack her. They obey, but their obedience is complicated by their own desire for the mother; they desire her for their own pleasure, denoted by their joy at their success, so that they share in the father's guilt by their carnality. The callous power prin-

ciple sent them off to die, for it now deserts them and they are left to
be punished, which they deserve. But in accepting their punishment,
they achieve a kind of redemption, for the sea is the maternal principle too, and it accepts them back, for they are hers, and assuages
their guilt."

P.155 "Very generalized beginning . . ." 1956 notebook; Bancroft.

P.156 "stumbled down the hall . . ." *Ibid.*

P.157 "She made in her throat . . ." *Ibid.*

P.157 "I went into . . ." *Ibid.*

P.158 "It was sexual impetuosity . . ." *Ibid.*

P.158 "When I was in my teens . . ." *Ibid.*

P.159 "Bit by bit . . ." *Ibid.*

P.159 "Things have happened . . ." Antoninus letter to Victor White,
Jan. 11, 1957.

P.161 "supported by an autobiographical . . ." "Prodigious Thrust"
manuscript.

P.161 "They read it . . ." Teiser interview.

P.162 "he was such an extreme . . ." Fr. Antoninus Wall, O.P., interview with Allen Campo, Nov. 6, 1975.

P.163 "For instance, we'd rise . . ." Hayes interview.

P.163 "That television set . . ." Teiser interview.

P.163 "He had with him . . ." Hayes interview.

P.164 "I went over to the church . . ." Antoninus letter to the LaPlacas,
Nov. 10, 1956.

P.165 "Every once in awhile . . ." Hayes interview.

P.165 "For me it was . . ." 1956 notebook; Bancroft.

P.166 "For all my advance . . ." Antoninus letter to Frank Sheed,
August 12, 1957.

CHAPTER EIGHT: The Rose of Solitude

P.168 "The term 'beat' . . . " Philip Whalen interview with the author,
May 7, 1985.

P.170 "I was on the stand . . ." 1962 notebook; Bancroft.

P.170 "probably the most profoundly . . ." See Rexroth, "San
Francisco Letter."

P.171 "reaction to the . . ." Afterword to *River-Root.*

P.172 "opened the way . . ." See Albert Gelpi, "Everson/Antoninus:
Contending with the Shadow," in *The Veritable Years.*

P.173 "everywhere anybody might be . . ." Steve Eisner interview with Allen Campo, Sept. 24, 1975.

P.173 "He kept staring . . ." *Ibid.*

P.174 "Beat Friar . . ." According to the editors of *Time*, "'Someone has said American poetry is divided into Smoothies and Shaggies. I'm a shaggy.' So says a poet who has been a Christian Scientist, agnostic, anarchist and conscientious objector. Yet today he wears the white tunic and black scapular of a Roman Catholic Dominican lay brother . . . . His poetry and his whole career may be way out, but his purpose is to move men way in to Christ." (May 25, 1959).

P.175 "a stir here . . ." Antoninus letter to White, Feb. 11, 1957.

P.175 "incident still lingered . . ." Further, as Antoninus related in his 1957 notebook (Bancroft), "Sunday night I talked with Fr. Blaise about *Thrust*, and we both thought a small private edition of the uncut version duplicated by hectograph might be wise since no imprimatur is required for that. I did not want to stir up a hornet's nest by a direct petition for permission, for often in the Order, at least in its present undisciplined state, formal permissions are embarrassing for the superiors to make. In the politically antagonistic factions of the house often only trouble results."

P.175 "I went to San Francisco . . ." 1959 notebook; Bancroft.

P.176 "he and a Jesuit priest . . ." Eisner interview.

P.177 "really very simple . . ." John Engles, "Two Religious Poets," *Poetry*, XCIV, 4 (Jan. 1962), 253–58.

P.177 "Rose brought . . ." Meltzer, 102.

P.178 "She was unlike anybody . . ." Hayes interview.

P.178 "How am I . . ." *Ibid.*

P.179 "The effect upon me . . ." 1960 notebook; Bancroft.

P.180 "She had this kind . . ." Hayes interview.

P.181 "In the afternoon . . ." 1959 notebook; Bancroft.

P.181 "I was able to talk . . ." Rose Tannlund interview with the 2uthor, Dec. 20, 1986.

P.182 "I have discovered . . ." Antoninus letter to Rose Tannlund, Jan. 25, 1961.

P.183 "The spiritual life . . ." Preface to *Rose of Solitude*.

P.183 "Every time something . . ." Tannlund interview.

P.183 "graphic homoerotic imaginings . . ." To complicate matters further, there is an implication in the 1957 notebooks that Everson's fear of "the natural homosexual element" originated in part in a homosexual encounter "between my 7th and 8th grades . . . . These relations were not of long duration. I don't think it happened more than 2 or 3 times at the most. I don't even remember exactly what it consisted of. I do know that I buggered him at least twice, but that the last time I remember doing it when I withdrew my penis there was dung clotted on it, and this revolted me. This image of dung on my penis I have never forgotten, and I suspect that it has something to do with my fierce projection against homosexuality." 1957 notebook (Oct. 24); Bancroft.

P.184 "I was a woman . . ." 1959 notebook; Bancroft.

P.184 "in 'The Encounter' and several other . . ." Gelpi, "Everson/ Antoninus."

P.186 "the cross . . ." C. G. Jung, *Symbols of Transformation* (Princeton, NJ: Princeton University Press, 1956), 269.

P.186 "Rose served . . ." Hayes interview.

P.186 "In the monastery . . ." Fr. William Ruddy, O.P., interview with Allen Campo, May 10, 1975.

P.187 "Our relationship . . ." Tannlund interview.

P.187 "The new Provincial . . ." Antoninus letter to Steve Eisner, Jan. 1961.

P.188 "It was clear . . ." Thomas P. McDonnell, "Poet from the West," *Commonweal*, LXXVIII, 1 (March 29, 1963), 13–4.

P.188 "God's own showman . . ." *Washington Daily News* (Nov. 18, 1964); *Columbia University Owl* (March 27, 1963); *The Dominican College Meadowlark* (Winter, 1967).

P.189 "these public appearances . . ." 1960 notebook; Bancroft.

P.189 "It was shambles . . ." *Ibid.*

P.190 "In defense of my style . . ." Antoninus letter to Czeslaw Milosz, Dec. 12, 1962.

P.191 "I have spent . . ." Antoninus letter to Lawrence Clark Powell, Jan. 19, 1962.

CHAPTER NINE: The Spirit and the Flesh

P.194 "I have served . . ." Antoninus letter to Fr. Basil Lamb, March 13, 1963.

P.194 "by the grace of God . . ." On Sept. 19, 1963, Antoninus wrote a series of letters to each of these schools.

P.197 "When a nation . . . ." "Tongs of Jeopardy," *Ramparts*, II, 5 (Spring 1964), 3–9.

P.198 "My vows-taking . . . ." Antoninus letter to Naomi Burton, Oct. 4, 1964.

P.199 "I made a big mistake . . . ." Wall interview.

P.200 "I had hoped to write . . . ." Antoninus letter to Albert Gelpi, Jan. 22, 1965.

P.200 "This is to say goodbye . . . ." Antoninus letter to Rose Tannlund, undated [1965].

P.201 "The feeling in the monastery . . . ." Ruddy interview.

P.204 "He said to the audience . . . ." *Ibid.*

P.204 "Annul in Me My Manhood," *The Crooked Lines of God.*

P.205 "a woman became hysterical . . . ." Ruddy interview.

P.205 "I understand . . . ." Antoninus letter to Susanna Rickson, April 12, 1966.

P.206 "Then too the humiliation . . . ." Antoninus to Susanna Rickson, April 16, 1966.

P.207 "Rose I worshipped . . . ." Antoninus to Susanna Rickson, July 26, 1966.

P.207 "I was so taken . . . ." Antoninus to Susanna Rickson, June 29, 1967.

P.208 "She was so radiant . . . ." Meltzer, 111–12.

P.209 "Antoninus was our house guest . . . ." Lawrence Clark Powell, *Life Goes On.*

P.210 "part of my thinking . . . ." Wall interview.

P.211 "hair down to his shoulders . . . ." According to the 1957 notebook, "As I went into the scullery the window was open and a cold blast of wind coming in from the north. I hurried back out into the warm refectory feeling harried, driven, and almost sick, as if I might come down with a cold. This caused me to reflect that everytime I have got a haircut here in the winter time I come down with a cold, which usually lays me up for several days. I began to investigate the psychological aspects of this."

"First was the castration complex. I remembered Neumann's correlation of hair-cutting with castration, baldness with impotence."

"When the cold blast hits my head I shrivel up—exposure. The shorn lamb, lack of protection; Samson, an inflation archetype if there ever was one. When I wore my hair long in Selma in the bad days before the draft, when the workers would ask me why I didn't cut it, I would jocularly reply, 'You know what happened to Samson!' There was a straight unconscious correlation between Samson and myself as proto-archetypal figures."

"Actually, the idea of long hair goes back to my mother. I was fascinated by her hair in infancy. She had it bobbed in the twenties about the time I crossed puberty, and no doubt it had a sense of loss, an alienating factor, a nostalgic conditioner. During the early forties, with the war coming on, when I was most insecure, I let my hair grow long. I wore it long through the war and after until I met a woman who eventually got me to cut my hair."

P.211 "Soon as we got settled . . ." *Ibid.*

P.211 "We went with . . ." *Ibid.*

P.212 "an article and photograph . . ." "Quidnunc: An Irishman's Diary," *The Irish Times*, August 27, 1969.

P.212 "we found ourselves . . ." Antoninus to Susanna Rickson, August 27, 1969.

P.213 "We got into London . . ." Antoninus to Susanna Rickson, August 31, 1969.

P.214 "I love you beautiful girl . . ." Antoninus to Susanna Rickson, Oct. 10, 1969.

P.214 'I think of you constantly . . ." Antoninus to Susanna Rickson, Nov. 21, 1969.

P.214 "When we started . . ." Eisner interview.

P.216 "Persephone smiles . . ." *Tendril in the Mesh.*

EPILOGUE: The Integral Years

P.217 "The next morning . . ." Hayes interview.

P.217 "People would quickly . . ." Wall interview.

P.218 "told me that it was . . ." Tannlund interview.

P.220 "Susanna: girl and bride . . ." *Man-Fate.*

P.220 "The poems expressed . . ." Everson letter to Laughlin, August 13, 1970.

P.220 "Instead of working . . ." Susanna Everson letter to Bren Baily, July 12, 1979.

P.221 "I had planned . . ." Everson letter to Laughlin.

P.222 "the literary heritage . . ." *Archetype West*, ix.

P.222 "Of course, regionalism . . ." *Ibid.*, xiv.

P.225 "an approach to ascesis . . ." Unpublished notes; Bancroft.

P.226 "The Santa Cruz effort . . ." Everson letter to Laughlin, Dec. 9, 1974.

P.226 "Bill asks . . ." Student evaluations; Literature Board, University of California, Santa Cruz.

P.226 "I had taken . . ." John Selby's preface to his unpublished interview with Everson; Bancroft.

P.226 "my principal reason . . ." Everson letter to Galen Williams, undated [1972].

P.228 "He had a badger skin . . ." Ruddy interview.

P.228 "When we talked . . ." Everson letter to John White Fox, August 12, 1972.

P.233 "Where the romanticists . . ." Everson letter to C. F. MacIntyre, undated [1940].

BIBLIOGRAPHY

I. WILLIAM EVERSON: PRIMARY WORKS

POETRY

These Are the Ravens. San Leandro: Greater West Publishing, 1935.
San Joaquin. Los Angeles: The Ward Ritchie Press, 1939.
The Masculine Dead. Prairie City: The Press of James A. Decker, 1942.
X War Elegies. Waldport: Untide Press, 1943.
The Waldport Poems. Waldport: Untide Press, 1944.
War Elegies. Waldport: Untide Press, 1944.
The Residual Years. Waldport: Untide Press, 1944.
poems: mcmxlii. Waldport: Untide Press, 1944.
The Residual Years. New York: New Directions, 1948.
A Privacy of Speech. Berkeley: The Equinox Press, 1948.
Triptych for the Living. Berkeley: The Seraphim Press, 1951.
An Age Insurgent. San Francisco: Blackfriars Publications, 1959.
The Crooked Lines of God. Detroit: University of Detroit Press, 1959.
The Year's Declension. Berkeley: Rare Books Department of the General
    Library at the University of California, 1961.
The Hazards of Holiness. Garden City: Doubleday, 1962.

The Poet Is Dead. San Francisco: The Auerhahn Press, 1964.

The Blowing of the Seed. New Haven: Henry W. Wenning, 1966.

Single Source. Berkeley: Oyez, 1966.

The Rose of Solitude. Garden City: Doubleday, 1967.

In the Fictive Wish. Berkeley: Oyez, 1967.

A Canticle to the Waterbirds. Berkeley: Eizo, 1968.

The Springing of the Blade. Reno: The Black Rock Press, 1968.

The Residual Years. New York: New Directions, 1968.

The City Does Not Die. Berkeley: Oyez, 1969.

The Last Crusade. Berkeley: Oyez, 1969.

Who Is She That Looketh Forth as the Morning. Santa Barbara: Capricorn Press, 1972.

Tendril in the Mesh. N.p.: Cayucos Books, 1973.

Black Hills. San Francisco: Didymous Press, 1973.

Man-Fate. New York: New Directions, 1974.

River-Root. Berkeley: Oyez, 1976.

The Mate-Flight of Eagles. Newcastle, CA: Blue Oak Press, 1977.

Rattlesnake August. Northridge, CA: Lord John Press, 1977.

The Veritable Years. Santa Barbara: Black Sparrow Press, 1978.

Blame It on the Jet Stream. Santa Cruz: The Lime Kiln Press, 1979.

The Masks of Drought. Santa Barbara: Black Sparrow Press, 1980.

Eastward the Armies. Aptos, CA: Labyrinth Editions, 1980.

Renegade Christmas. Northridge, CA: Lord John Press, 1984.

In Medias Res. San Francisco: Adrian Wilson Press, 1984.

PROSE

Robinson Jeffers: Fragments of an Older Fury. Berkeley: Oyez, 1968.

Archetype West: The Pacific Coast as a Literary Region. Berkeley: Oyez, 1976.

Earth Poetry: Selected Essays and Interviews. Ed. Lee Bartlett. Berkeley: Oyez, 1980.

Birth of a Poet: The Santa Cruz Meditations. Ed. Lee Bartlett. Santa Barbara: Black Sparrow Press, 1982.

On Writing the Waterbirds and Other Presentations: Collected Forewords and Afterwords. Ed. Lee Bartlett. Metuchen: Scarecrow Press, 1983.

The Excesses of God: Robinson Jeffers as a Religious Figure. Stanford: Stanford University Press, 1988.

EDITIONS

Novum Psalterium Pii XII. Los Angeles: Countess Estelle Doheny, 1955.
Cawdor/Medea by Robinson Jeffers. New York: New Directions, 1970.
Californians by Robinson Jeffers. N.p.: Cayucos Books, 1971.
The Alpine Christ by Robinson Jeffers. N.p.: Cayucos Books, 1973.
Tragedy Has Obligations by Robinson Jeffers. Santa Cruz: The Lime Kiln Press, 1973.
Brides of the South Wind by Robinson Jeffers. N.p.: Cayucos Books, 1974.
Granite & Cypress by Robinson Jeffers. Santa Cruz: The Lime Kiln Press, 1975.
The Double Axe by Robinson Jeffers. Ed. with Bill Hotchkiss. New York: Norton, 1977.
American Bard by Walt Whitman. New York: Viking, 1982.

II. SECONDARY WORKS

Allen, Donald. *The New American Poetry, 1945–1960*. New York: Grove Press, 1960.
Allen, Donald, and Warren Tallman. *The Poetics of the New American Poetry*. New York: Grove Press, 1973.
Bartlett, Lee, and Allan Campo. *William Everson: A Descriptive Bibliography, 1934–1976*. Metuchen: Scarecrow Press, 1977.
Bartlett, Lee. *The Beats: Essays in Criticism*. Jefferson: McFarland, 1981.
———."Creating the Autochthon: Kenneth Rexroth, William Everson, and The Residual Years." *Sagetrieb* 2:3 (1983), 57–69.
———."God's Crooked Lines: William Everson and C.G. Jung." *The Centennial Review* 27:4 (1983): 288–303.
———.*William Everson*. Boise: Boise State University, 1985.
———.*Talking Poetry: Conversations in the Workshop with Contemporary Poets*. Albuquerque: University of New Mexico Press, 1987.
Bertholf, Robert J., and Ian W. Reid. *Robert Duncan: Scales of the Marvelous*. New York: New Directions, 1979.
Blumenthal, Joseph. *The Printed Book in America*. Boston: David R. Godine, 1977.
Campo, Allan, David A. Carpenter, and Bill Hotchkiss. *William Everson: Poet from the San Joaquin*. Newcastle: Blue Oak Press, 1978.

Carpenter, David A. "William Everson: Peacemaker with Himself." *Concerning Poetry* 13:1 (1982): 19–34.

Cavanaugh, Brendon, O.P., Alfred Camillus Murphy, O.P., and Albert Doshner, O.P. "Brother Antoninus: A Symposium." *Dominicana* 68 (1963): 33–53.

Charters, Samuel. *Some Poems/Poets: Studies in American Underground Poetry Since 1945.* Berkeley: Oyez, 1971.

Connolly, Cyril. *Ideas and Places.* London: Weidenfeld and Nicolson, 1953.

Day, Dorothy. *Little By Little: The Selected Writings.* Robert Ellsberg, ed. New York: Alfred A. Knopf, 1983.

Dickey, James. *Babel to Byzantium.* New York: Grosset & Dunlap, 1968.

Faas, Ekbert. *Towards A New American Poetics: Essays & Interviews.* Santa Barbara: Black Sparrow Press, 1978.

———.*Young Robert Duncan: Portrait of the Poet as Homosexual in Society.* Santa Barbara: Black Sparrow Press, 1983.

Ferlinghetti, Lawrence, and Nancy J. Peters. *Literary San Francisco.* San Francisco: City Lights Books/Harper & Row, 1980.

Gelpi, Albert. "Everson/Antoninus: Contending with the Shadow." Afterword to *The Veritable Years.* Santa Barbara: Black Sparrow Press, 1978.

Gentry, Linnea, "On William Everson as Printer." *Fine Print* (July 1975).

Holland, Kenneth, and Frank Ernest Hill. *Youth in the CCC.* Washington, DC: American Council on Education, 1942.

Jung, C.G. *The Collected Works* (19 volumes). Princeton: Princeton University Press, 1953–79.

Kherdian, David. *Six Poets of the San Francisco Renaissance: Portraits and Checklists.* Fresno: Gilgia Press, 1967.

Lacey, Paul A. *The Inner War.* Philadelphia: Fortress Press, 1972.

Marusiak, Joe. "Where We Might Meet Each Other: An Appreciation of Galway Kinnell and William Everson." *Literary Review* 24 (1981): 355–70.

McFarland, J. Randall. *Centennial Selma.* The Selma Enterprise, 1980.

Meltzer, David. *Golden Gate: Interviews With 5 San Francisco Poets.* Berkeley: Wingbow Press, 1976.

Mills, Ralph J. *Contemporary American Poetry.* New York: Random House, 1965.

Neumann, Erich. *The Origins and History of Consciousness.* Princeton: Princeton University Press,1954.

Parkinson, Thomas. *Poets, Poems, Movements.* Ann Arbor: UMI Research Press, 1987.

Perkins, David. *A History of Modern Poetry: Modernism and After.* Cambridge: Harvard University Press, 1987.

Powell, James A. "Williams Everson (Brother Antoninus)." *The Beats: Literary Bohemians in Postwar America.* Ed. Ann Charters. Detroit: Gale, 1983.

Powell, Lawrence Clark. *Life Goes On.* Metuchen: Scarecrow Press, 1986.

Rexroth, Kenneth. *American Poetry in the Twentieth Century.* New York: Herder and Herder, 1971.

———.*World Outside the Window: The Selected Essays.* Ed. Brad Morrow. New York: New Directions, 1987.

Rizzo, Fred. "Brother Antoninus: Vates of Radical Catholicism." *Denver Quarterly* 3 (1969): 18–38.

Rosenthal, M.L. *The New Poets: American and British Poetry Since World War II.* New York: Oxford University Press, 1967.

Salmond, John A. *The Civilian Conservation Corps, 1933–1942.* Durham: Duke University Press, 1967.

Stafford, William E. *The Achievement of Brother Antoninus.* Glenview: Scott, Foreman and Co., 1967.

Taylor, Jacqueline A. *Civilian Public Service in Waldport, Oregon, 1941–1945.* Thesis, Department of History, University of Oregon, 1966.

Wakoski, Diane. "Neglected Poets 2: William Everson and Bad Taste." *American Poetry.* 2:1 (1984): 36–43.

White, Victor. *God and the Unconscious.* Cleveland: World Publishing Company, 1952.

INDEX

Agius, Fr. Joseph, 176
Aiken, Conrad, 95
Alioto, Joseph, 210
Alvarez, A., 213
American Libraries, 222
Angulo, Jaime de, 128
Anthony, St., 113
Aquinas, St. Thomas, 130
Ark, 53
Armstrong, Louis 74
Arthur, Gavin, 195
Atlantic Monthly, 18–19
Auden, W.H., 104
Augustine, St., 112, 116, 120, 147, 160, 197

Baudelaire, Charles, 44
Baxley, Joseph, 88
Beilenson, Peter, 106
Belloc, Hillary, 91
Benedict, St., 196
Bentley, Wilder, 88

Berryman, John, 105
Big Table, 172
Black Panther Party, 1
Blackfriars, 153
Blake, William, 108
Blank, Fr. Benedict, 128–29, 175
Blaser, Robin, 87, 99
Bloom, Harold, 105
Blumenthal, Joseph, 231
Bly, Robert, 224
Brecht, Bertholt, 188
Brody, Fawn, 132
Brooks, Cleanth, 96
Broughton, James, 95
Brown, Norman O., 224
Brown, Richard, 60, 87
Buel, Hubert, 15, 17, 20
Bukowski, Charles, 222
Bullough, Sebastian, 153
Bunyan, C.R., 44
Burke, John G., 222

Burroughs, William, 169
Burton, Naomi, 165, 167, 176, 198, 201

California Book Club Quarterly, The, 86, 138
Campbell, Joseph, 225
Campo, Allan, 228
Carothers, Kenneth, 56–58, 62, 64–65, 74–75, 93
Carpenter, Don, 182
Carroll, Paul, 172
Catholic Worker, The, 115–17
Christian Century, 68
Ciardi, John, 191
Circle, 68, 97
Civilian Conservation Corps (CCC), 13–15, 37–38, 76, 79
Civilian Public Service (CPS), 37–38, 40–44, 46, 49, 53, 59, 69, 72, 76–78, 85, 92, 98, 108, 110, 113, 158, 224
Clemens, Samuel, 96, 222
Coffield, Glen, 40–48, 51, 61–63, 69
Coleridge, Samuel Taylor, 146
Commonweal, 116, 188
Compass, The, 64, 66–67
Connolly, Cyril, 91–93
Cooney, James, 21–24
Curtin, Andrew, 15

Daily Californian, The, 190
Damien, Brother, 240–42
Dante, 185
Dawson, Muir, 138–39
Davidman, Joy, 19
Davis, Charles, 48
Day, Dorothy, 115–18
de Chardin, Pierre Teilhard, 228
Decker, James, 27–28
Dickey, James, 104, 107, 177
Dillon, George, 25–27
DiPrima, Diane, 227
Doheney, Countess, 138–39
Dolphin, The, 86

Donne, John, 104–05
Dreiser, Theodore, 53–55
Duffner, Fr. Aquinas, 150–52
Duggan, Fr., 117–20, 127, 163
Duncan, Robert, 21–25 27–28, 72, 75, 82–83, 87, 94, 99–100, 108–09, 124, 169–70, 210, 227, 233
Dupre, Vladimir, 66, 75

Earl, Broadus, 64,77
Earl, Hildegard, 77
Eberhart, Richard, 107
Eisner, Steve 172–73, 176, 187, 214, 221, 227
Eliade, Mircea, 225
Eliot, T.S., 28, 51, 95, 108, 146
Emerson, Ralph Waldo, 108, 226
Empson, William, 95
Engels, John, 177
Eshelman, William, 64, 68, 75–76, 78–80, 88, 137
Esquire, 19
Evergreen Review, 96, 101, 170–71
Everson, Edwa (Poulson), 9–10, 12–13, 15–18, 20–21, 25, 30–31, 38–43, 45–48, 51–53, 55–59, 62–63, 73, 75, 80, 84, 93, 108, 111–12, 149, 155, 177, 194, 206, 233
Everson, Francelia Marie (Herber), 4, 6, 15, 30–31, 237–40
Everson, Jude, 209, 215, 224
Everson, Lloyd Waldemar, 4–5, 7–9, 11, 15, 31
Everson, Louis Waldemar, 3–6, 8, 10, 15, 31–33, 58, 158, 237–40
Everson, Susanna (Rickson), 202–09, 211–16, 218–20, 224, 234
Everson, Vera Louise (Shorey), 5, 15, 21
Everson, William (works). "Age Insurgent, An" 176; *American Bard*, 229, 233; "Annul Me in My Manhood," 204–05;

"Approach, The," 24, 110; *Archetype West*, 222–23; "At the Edge," 95; "Attila," 28; "Big Shorts Are Coming, The," 11; "Black Hills, The," 228; *Blame It On the Jet Stream*, 229; "Blowing of the Seed, The," 84, 172, 205; "Blue Wind of September, The," 19; "Canticle to the Christ in the Holy Eucharist," 145; "Canticle to the Waterbirds, A," 123, 173, 188; "Chronicle of Division, The," 103, 108; "City Does Not Die, The," 210; "Clouds," 45; "Coast Thought," 28; *Crooked Lines of God, The*, 176, 184, 191; "Cutting the Firebreak," 232; "Dionysus and the Beat Generation," 175; "Do Not Brood For Long," 19; "Encounter, The," 123, 184, 212; "Falling of the Grain, The," 115, 161; "Feast Day," 22; "First Winter Storm," 103; "Fisheaters," 158; "Fog Days," 28; *Fragments of an Older Fury*, 210; "Frost Lay White on California, A," 142, 145; *Granite & Cypress*, 229–31; "Gypsy Dance," 12; *Hazards of Holiness, The*, 179, 198; "In the Dream's Recess," 95; *In the Fictive Wish*, 188; *Inceptions*, 221; "Internment (Rock Crusher), The," 43; "Jubilee for St. Peter Martyr, A," 144–45; "Kingfisher Flat," 232–33; "Knives, The," 29; "Latter-Day Handpress, The," 86; "Le Mal," 55; "Lines for the Last of a Gold Town," 23; "Magi, The," 116; "Making of the Cross, The," 115; *Man-Fate*, 220, 222, 227; "March," 110; *Masculine Dead, The*, 27, 29, 101; "Masculine Dead, The," 24,

29–30, 101; *Masks of Drought, The*, 232–33; "Massacre of the Holy Innocents, The," 115, 141, 144; "Months of Pep, The," 10; "Moongate," 232; "Muscat Pruning," 28–29; "October Tragedy," 16; "On the Anniversary of the Versailles Peace, 1936," 28; "Orion," 21, 29; "Outlaw," 91; *Poems*, 20; *poems:mcmxlii*, 73; "Poet Is Dead, The," 192; "Poetry and the Life of the Spirit," 188; "Printer as Contemplative, The," 138; *Privacy of Speech, A*, 89–90, 124, 172; "Prodigious Thrust," 147, 160, 165–67, 172, 198; *Psalter*, 133–40, 147, 148, 152; "Raid, The," 154; *Residual Years, The*, 100–02, 104–07, 174, 176, 210, 226; "Revolutionist, The," 91; *River-Root*, 171, 184; *Rose of Solitude, The*, 180, 183–87, 197, 199–202; *San Joaquin*, 21, 44, 101; "Savagery of Love, A," 145, 211; "Scout, The," 228; "Sides of a Mind, The," 29; *Single Source*, 210; "Sign, The," 26; "Sleep," 19; "Springing of the Blade, The," 87, 212; "Stranger, The," 93; "Stone Face Falls," 234; *X War Elegies*, 62; "Tendril in the Mesh," 205, 216, 220; *These Are the Ravens*, 18, 28, 101; *Tide-Turn: A Cycle of Renewal*, 222; "Time to Mourn, A," 227; *Tongs of Jeopardy*, 202, 227; *Tragedy Has Obligations*, 229; "Triptych for the Living," 95, 114, 124, 133; "To the Duck Hawk," 10; *Veritable Years, The*, 184, 232; *Waldport Poems, The*, 68, 100; *War Elegies*, 45, 47, 69, 101; "Watchers, The," 19; "We in the Fields," 29; *West to the*

Water, 229; *Who Is She That Looketh Forth as the Morning*, 222; "Who Lives Here Harbors Sorrow," 28, 102; "Winter Ascent, A," 107; "Winter Plowing," 19, 102; "Winter Solstice," 28.
Experimental Review, The, 21

Faas, Ekbert, 87
Farquhar, Samuel T., 88
Fearon, Fr., 201
Fellowship of Reconciliation (FOR), 49
Ferlinghetti, Lawrence, 175
Fiedler, Leslie, 105
Fitts, Dudley, 107
Fleuron, The, 87
Ford, Charles Henri, 44
Freeman, Ted, 88
Freud, Sigmund, 153–54, 159
Frost, Robert, 173, 205
Fugurhason, Mary, 48
Fulton, Fr. Joseph, 149–51, 162, 174, 176

Gahegan, Charles, 117–18
Gelpi, Albert, 172, 184, 200
George, Vic, 88
Gide, André, 51
Gill, Eric, 89, 114, 125, 155
Ginsberg, Allen, 170–71, 173
Gleason, Madeline, 95, 114, 169
Gould, Wallace, 103
Grabhorn Press, 106, 135, 229
Graves, Morris, 64–66
Groff, E., 44

Hackett, Harold, 40, 43–46, 49–53, 55, 57, 61–63, 69, 224
Hall, Dave, 61–62
Hallisey, Ruth, 128
Hampton, Edie Fitzpatrick, 203
Hampton, Fred, 1
Happold, F.C., 226

Harmon, Jim, 53–55
Harper's, 18
Hart, James, 88
Harte, Bret, 222
Hartman, Jane, 153–54
Hawley, Dorothy, 219
Hawley, Robert, 215, 219, 223–24
Hawthorne, Nathaniel, 51
Hayes, Fr. Finnbar, 132–33, 136–37, 140–43, 149, 162–63, 178, 180, 186, 193, 233
Henrich, Edith, 95
Herber, William, 26–27, 235–36
Herr, Jane, 82
Hershey, General, 72
Hill, Lewis, 145–46
Hinckle, Warren, 176
Hoffman, Hans A., 19, 21, 28
Horizon, 91–92
Hoyem, Andrew, 199
Huxley, Aldous, 51

Illiterati, The, 51, 65, 67–68, 79
Imprint: Oregon, 66
Irish Times, The, 212
Isherwood, Christopher, 42

Jackson, David, 64
James, Clayton, 64–66, 68, 72, 76–77
James, Henry, 147
Jarrell, Randall, 105
Jeffers, Robinson, 16, 18, 20, 22–23, 28–29, 41, 101–03, 108–09, 147, 191–92, 227, 229–30, 233
Jerome, St., 184
Jones, Ernest, 159
Joyce, James, 136
Jung, Carl Gustav, 111, 153, 157, 179, 183, 186, 195–96, 222, 226
Justema, William, 95

Kahn, Michael, 223
Kalal, Joe, 67–68, 73, 88
Kane, John Victor, 133
Keaton, Morris, 60

Kennedy, John F., 197–98
Kenyon Review, 98
Kerouac, Jack, 168, 173, 198
Kesey, Ken, 222
Kinsella, Thomas, 212
Kirchner, Leon, 109
Kosbab, Earl, 49–50, 69

Lamantia, Philip, 44, 87, 91–92, 96, 170
Lamb, Fr. Basil, 194
LaPlaca, Mickey, 154, 163–64
Laughlin, James, 100, 105–06, 221, 226
Lawrence, D.H., 82, 94–97, 105, 112, 125, 159, 223
Leavis, F.R., 159
LeBlanc, Peter, 227
Leite, George, 97–98
Libertarian Circle, The, 94
Life, 170
Lime Kiln Press, 229–31
Lincoln, Abraham, 147
Lincoln County Times, The, 62
Lindbergh, Charles, 6
Lindsay, Vachel, 41
Literary Behavior, 99
London, Jack, 222
Longavan, Don, 230
Lowell, Robert, 107
Lowrie, Walter, 44
Loy, Mina, 97
Lubin, Hal, 83

MacDonald, Dwight, 99
MacIntyre, C.F., 27, 101, 233
Magnet, The, 10
Magnus, Albertus, 130
Malkiel, Maria-Rosa Lida, 110
Marcus, Morton, 231
Marcuse, Herbert, 153–54
Markee, Cris, 202–05
Markee, Chuck, 203
Markham, Edwin, 96
Martyr, St. Peter, 144

Masses, The, 116
Maurin, Peter, 116
McAlmon, Robert, 97
McClure, Michael, 170
McCool, Carroll, 118–22, 180
McDonnell, Thomas, 188
McDougal, Marsha, 224
McGlynn, Fr. Charles, 176, 221
McIntyre, Cardinal, 140
McKelvy, Stuart, 15
Meadowlark, 189
Meagher, Fr., 127, 145, 201
Meltzer, David, 53, 208
Melville, Herman, 108
Merton, Thomas, 115, 146, 160, 176, 186
Miles, Josephine, 28, 97, 107
Miller, Henry, 44, 46, 97
Miller, Joaquin, 228
Mills, Richard, C., 40, 49–50, 59–61, 63, 69–71, 78
Milosz, Czeslaw, 190
Milton, John, 104
Mitty, Archbishop John, 174, 176, 194
Monroe, Harriet, 25
Montague, John, 212
Montague, Richard, 99
Moore, Harry T., 25
Moore, Richard, 204
Morris, William, 109

Nash, John Henry, 229
Nation, The, 68, 177
National Council of Religious Objectors (NCRO), 59, 78–79
Neumann, Erich, 159, 195
New Republic, 19
New York Times Book Review, 168
New Yorker, The, 19
Nichols, Terry, 195–96
Nin, Anaïs, 25, 97
Nixon, Richard, 196
Nomland, Kemper, 44, 47, 51, 61, 68, 70, 75, 80

Norris, Frank, 222
Norse, Harold, 97
Now, 91

O'Brien, David, 116
Oregonian, 78
Osborn, Fr. Leo, 120–27
Oswald, Lee Harvey, 198
Ottsman, Ed, 81
Owl, 189

Page, Homer Gordon, 109
Parkinson, Thomas, 83, 94, 97, 192, 202
Parmisano, Fr., 241
Parr, Jack, 174
Partisan Review, 105
Pascal, Blaise, 160
Patchen, Kenneth, 48, 73, 75, 77, 88, 97, 105,
Perry, Raymond, 130
Phoenix, The, 21–22
Poetry, 19, 21, 25–27, 68, 177
Politics, 98
Ponch, Martin, 64, 67
Porter, Bern, 97
Pound, Ezra, 23, 95, 227
Powell, Lawrence Clark, 20–21, 44, 86, 101, 107, 165, 191, 209
Print, 86

Ramparts, 176
Ransom, John Crowe, 96, 98
Reagan, Ronald, 196
Reich, Wilhelm, 77, 153
Rexroth, Andree, 96
Rexroth, Kenneth, 75, 81–82, 87, 91–110, 124, 170, 177, 182–83, 233
Rexroth, Marie, 96
Rickson, Susanna (see Everson, Susanna)
Riding, Laura, 95
Rimbaud, Arthur, 55
Ritchie, Ward, 21

Ritual, 21
Robinson, Fr. Louis, 193
Roethke, Theodore, 185
Rolling Stones, 1
Roosevelt, Franklin D., 13, 72
Rosenthal, M.L., 192
Row, Harold, 63
Rubin, Jerry, 70, 78
Ruby, Jack, 198
Ruddy, Fr. William, 186, 201, 204
Rudhyar, Dane, 44, 197
Rukeyser, Muriel, 95
Russell, Sanders, 95, 99

San Francisco Chronicle, 1, 192
Sandburg, Carl, 103
Saturday Review, 18, 19, 107, 191
Say, Allen, 219
Scanlon, Fr. Paul, 215, 218
Schafer, Helen, 10
Schauer, Fr. Blaise, 142–43, 154, 217, 233
Schevill, James, 191
Schorer, Mark, 99
Scribner's, 18
Seimons, Larry, 45–46, 61–62, 67, 69
Sewanee Review, 96, 177
Shakespeare, William, 150
Shapiro, Karl, 232
Sheed, Frank, 164–67
Sheets, Kermit, 61–64,
Signature, 86
Sitwell, Edith, 81
Sloan, Jacob, 68
Smith, Page, 224
Snyder, Gary, 100, 109, 199, 223
Sophocles, 159
Spanner, Virginia, 187
Spender, Stephen, 95
Spicer, Jack, 87, 94–95, 99, 168
Stars and Stripes, 44
Stein, Gertrude, 26
Steinbeck, John, 222
Stegner, Wallace, 109
Stephen, Ruth, 107

Sullivan, Jack, 212
Swab, Gustav, 158
Symmes, Robert (see Robert Duncan)

Tannlund, Rose Moreno, 177–87,
    194, 199–202, 206, 218–19, 233
Tate, James, 212
Teiser, Ruth, 139
Teresa of Avila, St., 119, 182
Thomas, Fr. Leo, 140, 142–43,
    163–64, 217, 241
Thomas, Norman, 70
Thoreau, Henry David, 108, 147
Tide, 44–45
Time, 174
Times (London), 213
Truman, Harry S., 76
Tyler, Hamilton, 47, 72–73, 80–84,
    93, 97
Tyler, Mary, 72–73, 80–84, 93
Tyler, Parker, 44

Untide, 45–47, 50, 67, 77

Vann, Gerald, 153, 195
Verlaine, Paul, 55
View, 44
Villa, Pancho, 143

Wakoski, Diane, 232
Walker, Robert, 54
Wall, Fr. Albert, 137

Wall, Fr. Antoninus, 162, 193, 199,
    210–14, 233
Wall Street Journal, 175
Washington Daily News, 188
Watkins, Lee, 18, 20–21, 39, 58, 62,
    72, 75, 81–82, 97, 233
Watkins, Milicent, 18, 39, 62, 81–82,
    97
Watts, Alan, 175
Welch, Lew, 223
Wellisch, Eric, 158
Westward, 19
Whalen, Philip, 168, 182, 223
White, Fr. Victor, 153, 157, 159,
    161, 166, 175, 195, 233
Whitman, Walt, 29, 108, 147, 229
Williams, Galen, 226
Williams, William Carlos, 97, 105,
    223
Wilson, Adrian, 64, 72
Wilson, Edmund, 209
Winchell, Walter, 62
Winslow, Yvonne, 179–80, 185
Wolf, Leonard, 99, 169
Woodcock, George, 79
Wordsworth, William, 29, 35

Yale Review, 19
Yeats, William Butler, 95

Zimmer, Heinrich, 225